Cohabitation and Co-ownership Precedents

Cohabitation and Co-ownership Precedents

Denzil Lush BA, MA, LLM
Solicitor, Exeter

Family Law
1993

Family Law is a publishing imprint of
Jordan Publishing Limited
21 St Thomas Street
Bristol BS1 6JS

British Library Cataloguing-in-Publication Data
A catalogue record for this book is available from the British Library.

ISBN 0-85308-137-9

Typeset by Wyvern Typesetting Ltd, Bristol
Printed in Great Britain at The Bath Press, Bath

CONTENTS

TABLE OF CASES

References in the right-hand column are to page numbers.

TABLE OF STATUTES

References in the right-hand column are to page numbers.

TABLE OF STATUTORY INSTRUMENTS

References in the right-hand column are to page numbers

INTRODUCTION

In the last twenty years many books and articles have been written about cohabitation. Some have attempted to define it, and some have analysed its prevalence. Others have examined the reasons why people choose to live together, rather than to marry. There have been numerous historical, socio-logical and comparative law studies, but only a handful of these publications has explored the documentary aspects of cohabitation and co-ownership.

This book of precedents is divided into five chapters: Declarations of Trust; Cohabitation Contracts; Children; Wills; and Miscellaneous Docu-ments. Each of these areas has its own peculiar difficulties, some of which are outlined in the introductory text to each chapter. The purpose of this general introduction is to draw attention to one or two problems of a more fundamental nature.

The law relating to co-ownership requires a radical overhaul. England and Wales are still largely governed by property laws passed in the 1920s, many of which were consolidatory at the time. In 1925 very few people owned their own homes, and those who did would have considered it untraditional to purchase a house in joint names. The trust for sale, the power to postpone sale, the need to enlarge the trustees' powers, and the doctrine of conversion are fictitious and anachronistic. Worst of all, they are confusing to the ordinary home-buyer.

Other aspects of co-ownership have not received the scrutiny they deserve. There has been no serious investigation of the correct method of quantifying beneficial interests; at least, none from which one can extract principles of universal application. Similarly, there has been no in-depth analysis of the various predicaments which co-owners may experience at one time or another.

Some commentators regard the emergence of cohabitation contracts as a vindication of Sir Henry Maine's famous generalisation in *Ancient Law*, Chapter 5, that 'the movement of progressive societies has hitherto been a movement from status to contract'. The pioneers in this field – mostly, and understandably, women – have promoted the contract as almost a *sine qua non* of cohabitation or, at least, as some sort of panacea. Both cases are overstated. It is difficult to convince many cohabitees of the wisdom of declaring their interests in jointly owned property; fewer still are willing to enter into a full-blown cohabitation contract. The fact that such contracts exist, that there is considered to be a need for them, and that there is mounting pressure on Parliament to introduce legislation which will make them enforceable, indicates an underlying dissatisfaction with the existing legal and equitable remedies available to cohabitees. Satisfactory laws ought to produce satisfactory solutions. An Act which validated cohabitation contracts would simply be treating the symptoms, without actually tackling the cause.

In theory, there should be no difference between the wills of a married couple and those of an unmarried couple and, in practice, there is very little difference. The married and unmarried alike experience the same quandary when their family relationships become particularly complex. Partners usually wish to provide for the survivor, perhaps for life or until he or she enters into a new union, and the ultimate destinations of their respective estates may be entirely different. To a layman these wishes seem simple and straightforward and, most importantly, fair; but there is no foolproof machinery to implement them in law. 'Mutual Wills', in the legal sense of the term, are fraught with complications. A trust is sometimes inappropriate, inconvenient or inefficient and, although the provisions of the Settled Land Act 1925 might have suited someone with dynastic aspirations at the beginning of this century, they will be of limited assistance to anyone wishing to provide a home for a partner in the next century. The Inheritance (Provision for Family and Dependants) Act 1975 contained a welcome provision. It allowed a cohabitee, for the first time, to apply to the court for discretionary provision out of the deceased partner's estate. But, in order to succeed, the survivor has to prove that he or she was being maintained by the deceased, and that the deceased was making a substantial contribution in money or money's worth towards his or her reasonable needs. This strict requirement of dependence has had the unfortunate, and probably unintentional, effect of reducing the Act into little more than a 'sponger's charter'.

During the last few years there has been an enormous amount of legislative activity affecting children. Partly as a result of this, but mainly because of the basic principle that the child's welfare should always be a determining factor, there is relatively little scope for private agreements between the parents. Accordingly, the selection of precedents in the 'Children' section (Chapter 3) is minimal.

This book attempts to be neutral without being impassive or inert. Apart from the comments above, it is politically neutral. It also seeks to be morally neutral, gender neutral, orientation neutral and neutral in terms of the age and socio-economic background of those to whom its precedents might apply. It is hoped that the precedents will prove to be user-friendly, not only to those who prepare the documents but also to those who choose to live or die by them.

CHAPTER 1: DECLARATIONS OF TRUST

INDEX

Forms   74

PART 1: INTRODUCTORY TEXT

Introduction

An express declaration of trust in respect of land is an instrument in writing, which is signed by the person or persons competent to declare the trust and which records the beneficial interests of those who are entitled to the land, its net proceeds of sale and its net income until sale.[1]

In the absence of an express declaration of trust, it is open to anyone claiming a beneficial interest in the land to rely on the doctrines of implied trusts, resulting trusts and constructive trusts, which are exempt from the written formalities.[2] An interest could also be claimed on the basis of proprietory estoppel[3] or contract.[4]

---

1 Law of Property Act 1925, s 53(1)(b) (see below).
2 Ibid, s 53(2).
3 As in *Pascoe v Turner* [1979] 1 WLR 431.
4 As in *Tanner v Tanner* [1975] 1 WLR 1346.

Effects of an Express Declaration of Trust

Section 53(1)(b) of the Law of Property Act 1925 states that:

> 'a declaration of trust respecting any land or any interest therein must be manifested and proved by some writing signed by some person who is able to declare such trust or by his will.'

The trust does not need to be declared in writing at the time of its creation. A subsequent declaration will suffice, provided that it is in existence before any action is brought.[1]

Although there is no legal requirement that there should be more than one deed, it is considered better practice to keep the trusts off the title.[2] So, generally, there will be two deeds: one (the transfer) vesting the legal estate in a sole owner or in the trustees for sale; and the other (the declaration of trust) setting out the beneficial interests.

An express declaration of trust which comprehensively declares the beneficial interests in the property and its proceeds of sale is conclusive unless and until it is varied by those who are competent to vary it, or it is rectified or set aside on the grounds of fraud or mistake.[3] However, such a declaration is only conclusive as to the position at the time when the trust is declared.[4] Subsequent events may cause the beneficial interests to vary.

An express declaration of trust can be varied provided that the variation is manifested and proved by an instrument in writing signed by the person or persons able to vary the original trusts.[5] The new trusts will then operate *proprio vigore* by virtue of the new instrument.[6] The beneficial interests can also be varied by an order of the court.[7]

---

1 *Rochefoucauld v Boustead* [1897] 1 Ch 196 at 206.
2 'The declaration of beneficial trusts could perfectly well have been contained in a separate document altogether off the face of the title to the land, and many conveyancers would regard that as the more proper method of proceeding' (*Wilson v Wilson* [1969] 3 All ER 945 at 948H, per Buckley J).
3 *Goodman v Gallant* [1986] 1 FLR 513 at 517C.
4 'If that document declares not merely in whom the legal title is to vest but in whom the beneficial title is to vest, that necessarily concludes the question of title as between the (co-owners) for all time, and in the absence of fraud or mistake at the time of the transaction the parties cannot go behind it at any time thereafter even on death or the break-up of the marriage' (*Pettitt v Pettitt* [1970] AC 777 at 813E, per Lord Upjohn).
5 'The trust and the equitable interests arising under it cannot be changed except with the consent of all interested parties' (*Cowcher v Cowcher* [1972] 1 All ER 943 at 950f, per Bagnall J).
6 *Re Holmden's Settlement Trusts* [1968] AC 685 at 713D, per Lord Wilberforce.
7 For example: Matrimonial Causes Act 1973, s 24; Inheritance (Provision for Family and Dependants) Act 1975, s 9; Insolvency Act 1986, s 339; Children Act 1989, Sch 1. Note also the effect of the Income Support (General) Regulations 1987, SI 1987/1967, reg 52, and the similar regulations affecting family credit and housing benefit. Where the claimant and one or more other persons are beneficially entitled in possession to property, they are treated as being entitled in equal shares.

Land Registry Forms[1]

Since 1 December 1990 every district in England and Wales has been an area of compulsory registration of title.[2]

The Land Registry is not interested in trusts and, as far as possible, any reference to a trust must be excluded from the registers.[3]

Except where joint proprietors are beneficial joint tenants, in order to give effect to the concurrent or successive interests in the land they hold, joint proprietors should apply for the entry of the appropriate restriction on the register.[4]

The standard form of transfer to joint proprietors (Land Registry Form 19(JP)), was introduced in 1975.[5] It contains a declaration: 'The transferees declare that the survivor of them (can)/(cannot) give a valid receipt for capital money arising on a disposition of the land'.[6] The inappropriate alternative should be deleted. Often it is not. The transfer should also be executed by the transferees. Again, often it is not,[7] particularly where no indemnity covenant is given. The standard forms of application to register dealings (Form A4 for dealings with the whole of titles, Form A5 for dealings with part of titles other than the grant of a lease) contain the question, to be answered by the applicant or practitioner, 'Can the survivor of them give a receipt for capital money arising on a disposition of the land?' In each case (Forms 19(JP), A4 and A5) the affirmative is designed to establish that the transferees are beneficial joint tenants. The negative is intended to establish that the transferees are not beneficial joint tenants, and constitutes an application for the entry of the obligatory restriction.

On its own, the declaration in Form 19(JP) does not constitute a declaration of trust.[8] The court has recommended that, in the case of a beneficial joint tenancy, words to the effect of 'to hold unto themselves as joint tenants beneficially' should be expressly inserted in the transfer.[9] In the case of a beneficial tenancy in common, it is considered better practice to declare the beneficial interests in an instrument entirely separate from the transfer itself.[10] In any event, the transfer is usually 'swallowed up' by the Land Registry.[11]

---

1 See, generally, Ruoff and Roper *Registered Conveyancing* (Sweet & Maxwell, 1991); and Ruoff and Pryer *Land Registration Handbook: Forms and Practice* (Sweet & Maxwell, 1990).

2 Registration of Title Order 1989, SI 1989/1347. Registration of title to land was introduced in Scotland by the Land Registration (Scotland) Act 1979.

3 Land Registration Act 1925, s 74.

4 Form 62 (Land Registration Rules 1925, SI 1925/1093, r 213, as amended by the Land Registration Rules 1989, SI 1989/801, r 6). See also, the Land Registration Act 1925, s 58(3).

5 The announcement of the Chief Land Registrar dated 31 December 1974 is set out in *Harwood v Harwood* [1991] 2 FLR 274 at 287B.

6 Designed to give effect to the thinking behind the Law of Property Act 1925, s 27(2).

7 As in the cases of *Robinson v Robinson* [1976] 241 EG 153, and *Re Gorman (A Bankrupt) ex parte Trustee of The Bankrupt v The Bankrupt* [1990] 1 WLR 616. In *Taylor and Harman v Warners* (unreported) 21 July 1987, the only indication of the transferees' intentions concerning the beneficial ownership was an affirmative answer on Land Registry Form A5. See *The Law Society's Gazette* 29 June 1988, at pp 26 and 27, for a summary of the facts and judgment.

8 *Harwood v Harwood* [1991] 2 FLR 274 at 289C, per Slade LJ. Harwood was distinguished in *Re Gorman (A Bankrupt)* (above), and *Huntingford v Hobbs* [1992] EGCS 38.

9 *Harwood v Harwood* [1991] 2 FLR 274 at 288F, per Slade LJ.

10 *Wilson v Wilson* [1969] 3 All ER 945 at 948.

11 Land Registration Rules 1925, SI 1925/1093, r 90.

The Legal Adviser's Duty

Anyone who acts for a purchaser has a duty to enquire whether any other person has contributed to the purchase price or is otherwise likely to be beneficially interested in the property.[1]

Anyone who acts for two or more persons who are purchasing a property has a duty to:

1 explain the differences between beneficial joint tenancies and ten ucies in common;[2]

2 assess the advantages and disadvantages of each type of beneficial
   ownership;
3 consider the preference of one type of beneficial ownership over the other
   in the light of all the circumstances; and
4 alert the purchasers to risks.[3]

In order to give reasoned advice, the practitioner will require full details
of the contributions already made, or yet to be made, towards the purchase
price and purchase costs, information about the co-owners' finances and
relationship, and a clear idea of their intentions with regard to any mortgage
payments.

In the course of making such enquiries, the legal adviser may sense that
there is, or could be, a conflict of interests between the purchasers. If this is
the case, the adviser should not continue to act for both or all parties.[4]

Having established what the parties intend, the practitioner has a duty to
record those intentions properly in order to give them effect.[5] In most cases,
the proper documentation will consist of an express declaration of trust,
contained in a separate instrument altogether off the face of the title to the
land.[6] In some cases, additional documents, such as wills, may need to be
prepared.

A practitioner who fails in these duties could be liable for damages in
negligence.[7] On several occasions the courts have stated that it is deplorable
that solicitors and licensed conveyancers should fail to find out and declare
the beneficial interests when a property is being acquired.[8]

---

1 *City of London Building Society v Flegg* [1988] AC 54.
2 *Taylor and Harman v Warners* (unreported) 21 July 1987. Although this decision of Warner
   J is unreported, a summary of the facts and judgment is given by Ross Crail in *The Law
   Society's Gazette* 29 June 1988, at pp 26 and 27. Warner J said that merely to inform the
   purchasers of the survivorship right in a beneficial joint tenancy is 'perfunctory'.
3 The practitioner should, according to Warner J (ibid at p 27) '. . . have regard to the
   dictum of Bingham LJ in *County Personnel (Employment Agency) Ltd v Alan R Pulver & Co*
   [1987] 1 WLR 916, namely: 'If in the exercise of a reasonable professional judgment a
   solicitor is or should be alerted to risks which might elude even an intelligent layman,
   then plainly it is his duty to advise the client of these risks and explore the matter
   further.'
4 The Law Society's *Guide to the Professional Conduct of Solicitors* (1990) states, under
   Principle 11.03, that: 'a solicitor or firm of solicitors must not continue to act for two or
   more clients where a conflict of interests arises between those clients'.
5 *Taylor and Harman v Warners* (unreported) 21 July 1987: '. . . it was common ground
   between counsel that it is a solicitor's duty to ascertain the parties' intentions with regard
   to the beneficial ownership of the property and give effect to them' (*The Law Society's
   Gazette* 29 June 1988, at p 27).
6 'The declaration of beneficial trusts could perfectly well have been contained in a separate
   document altogether off the face of the title to the land, and many conveyancers would
   regard that as the more proper method of proceeding' (*Wilson v Wilson* [1969] 3 All ER
   945 at 948H, per Buckley J).
7 Threatened by Dillon LJ in *Walker v Hall* [1984] FLR 126 at 129E. 'The significance of
   (*Taylor and Harman v Warners*) lay in the solicitor's being held guilty of negligence' *The
   Law Society's Gazette* 29 June 1988, at p 27. However, it is not clear what damages would

be available if such an action were to succeed: see MJ Sookias, J Cole, and RL Price 'Conveyancers Beware the Cohabitee', *The Law Society's Gazette* 6 May 1987, at p 1309.

8 *Cowcher v Cowcher* [1972] 1 All ER 943 at 959, per Bagnall J. *Bernard v Josephs* (1983) FLR 178 at 187F, per Griffiths LJ. *Walker v Hall* [1984] FLR 126 at 129E, per Dillon LJ. *Springette v Defoe* (1992) *The Independent*, March 24, per Dillon LJ.

Why is there Reticence about Declaring the Beneficial Interests?

It is obvious that, despite several stern judicial warnings, many practitioners show a marked reluctance to ascertain and declare the beneficial interests of joint proprietors. The following observations are not an apologia, but an attempt to identify some of the social, psychological, financial and drafting problems which, in combination, tend to militate against an express declaration of the beneficial interests.

1   In most cases the purchasers themselves give no consideration to the question of beneficial ownership when they acquire the property.[1]

2   To declare the trusts might well be construed as demonstrating a lack of trust. It could be taken as an assumption that the relationship will fail, sooner or later, and to insist on declaring the trusts could even 'rock the boat'.[2]

3   It is necessary to ask probing personal questions. To ask them can be embarrassing for the practitioner: to answer them can be embarrassing for the clients. Of course, similar questions would be asked at the end of the relationship, but at the start of a relationship some of these enquiries might be considered inappropriate or even offensive.

4   Some practitioners feel that the exercise serves little useful purpose where the couple intend eventually to get married, because the court can make whatever property adjustment order it thinks fit in a matrimonial action[3] or in family proceedings.[4]

5   There are various ways of calculating the beneficial interests[5]. It may be hard to decide, when a couple purchases, which method of calculation will produce the fairest result when they come to sell.

6   Family finances are often pooled, which can make it difficult to pinpoint the exact contributions made by either party towards the mortgage payments.

7   There have been one or two judicial statements to the effect that shares can only be assessed arithmetically when the property is bought outright, and that there is no place for mathematical calculations where (as is practically always the case) the property is purchased with the aid of a mortgage.[6] One Lord Justice of Appeal has even acknowledged that 'there is of course an air of unreality about the whole exercise'.[7]

8   The potential immutability of a declaration of trust is often an inhibiting factor. Having 'fixed' the beneficial interests on acquisition, what happens if the co-owners' circumstances change? In theory, another declaration of trust should be executed to record the variation, but in practice it is unlikely to happen. Perhaps a resulting trust or a constructive trust, which might have arisen anyway in the absence of an express declaration, would have been a more satisfactory solution in the first place.

9   There is fierce competition to cut purchase costs to a minimum, particularly in the first-time buyers' market. Proper advice and documentation concerning the beneficial interests can add substantially to these costs.[8]

10 Sometimes there is a conflict, or a potential conflict of interests between the buyers. The need to obtain independent legal advice would further increase the costs.

11 Declarations of trust are 'inter-disciplinary'. They do not fall completely or comfortably within the province of a conveyancer, a trust lawyer, or a family lawyer. It is sometimes difficult to establish who is best suited to advise on, negotiate, or draft a declaration. Having to refer to several people in the same firm could have a knock-on effect in terms of costs.

12 Many lawyers do not enquire about and declare the beneficial interests of their clients, and there is a mistaken belief that a practitioner will not be guilty of negligence if he or she acts in accordance with a practice accepted as proper by a responsible body of men and women skilled in this particular area of the law.[9]

---

1 'When two people are about to be married and are negotiating for a matrimonial home it does not naturally enter the head of either to enquire carefully, still less to agree, what should happen to the house if the marriage comes to grief' (*Re Rogers' Question* [1948] 1 All ER 328, per Evershed LJ).
   'In a great many cases, perhaps in the vast majority, no consideration will have been given by the parties . . . to the question of beneficial ownership of the home at the time that it is being acquired' (*Gissing v Gissing* [1970] 2 All ER 780 at 785, per Viscount Dilhorne).
2 Compare: 'I cannot think that connubial harmony would be unduly jeopardized' (*Cowcher v Cowcher* [1972] 1 All ER 943 at 959h, per Bagnall J).
3 Matrimonial Causes Act 1973, s 24.
4 Children Act 1989, Sch 1.
5 See Precedents 10 to 19 at pp 27 to 42 below.
6 'Where the house is bought outright and not on mortgage, the extent of their respective shares will depend upon a more-or-less precise arithmetical calculation of the extent of their contributions to the purchase price. Where, on the other hand, and as is more usual nowadays, the house is bought with the aid of a mortgage, then the court has to assess each of the parties' respective contributions in a broad sense' (*Burns v Burns* [1984] FLR 216 at 241G, per May LJ).
7 Griffiths LJ in *Bernard v Josephs* (1983) FLR 178 at 188B.
8 Compare: 'The additional costs would be insignificant' (*Cowcher v Cowcher* [1972] 1 All ER 943 at 959h, per Bagnall J).
9 The principle that a practitioner is not guilty of negligence if he or she acts in accordance with a practice accepted as proper by a responsible body of men and women skilled in

that particular art was established in the medical negligence case *Bolam v Friern Hospital Management Committee* [1957] 1 WLR 582. Defence submissions based on Bolam were rejected by Warner J in *Taylor and Harman v Warners* (unreported) 21 July 1987 (but see *The Law Society's Gazette* 29 June 1988, at p 27).

The Person who 'Moves In'

Legal problems arise when one person moves in with another and, almost invariably, their respective legal advisers are unaware of the situation. If the incomer contributes towards the homeowner's mortgage payments, or pays for repairs and improvements to the property, a resulting, implied or constructive trust may be created, or the doctrine of estoppel may apply. Since Lord Denning's retirement in 1982, the court's approach to these issues has been more conservative and orthodox.[1] It would appear that for any such claim to succeed nowadays there must be evidence of an intention inferring joint ownership[2] and evidence that the claimant acted to his or her detriment in reliance on a belief that he or she was, or would be, entitled to a beneficial interest in the property.[3] Detriment is now restricted to pure economic loss.[4]

A conflict of interests between the parties is more likely to occur where one person moves in with the other, than in a straightforward, outright purchase by both of them. The adviser acting for the incomer would probably require the homeowner to create a beneficial tenancy in common.[5] The adviser acting for the homeowner would probably require the incomer to execute a deed relinquishing any interest in the property.[6]

1 *Burns v Burns* [1984] Ch 317.
2 *Grant v Edwards* [1986] Ch 638.
3 *Midland Bank PLC v Dobson and Dobson* [1986] 1 FLR 171.
4 *Thomas v Fuller-Brown* [1988] 1 FLR 237; *Lloyds Bank PLC v Rosset* [1991] 1 AC 107.
5 See Precedent 47(b) at p 85 below.
6 See Precedent 47(a) at p 84 below.

Fixed Shares and Floating Shares

Usually, the co-owners' shares of the net proceeds of sale are ascertained or fixed at the time of purchase.[1] In this book, such shares are referred to as *fixed shares*.

In the absence of any deed of variation executed by those who are competent to vary the original trusts, and in the absence of any court order, fixed shares remain static throughout the duration of the trust for sale.[2]

Alternatively, and more unusually in practice, the ascertainment of the shares can be deferred until the property is sold, and then determined in the light of the actual contributions made by either party while the trust for sale subsisted.[3] In this book, such shares are referred to as *floating shares*.[4]

The effect of executing a declaration of trust which creates floating shares is much the same as expressly creating a resulting trust and a constructive trust at the outset.

---

1 'In the absence of any special circumstances . . . the time at which the beneficial interest crystallises is the time of the acquisition' (*Bernard v Josephs* (1983) FLR 178 at 188F, per Griffiths LJ).

2 *Pettitt v Pettitt* [1970] AC 777 at 813E.

3 'There is nothing inherently improbable in their acting on the understanding that the wife should be entitled to a share which was not quantified immediately on the acquisition of the home, but should be left to be determined when the mortgage was repaid or the property disposed of, on the basis of what would be fair having regard to the total contributions, direct or indirect, which each spouse had made by that date' (*Gissing v Gissing* [1970] 2 All ER 780 at 793d, per Lord Diplock).

4 The expression 'floating shares' is not a technical term. They could be referred to as, say, 'deferred shares'. When floating shares crystallise, they become fixed. See, generally, Peter Sparkes 'The Quantification of Beneficial Interests: Problems Arising from Contributions to Deposits, Mortgage Advances and Mortgage Instalments', Oxford Journal of Legal Studies, Vol 11, No 1 (1991), at pp 39 to 62.

The Advantages of Fixed Shares

Ascertaining or 'fixing' the co-owners' shares of the net proceeds of sale when they purchase the property has a number of advantages.[1] They include the following.

1 Certainty. The position is clear from the start.

2 At any given time each co-owner can work out approximately how much he or she would be entitled to receive if the property were sold.

3 Simplicity. All that is needed to work out 'who gets what' is a completion statement when the property is sold or – during the subsistence of the trust – a current valuation of the property and a mortgage redemption statement or a statement of the surrender value of any mortgage-linked insurance policy.

4 Convenience. There is less paperwork needed than for floating shares. There is no need for the co-owners to keep receipts and elaborate accounts as evidence of their respective contributions.

5 If the co-owners' circumstances change (eg if their contributions towards the mortgage payments vary, or if they contribute disproportionately towards the cost of any repairs and improvements to the property) the imbalance can easily be rectified by means of a supplemental declaration of trust.

6 The fixed share system enables one co-owner to confer a gratuitous benefit on the other – if that is the intention.[2]

---

1 For the distinction between fixed shares and floating shares, see above. For a discussion of the disadvantages of fixed shares, see below.
2 For example, where the co-owners declare themselves to be beneficial joint tenants or beneficial tenants in common in equal shares, and one co-owner has contributed substantially more than the other towards the purchase price or the mortgage payments.

The Disadvantages of Fixed Shares

The fixed-share system is not without its disadvantages.[1]

1 Fixed shares are potentially immutable. They conclude the question of title between the co-owners for all time 'and in the absence of fraud or mistake at the time of the transaction the parties cannot go behind (the declaration of trust) at any time thereafter, even on death or the (breakdown of their relationship)'.[2]

2 Circumstances change. What seemed fair and reasonable when the property was purchased may be quite unconscionable when the time comes to sell it.

3 Often it requires each co-owner to commit himself to paying a specified share of the mortgage payments. For various reasons, one or other co-owner may be unable or unwilling to keep up those payments.

4 It may be necessary to keep the fixed shares under constant review.

5 In practice, it is unlikely that the co-owners will execute a supplemental declaration of trust if their contributions vary. Inviting one's partner to enter into a further declaration could 'rock the boat'. It may involve some expenditure on valuation fees. It will almost certainly involve paying more legal fees.

6 There are several ways of calculating fixed shares. It is not easy to decide at the outset which method will produce the fairest result when the property is sold. One method of calculation might favour one partner, while another method might favour the other. Occasionally, the differences between the various formulae can produce perverse results.[3]

7 Problems arise over post-separation contributions, particularly where one co-owner has abandoned the property and stopped making any further contribution towards the mortgage payments.

8 It is not entirely clear when the fixed shares should 'crystallise' if the couple separate. Should they crystallise on the date of separation or on the date when the property is eventually sold? The Court of Appeal has experienced difficulties in answering these questions.[4]

1 For the distinction between fixed shares and floating shares, see above.
2 *Pettitt v Pettitt* [1970] AC 777 at 813E, per Lord Upjohn.
3 See Precedents 10 to 14 at pp 27 and 32 below and footnotes thereto.
4 In *Hall v Hall* (1982) FLR 379, the court held that the plaintiff was entitled to a share of
   the equity valued at the date on which the relationship ended. This decision was
   explained and distinguished in *Gordon v Douce* [1983] 1 WLR 563. In *Turton v Turton*
   [1988] 1 FLR 23 it was held that 'unless there is some express declaration or agreement to
   the effect that the parties' respective beneficial shares are to be valued at the time of their
   separation . . . the parties' beneficial interests would always have to be regarded in the
   normal way under a trust for sale, with the effect that they would endure until such time
   as the property is sold, and that they will then attach to the proceeds of sale' (at p 34A,
   per Kerr LJ).

The Advantages of Floating Shares

Floating shares may be considered preferable to fixed shares for the following reasons.[1]

1   The concept is more equitable, in theory at least.

2   'Who gets what?' depends on 'who paid what?'

3   There should be no need to keep floating shares under constant review.

4   Any variations in the co-owners' contributions will automatically be
     taken into account. There is no need to execute a supplemental declara-
     tion of trust or to suffer the expense and potential acrimony which that
     might involve.

5   The contributions made by each party will be examined retrospectively
     from the date on which the property was sold or from the date on which
     the co-owners separated, in much the same way that a court is able to
     look back with the benefit of hindsight on all the relevant facts.[2]

6   There should be less difficulty over post-separation contributions.[3]

7   Any possible need to apply to the court for a declaration of trust to be
     rectified or set aside on the grounds of fraud or mistake is virtually
     eliminated.

8   There should be less likelihood of one co-owner inadvertently confer-
     ring a gratuitous benefit on the other.

9   Although it is argued that the mathematics of calculating floating shares
     are complex, in reality – given all the relevant information and a reliable
     calculator – the exercise should not take very much longer than the
     calculation of fixed shares, and is well within the capacity of anyone of
     average intelligence.[4]

10   The contention that the co-owners would find it more difficult to
     pinpoint their exact entitlement at any given time is, it is submitted,
     artificial: such calculations are generally not a matter of regular concern.

11 The suggestion that co-owners do not keep the receipts and accounts which floating shares require them to maintain is not always true in practice. Even the most cursory glance at the reported cases will reveal that on the breakdown of a relationship most parties know exactly who paid what and when.[5]

---

1 For the distinction between fixed shares and floating shares, see above. For a discussion of some of the disadvantages of floating shares, see above.
2 *Gissing v Gissing* [1970] 2 All ER 780 at 793.
3 For the difficulties over post-separation contributions, see p 14 above, footnote 4.
4 See Precedents 15 to 18 at pp 32 to 41 below.
5 For instance: Harold John Pettitt, 'an experienced estate agent's negotiator' said: 'I estimate that I have performed work and supplied material to the value of £723.17s.0d ... HJP2 (is) a Schedule setting out how this sum is made up' (*Pettitt v Pettitt* [1970] AC 777 at 780F). 'In 1951 when the house was purchased she spent about £190 on buying furniture and a cooker and a refrigerator for it. She also spent about £30 for improving the lawn' (*Gissing v Gissing* [1970] 2 All ER 780 at 794).

The Disadvantages of Floating Shares

Floating shares have their drawbacks.[1]

1 There is less certainty. A co-owner may find it difficult to quantify his or her entitlement at any time.[2]

2 Co-owners must keep accounts, receipts and statements, showing who paid what and when. In many cases it is unlikely that they will do so.[3]

3 Even if they do keep accounts, the couple could still disagree about the contributions made, especially if they came from a joint account.

4 The calculations are more complicated than the calculation of fixed shares.

5 It is difficult to know where to draw the line with repairs and improvements, eg what repairs should affect the beneficial interests, and what repairs are *de minimis* and irrelevant?

6 Although floating shares reflect the direct cash contributions made by each co-owner, inflation can play havoc with the equities. For example, payment of £1,000 by co-owner A when the property was purchased in 1974 would probably, in real terms, be worth five times as much as a payment of £1,000 made by co-owner B towards improvements to the property in 1993.[4]

7 Cash contributions towards repairs and improvements are not always identical to the enhancement value; the co-owners might disagree about the extent to which the value of the property has been enhanced.[5]

8 Floating shares can only exist in the context of a beneficial tenancy in

common. Accordingly, they are subject to any perceived disadvantages to which tenancies in common are themselves subject.

9   There is less scope for mutual dependence. For example, floating shares would prejudice a female co-owner who had left work in order to have a baby or to look after children, and who was unable to make any financial contribution towards the mortgage payments or any repairs or improvements to the property.

10 Two methods of calculating floating shares are described in this book. One is the simple addition of each co-owner's contributions, and an apportionment of the net proceeds of sale pro rata.[6] The other identifies the extent to which any change in the value of the property is attributable to a co-owner's lump-sum contributions and his or her mortgage-related contributions.[7] These methods will produce different results: sometimes, substantially different results.[8]

11 An injustice might occur if one co-owner pays the mortgage (which will affect his or her beneficial interest) and the other co-owner pays the other outgoings which do not affect any beneficial interests.

---

1   For the distinction between fixed shares and floating shares, see above. For a discussion of some of the advantages of floating shares, see above.
2   But see point 10, at p 14 above.
3   But see point 11, at p 15 above.
4   Alluded to by Nicholls LJ in *Passee v Passee* [1988] 1 FLR 263 at 271.
5   In *Pettitt v Pettitt* [1970] AC 777 at 780, the wife was not prepared to concede that her husband's expenditure of £723.17s had increased the value of Tinker's Cottage by £1,000.
6   See Precedent 16 at p 33 below.
7   See Precedent 18a (narrative) and 18b (tabular) at pp 35 and 38 below.
8   See Precedent 18a, footnote 1 at p 35 below.

Fractions, Percentages and Ratios

Fixed shares are usually expressed as fractions or percentages of the sale price or the net proceeds of sale. Occasionally, they appear as ratios. When quoting fractions there is a tendency to reduce them to the lowest common denominator, but this could diminish the understanding of the document for the sake of visual amenity. In the final analysis, how one expresses the shares is a balancing act. Which method is easier to understand, and which is more elegant or less perverse?[1]

---

1   *Example*: Vic and Doris buy a bungalow for £56,000. Vic pays £40,000, and Doris pays £16,000. A declaration of trust which states that Vic is entitled to 71.4286 per cent of the net proceeds of sale and that Doris is entitled to 28.5714 per cent would be entirely accurate, but rather bizarre. A declaration which states that Vic is entitled to 40/56ths and Doris 16/56ths, would be much easier to reconcile with the original contributions:

probably easier to reconcile than reducing the fractions to the lowest common denominator – Vic 5/7ths and Doris 2/7ths.

Example: Pete and Angie buy a house for £73,850. Pete contributes £47,264, and Angie contributes £26,586. A declaration of trust, which provides that Pete is entitled to receive 47,264/73,850ths and Angie 26,586/73,850ths of the net proceeds of sale would be precise but a little clumsy. It would be much better to say that Pete will receive 64 per cent and Angie 36 per cent.

Shares of the Sale Price and Shares of the Net Proceeds of Sale

The sale or disposal of a property usually comprises four cash elements:

1 the sale price itself;
2 the amount required to redeem the mortgage;
3 the incidental costs of the sale; and
4 the net proceeds of sale.

A statement in a declaration of trust to the effect that one co-owner will receive 75 per cent of the sale price and the other co-owner will receive 25 per cent of the sale price is, on its own, deficient, because it fails to take into account the co-owners' liability for the payment of the sale costs or for the redemption of the mortgage, if there is one. So, any reference to the sale price should be followed by some indication as to how the deductions are to be apportioned between the co-owners.

'The net proceeds of sale', on the other hand, generally refers to the balance of the sale price remaining after all the deductions have been made. So, in principle, the expression 'net proceeds of sale' should be preceded by some indication as to how the deductions were apportioned between the co-owners. In isolation, a statement that one co-owner will receive three-quarters, and the other co-owner one-quarter, of the net proceeds of sale, assumes that the sale costs and the amount required to redeem the mortgage have already been deducted from the sale price in those proportions.

The acquisition of a property also usually consists of four distinct cash elements:

1 the purchase price;
2 the mortgage advance;
3 the incidental purchase costs; and
4 the co-owners' down payments or cash contributions.

A common mistake is to correlate the co-owners' down payments – their cash contributions towards the purchase price – and their eventual shares of the net proceeds of sale. It is only safe to correlate the co-owners' original contributions to their shares of the net proceeds of sale where:

1 there is no mortgage; or

2 there is a mortgage, but the co-owners intend to contribute towards the mortgage payments in exactly the same proportions as their down payments bear to each other; and

3 they also intend to pay the sale costs in exactly the same proportions as their down payments bear to each other.

It is recommended that wherever there is a mortgage, the shares of the co-owners should be expressed as a fraction or percentage of the sale price, *less* a fraction or percentage of the amount required to redeem the mortgage, *less* a fraction or percentage of the incidental costs of selling the property.

It is important to remember both the purchase costs and the sale costs. Often they are overlooked.

How to Use these Precedents

The following section contains a considerable number of individual clauses and comparatively few complete precedents. The individual clauses can be pieced together, like a jigsaw, to form a complete declaration of trust which, it is envisaged, will assume the following structure, or something similar:

1 commencement and date;[1]
2 recitals (both of fact and intention);[2]
3 trusts;[3]
4 shares (either fixed shares[4] or floating shares[5]);
5 a clause introducing the contingencies.[6] In other words, 'What happens if . . . ?' It is recommended that the provisions for each contingency are set out in a separate Schedule at the end of the declaration;
6 general, miscellaneous clauses;[7]
7 Schedules;[8]
8 attestation clause.[9]

There are two types of complete precedent: the short form and the long form. The short forms tend to combine the recitals, trusts and shares in the context of the co-owners jointly and each co-owner separately.[10] The short forms do not provide for any contingencies, although Schedules setting them out could very easily be appended to any of the short form precedents. The long form precedents are really no more than illustrations of the effect of combining any number of individual clauses.[11]

---

1 Precedent 1 at p 19 below.
2 Precedents 2, 3 and 4 at pp 19 to 21 below.
3 Precedents 5 to 9 at pp 23 to 26 below.
4 Precedents 10 to 14 at pp 27 to 32 below.
5 Precedents 15 to 19 at pp 32 to 42 below.
6 Precedent 20 at p 43 below.
7 Precedents 21 to 31 at pp 45 to 52 below.
8 Precedents 33 to 45 at pp 54 to 73 below.
9 Precedent 32 at p 52 below.

PART 2: PRECEDENTS

Clauses

A Commencement and Recitals

1 COMMENCEMENT AND DATE[1]

THIS DECLARATION OF TRUST is made on (*date*)
BETWEEN 'the co-owners' (1) (*name 1*) of (*address*) ('*name 1*') and (2) (*name 2*) (also) of (*address*) ('*name 2*').

IT IS AGREED AND DECLARED as follows:

---

1 Law of Property Act 1925, s 53(1)(b), states that 'a declaration of trust respecting any land or any interest therein must be manifested and proved by some writing signed by some person who is able to declare such trust or by his will'.

    Although it is imperative that the declaration of trust be in writing, it is not essential that it should be a deed.

    Stamp Act 1891," Sch 1 (as amended), states that a 'declaration of any use or trust of or concerning any property by any writing not being a will, or an instrument chargeable with ad valorem duty as a unit trust instrument' is chargeable to 50p stamp duty.

---

2 RECITALS OF FACT

(a) Purchase of property[1]

Recitals

- The co-owners are the proprietors of (*address*) ('the property').

- Title to the property is registered at the Land Registry under title number (*number*).

- The co-owners purchased the property on (*completion date*).[2]

- The co-owners purchased the property for £

- The incidental costs of purchasing the property came to £

- (*Name 1*) paid £   towards the purchase price and purchase costs.

- (*Name 2*) paid £   towards the purchase price and purchase costs.

- The co-owners obtained an advance of £   from and have mortgaged the property to (*lender*) ('the mortgage').[3]

---

1 For the effect of recitals on the construction of an instrument, see, generally, *Halsbury's Laws of England* (Butterworths) 4th Edn, Vol 12, at paras 1509 to 1515.
2 The completion date is probably preferable to the date on which contracts were exchanged.
3 For separate recitals relating to the mortgage, see **(b)** below.

(b) Mortgage of property[1]

- The mortgage is a repayment mortgage.

- The mortgage is an endowment mortgage.

- (*Name 1*) has taken out an endowment policy on (his)/(her) life with (*insurance company*) numbered (*number*).

- The endowment policy is (assigned to)/(deposited with)/(neither assigned to nor deposited with) (*lender*).

- The co-owners entered into a mortgage indemnity policy for a single premium of £   (which will be added to the mortgage and repaid over the mortgage term) [*OR*] (of which (*name 1*) paid £   and (*name 2*) paid £

---

1 There are so many possible variables that only a small selection has been included here. Perhaps the facts relating to the mortgage are less important than the co-owners' intentions regarding the mortgage payments (see Precedent 4(a) at p 21 below).

(c) The underlying purpose of the trust[1]

- The co-owners purchased the property for their joint occupation.[2]

- The co-owners purchased the property in order to provide a home for themselves and their (respective) children.[3]

- The co-owners purchased the property as an investment.

---

1 The underlying purpose of the trust for sale could be an important consideration in any possible, future application to the court for an order under the Law of Property Act 1925, s 30. The courts have progressively developed this theme since *Re Buchanan-Wollaston's Conveyance* [1939] Ch 738. See, generally, M P Thompson *Co-Ownership* (Sweet & Maxwell, 1988) at pp 54 to 56.
2 The court is more likely to order a sale where no children are involved and the parties

have simply purchased the property for their joint occupation (*Smith v Smith* (1976) 120 SJ 100).

3 'If there were young children, the position would be different. One of the purposes of the trust would no doubt have been to provide a home for them, and whilst that purpose still existed a sale would not generally be ordered' (*Rawlings v Rawlings* [1964] P 398 at 419, per Salmon LJ). See also *Re Evers' Trust* [1980] 1 WLR 1327.

3 RECITALS OF FACT AND INTENTION: THIRD PARTY CONTRIBUTIONS[1]

- (*Name 3*) paid £   towards the purchase price and purchase costs with the intention of acquiring a beneficial interest in the property.

- (*The co-owners*) [OR] (*Name 1* and *name 2*) acknowledge that the payment of £   made by (*name 3*) towards the purchase price and purchase costs was neither a loan nor a gift to them but was made with the express intention that (he)/(she) would acquire a beneficial interest in the property.

1 The law presumes a resulting trust in favour of the third party unless that presumption is rebutted by evidence that the third party intended to make a gift or a loan without acquiring any beneficial interest (*Sekhon v Alissa* [1989] 2 FLR 94).

4 RECITALS OF INTENTION

(a) Mortgage payments[1]

- The co-owners intend to contribute equally towards the mortgage payments.

[OR]

- The co-owners intend that their contributions towards the mortgage payments will be treated as equal, regardless of any inequality that may exist at any time.

[OR]

- (*Name 1*) intends to pay   per cent of the mortgage payments.

- (*Name 2*) intends to pay   per cent of the mortgage payments.

[OR]

- The co-owners intend to contribute towards the mortgage payments in the proportions that their respective incomes bear to each other, or in such other proportions as they may from time to time agree.

1 It is very important to ascertain the co-owners' intentions regarding the mortgage payments. Without any clear intentions in this respect it would be unwise to channel them into holding fixed shares of the net proceeds of sale, but see Precedent 14 at p 31 below. For a definition of 'the mortgage payments', see Precedent 29(f) at p 50 below.

(b) Co-owners intend to marry each other: provisions of this declaration to apply despite marriage[1]

- The co-owners are engaged to be married to each other.[2]

[OR]

- The co-owners expect to marry each other.

[AND]

- The co-owners intend that the provisions of this Declaration of Trust will apply regardless of their marriage and its possible dissolution.[3]

1 **Warning**. The effect of this clause is to turn the declaration of trust into a form of antenuptial agreement, the legal status of which is not recognised in England and Wales. For The Law Society's Family Law Committee's recommendations on the legalisation of antenuptial agreements, see 'Maintenance and Capital Provision on Divorce' The Law Society Legal Practice Directorate (May 1991). See, generally, p 299 below.
2 For provisions relating to the property of engaged couples, or couples who have been engaged to each other within the last three years, see the Law Reform (Miscellaneous Provisions) Act 1970, s 2.
3 For property adjustment orders in connection with divorce proceedings, see the Matrimonial Causes Act 1973, s 24. For the effect of contributions by a spouse in money or money's worth to the improvement of property, see the Matrimonial Proceedings and Property Act 1970, s 37.

B *Trusts*

5 THE STANDARD TRUSTS[1]

Trusts

The co-owners (declare that they):

1 hold the property on trust to sell it;[2]

2 have power to postpone the sale;[3]

3 have powers to deal with the property which are equal to those of a sole beneficial owner;[4]

4 hold the property and its net proceeds of sale[5] (and its net income until sale)[6] in trust for themselves (*and any third party, if appropriate*)[7] as beneficial (joint tenants)[8]/(tenants in common)[9]/(regardless of their actual contributions towards acquiring, financing and improving the property).[10]

---

1 This precedent sets out the standard trust for sale, the power to postpone the sale, the enlargement of the trustees' powers, and states whether the co-owners hold as beneficial joint tenants or beneficial tenants in common. Arguably, the first three subclauses are not essential.

2 A trust for sale is normally imposed whenever two or more persons are entitled to land as beneficial joint tenants or beneficial tenants in common (Law of Property Act 1925, ss 36(1) and 34(2)).

3 Although a trust for sale is technically 'immediate' and 'binding' it is construed as a trust for sale with power to postpone the sale (Law of Property Act 1925, s 25).

4 Trustees for sale have all the powers conferred by statute on a tenant for life and on the trustees of a settlement (Law of Property Act 1925, s 28(1)). However, these powers do not authorise the mortgage of the property in order to raise the purchase price (*Re Suenson-Taylor's Settlement* [1974] 1 WLR 1280). To overcome possible objections from mortgagees it has become customary to include a clause enlarging the trustees' powers. Admittedly, where the trustees are also the persons who are absolutely and beneficially entitled to the property, a specific extension of their powers may be considered unnecessary. The Law Commission has recommended that trustees for sale should be given all the powers over the land of an absolute owner (Law Com Working Paper No 94 'Trusts of Land' (1986), at para 7.5).

5 The Law of Property Act 1925, s 35, when defining 'the statutory trusts', refers to 'the net proceeds of sale, after payment of costs' and to 'the net rents and profits until sale after payment of rates, taxes, costs of insurance, repairs, and other outgoings'. The statutory definition of 'the net proceeds of sale' may be considered vague or unsatisfactory, and it might be considered necessary to provide an alternative definition in the declaration of trust. See Precedent 29 (d) at p 50 below.

6 The phrase 'the net income until sale' should be deleted if the net proceeds of sale and the net income until sale are enjoyed in differing shares. See Precedent 21 at p 45 below.

7 The name of anyone else who is beneficially interested should be inserted, for example someone who has contributed to the purchase price with the intention of acquiring a beneficial interest, rather than with the intention of making a gift or a loan.

8 'Joint tenants' and 'tenants in common' are alternatives. One must be deleted. See *Joyce v Barker Bros* (1980) *The Times*, February 26, where a conveyance stated that the purchasers were joint tenants and tenants in common.

9 This precedent assumes that in the case of a beneficial tenancy in common the shares will be set out in a separate clause. Sometimes the method of calculating the shares is lengthy and complex, and in such cases it may be preferable to separate the clauses relating to the shares and the trusts. If, however, the shares are simple and straightforward (for example, 'in equal shares') they could be dealt with in this clause, without the need for a separate clause.

10 The words 'regardless of their actual contributions . . . etc' are not essential. They are unnecessary if the co-owners hold floating shares. Their inclusion may be considered useful where one co-owner is likely to confer a gratuitous benefit on the other.

6 CO-OWNERS TO BE JOINT TENANTS UNTIL SEVERANCE AND TENANTS IN COMMON IN UNEQUAL SHARES AFTER SEVERANCE[1]

Trusts[2]

The co-owners (declare that they):

1 hold the property on trust to sell it;

2 have power to postpone the sale;

3 have powers to deal with the property which are equal to those of a sole beneficial owner;

4 hold the property and its net proceeds of sale and its net income until sale in trust for themselves as beneficial joint tenants until the beneficial joint tenancy is severed (regardless of their actual contributions towards acquiring, financing and improving the property);[3]

5 will hold the property and its net proceeds of sale (and its net income until sale)[4] in trust for themselves as beneficial tenants in common in the shares set out below[5] after the beneficial joint tenancy has been severed.

---

1 This is, presumably, the sort of declaration of trust Slade LJ had in mind when he said that 'it would no doubt be possible for a trust in terms to provide that the beneficial interests of two parties should be equivalent to those of joint tenants unless and until severance occurred, but that in the event of severance their interests should be otherwise than in equal shares' (*Goodman v Gallant* [1986] 1 FLR 513 at 525C).

2 See, generally, the footnotes to Precedent 5 above.

3 See Precedent 5, footnote 10 above.

4 See Precedent 5, footnote 6 above.

5 These shares could be fixed or floating.

7 CO-OWNERS TO BE TENANTS IN COMMON UNTIL THEIR MARRIAGE AND SUBSEQUENTLY JOINT TENANTS[1]

Trusts[2]

The co-owners (declare that they):

1 hold the property on trust to sell it;

2 have power to postpone the sale;

3 have powers to deal with the property which are equal to those of a sole beneficial owner;

4 hold the property and its net proceeds of sale (and its net income until sale)[3] in trust for themselves as beneficial tenants in common (in the shares set out below)[4] until the solemnisation of their intended marriage;

5 will hold the property and its net proceeds of sale and its net income until sale in trust for themselves as beneficial joint tenants after their intended marriage has been solemnised (regardless of their actual contributions towards acquiring, financing and improving the property).[5]

---

1 The effect of the inheritance tax exemptions must be considered, ie transfers between spouses, the Inheritance Tax Act 1984, s 18, and gifts in consideration of marriage (ibid, s 22). Note also the effect of the Insolvency Act 1986, s 339, in respect of transactions at an undervalue.

2 See, generally, the footnotes to Precedent 5 at p 23 above.

3 See the comments in Precedent 5, footnote 6 at p 24 above.

4 The shares could be fixed or floating. If the co-owners hold 'in equal shares' it would be preferable to insert those words here instead of 'in the shares set out below', thus avoiding the need for an additional clause.

5 See Precedent 5, footnote 10 at p 24 above.

---

8 SHARES OF THE NET PROCEEDS OF SALE DIFFER FROM THOSE OF THE NET INCOME UNTIL SALE

Trusts[1]

The co-owners (declare that they):

1 hold the property on trust to sell it;

2 have power to postpone the sale;

3 have powers to deal with the property which are equal to those of a sole beneficial owner;

4 hold the net proceeds of sale in trust for themselves as beneficial tenants in

common (in the shares set out in Clause   ) (regardless of their actual contributions towards acquiring, financing and improving the property);

5 hold the net income until sale in trust for themselves as beneficial tenants in common (in the shares set out in Clause   )[2] regardless of the manner in which the net proceeds of sale will be divided between them.

---

1 See, generally, the footnotes to Precedent 5 at p 23 above.
2 See Precedent 21 at p 45 below.

---

9 DEFERRED TRUST FOR SALE: '*MESHER*' AND '*MARTIN*'-TYPE TRUSTS[1]

Trusts

The co-owners (declare that they):

1 hold the property on trust to sell it;

2 have powers to deal with the property which are equal to those of a sole beneficial owner;

3 have power to postpone the sale;

4 will postpone the sale, unless they agree otherwise or unless the court orders otherwise, until the first of these events occurs:

    4.1 (*child's name*) [OR] (the youngest child of the family) attains the age of 18 or completes (his)/(her)/(his or her) full-time secondary education, whichever is later; or

    4.2 the co-owner with whom (*child's name*) [OR] (the youngest child of the family) lives in the property marries or cohabits;[2]

5 hold the property and its net proceeds of sale (and its net income until sale) in trust for themselves as beneficial tenants in common in the shares set out below.

---

1 An order of the court whereby the sale of a matrimonial home is postponed until the youngest child of the family is aged 18, or some other age, is usually known as a '*Mesher* Order' (*Mesher v Mesher* [1980] 1 All ER 126). Although it was not reported until 1980, the case was, in fact, heard by the Court of Appeal on 12 February 1973. An order of the court whereby the sale is postponed until the wife dies, remarries or cohabits, is usually known as a '*Martin* Order' (*Martin v Martin* [1978] Fam 12). For a discussion of 'the rise and fall of the *Mesher* Order' and for consideration as to where it might still provide the best solution, see *Clutton v Clutton* [1991] 1 All ER 340 at 345, per Lloyd LJ.
2 The word 'cohabits' tends to defy definition (see p 188 below and Chapter 4, Precedent 31 at p 217 below).

C Shares

10 FIXED SHARES: EXPRESSED AS FRACTIONS OR PERCENTAGES OF THE NET PROCEEDS OF SALE[1]

Shares

When the property is sold (*name 1*) will receive (*fraction or percentage*)[2] of the net proceeds of sale and (*name 2*) will receive (*fraction or percentage*) of the net proceeds of sale.[3]

---

1 **Warning**. Care should be taken when expressing the co-owners' shares as fractions or percentages of the net proceeds of sale. It is only safe to do so if: (a) there is no mortgage; or (b) they contribute to the mortgage payments in fractions or percentages which are identical to their respective entitlements out of the net proceeds of sale; and (c) they intend to pay the sale costs in the same fractions or percentages.

Example
Karen and Simon bought a house for £88,500. The purchase costs amounted to £1,500. Karen contributed £30,000, Simon contributed £10,000. They obtained a mortgage advance of £50,000 and contributed equally to the mortgage payments. They intended to share the sale costs equally. Five years later they sold the house for £130,000. The sale costs amounted to £4,000. The amount required to redeem the mortgage was £46,000. The net proceeds of sale came to £80,000. Who got what?

Wrong solution
Karen and Simon had executed a declaration of trust which said that Karen would receive 75 per cent of the net proceeds of sale and Simon would receive 25 per cent. These percentages reflected their original contributions to the purchase price (Karen £30,000 and Simon £10,000). It was a mistake to correlate their contributions to their entitlements from the net proceeds of sale because these percentages fail to take into account the shared responsibility for the mortgage payments and the sale costs. Karen ended up with £60,000, and Simon £20,000.

Wrong solution
Karen and Simon executed a declaration of trust which stated that Karen would receive 55/90ths of the net proceeds of sale and Simon would receive 35/90ths. In each case the denominator (90) represents £90,000 (the purchase price of £88,500 plus the purchase costs of £1,500). In Karen's case the numerator (55) represents £55,000 (her original contribution of £30,000 plus £25,000, half of the mortgage advance). In Simon's case, the numerator (35) represents £10,000 plus £25,000. On this basis, Karen ended up with £48,889 and Simon with £31,111.
    This formula will only work if the mortgage debt is repaid over its full term. Say, for example, Karen and Simon had split up shortly after they bought the house, and had sold it for £93,000. The sale costs came to £3,000, and the amount required to redeem the mortgage was the same as the original advance, £50,000. The net proceeds of sale would have been £40,000 and, in effect, the couple would be back to square one in terms of the

combined total of their original contributions. The application of this formula would mean that Karen would receive £24,444 and Simon £15,556.

Suggested solution

It would have been better if Karen and Simon had executed a declaration of trust which stated that Karen would receive 55/90ths of the sale price, *less* half of the amount required to redeem the mortgage, *less* half of the sale costs. Simon would receive 35/90ths of the sale price *less* half of the amount required to redeem the mortgage, *less* half of the sale costs. On this basis Karen would receive (£79,444 − £23,000 − £2,000) = £54,444. Simon would receive (£50,556 − £23,000 − £2,000) = £25,556.

Even this solution is not perfect. Problems would arise if the couple failed to pay the mortgage in equal shares, or if only one of them contributed towards repairs and improvements to the property.

2 In the case of fractions, the combined total of the numerators must be the same as the denominator. In the case of percentages, the combined total must be 100.

3 It may be considered prudent to define 'net proceeds of sale' (see Precedent 29(d) at p 50 below).

---

11 FIXED SHARES: EXPRESSED AS A FIXED SHARE OF THE SALE PRICE, LESS A FIXED SHARE OF THE AMOUNT REQUIRED TO REDEEM THE MORTGAGE, LESS A FIXED SHARE OF THE SALE COSTS[1]

Shares

When the property is sold:

1 (*name 1*) will receive (*fraction or percentage*)[2] of the sale price[3] less:

  1.1 (*fraction or percentage*)[4] of the amount required to redeem the mortgage;[5] and

  1.2 (*fraction or percentage*)[6] of the incidental costs of selling the property;

2 (*name 2*) will receive (*fraction or percentage*)[2] of the sale price[3] less:

  2.1 (*fraction or percentage*)[4] of the amount required to redeem the mortgage;[5] and

  2.2 (*fraction or percentage*)[6] of the incidental costs of selling the property;

3 if the total amount to be deducted from one co-owner's share of the sale price exceeds the value of that share then the excess will be paid from the other co-owner's share.[7]

---

1 For an illustration of how this formula works, see the suggested solution in Precedent 10, above.

2 The denominator will, presumably, represent the purchase price plus the purchase costs. The numerator will represent the co-owner's original contribution, plus the share of the mortgage debt for which he or she is assuming responsibility.

3 For a definition of 'the sale price', see Precedent 29(a) at p 49 below.

4 The denominator will, presumably, represent the mortgage advance itself; and the

numerator will represent the extent to which the co-owner assumes responsibility for the mortgage payments.

5 For a definition of 'the amount required to redeem the mortgage', see Precedent 29(b) at p 49 below.

6 If the co-owners intend to share the sale costs equally, insert one half or 50 per cent, as the case may be.

7 This subclause provides for the possibility that the property has gone down in value, or the mortgage debt exceeds the market value. One co-owner will be liable for the excess of the other co-owner's debt.

Example

Rick and Samantha bought a house for £57,000. The purchase costs came to £1,000. Rick contributed £4,000 and Samantha contributed £10,000. They took out a mortgage of £44,000. Rick assumed responsibility for three-quarters of the mortgage payments and Samantha assumed responsibility for one-quarter of the mortgage payments. Two years later they sold the house for £48,000. The amount required to redeem the mortgage was £43,500. The sale costs came to £1,500 and the net proceeds of sale were £3,000. Who got what?

They had signed a declaration of trust which said that Rick would receive 37/58ths of the sale price *less* three-quarters of the amount required to redeem the mortgage, *less* one half of the sale costs. It said that Samantha would receive 21/58ths of the sale price, *less* one quarter of the amount required to redeem the mortgage, *less* one half of the sale costs.

On that basis Rick would receive (£30,620−£32,625−£750). The result is a minus sum: −£2,755. Samantha would receive (£17,380−£10,875−£750) = £5,755.

Their declaration of trust also stated that if the total amount to be deducted from one co-owner's share of the sale price exceeded the value of that share, then the excess would be paid from the other co-owner's share. So Samantha paid Rick's shortfall of £2,755, and was entitled to retain all of the net proceeds of sale (£3,000).

---

12 FIXED SHARES: REFUND OF ORIGINAL CONTRIBUTIONS: PROVISION FOR ABATEMENT: FIXED SHARES OF THE BALANCE OF THE NET PROCEEDS OF SALE[1]

Shares

When the property is sold:

1 (*name 1*) will receive a refund of (his)/(her) original contribution of £   towards the purchase price and the purchase costs;

2 (*name 2*) will receive a refund of (his)/(her) original contribution of £   towards the purchase price and the purchase costs;

3 if the net proceeds of sale are insufficient to refund the co-owners' original contributions fully, the contributions will abate (in the proportions that they bear to each other)[2] [*OR*] (equally);

4 when the original contributions have been refunded the remaining balance of the net proceeds of sale will be divided as to (*fraction or percentage*)[3] for (*name 1*) and (*fraction or percentage*)[3] for (*name 2*).

1 For a variation of this formula, see Precedent 13 below.

Example

Karen and Simon bought a house for £88,500. The purchase costs amounted to £1,500. Karen contributed £30,000 and Simon contributed £10,000. They obtained a mortgage advance of £50,000 and contributed equally to the mortgage payments. They agreed to share the sale costs equally. Five years later they sold the house for £130,000. The sale costs totalled £4,000. The amount required to redeem the mortgage was £46,000. The net proceeds of sale were £80,000. Who got what?

When they bought the house, Karen and Simon executed a declaration of trust which said that each of them would get back his or her original contribution, and that the balance of the net proceeds of sale would be divided equally between them. Therefore, Karen was refunded her £30,000. Simon was refunded his £10,000. The balance of the net proceeds (£40,000) was divided equally between them. Karen received, in total, £50,000 and Simon received £30,000.

The problem with applying this formula is more noticeable in Karen's case. Her original contribution has remained stationary, or stagnated. The value of the property has increased by about 47 per cent, and in real terms her original contribution of £30,000 should have grown to roughly £44,000.

Compare the suggested solution in Precedent 10, footnote 1 at p 27 above where the facts are identical and the example in the footnote to Precedent 13 below, where the original contribution is credited with interest.

2 A provision for abatement is necessary to cover any possible downturn in property values.

Example

The facts are similar to those in footnote 1 above, except that the property was sold for £76,000. The amount required to redeem the mortgage was £46,000. The sale costs came to £2,000 and the net proceeds of sale were £28,000, representing an overall loss of £12,000.

The declaration of trust provided that the original contributions would abate in the proportions that they bear to each other. So, Karen's original contribution of £30,000 was reduced to £21,000; and Simon's original contribution of £10,000 was reduced to £7,000.

If the declaration of trust had stated that their original contributions would abate equally, Karen would have received £24,000, and Simon would have ended up with £4,000. In other words, their net loss of £12,000 would have been shared by them equally.

3 The denominator will, presumably, represent the mortgage debt and the sale costs. The numerator will reflect the extent to which each co-owner assumes responsibility for the mortgage and the sale costs.

---

13 FIXED SHARES: REFUND OF ORIGINAL CONTRIBUTIONS PLUS INTEREST: PROVISION FOR ABATEMENT: FIXED SHARES OF THE BALANCE OF THE NET PROCEEDS OF SALE[1]

Shares

When the property is sold:

1 (*name 1*) will receive a refund of (his)/(her) original contribution of

£   towards the purchase price and the purchase costs *plus* (simple) interest at a rate of (7) per cent per year from the date (on which the purchase of the property was completed) [*OR*] (of this Declaration of Trust) to the date on which the refund of the contribution is made;

2 (*name 2*) will receive a refund of (his)/(her) original contribution of £   towards the purchase price and the purchase costs *plus* (simple) interest at a rate of (7) per cent per year from the date (on which the purchase of the property was completed) [*OR*] (of this Declaration of Trust) to the date on which the refund of the contribution is made;

3 if the net proceeds of sale are insufficient to refund the co-owners' original contributions plus interest, the original contributions and the interest on them will abate (in the proportions that they bear to each other) [*OR*] (equally);

4 subject to the above, the remaining balance of the net proceeds of sale will be divided as to (*fraction or percentage*) for (*name 1*) and (*fraction or percentage*) for (*name 2*).

---

1 See the footnotes to Precedent 12 above.

Example

The facts are identical to those in the example given in Precedent 12, footnote 1 above, except that Karen and Simon's declaration of trust said that they would be entitled to simple interest at seven per cent a year. Karen receives her original contribution of £30,000, plus £10,500 in interest, plus £13,000 (half of the remaining balance); a total of £53,500. Simon receives a total of £26,500 (his contribution of £10,000, plus £3,500 in interest, plus £13,000 (half the remaining balance)).

---

14 FIXED SHARES: REFUND OF ORIGINAL CONTRIBUTION EXPRESSED AS A FRACTION OR PERCENTAGE OF THE SALE PRICE: ALTERNATIVE PROVISIONS FOR THE DIVISION OF THE BALANCE OF THE NET PROCEEDS OF SALE[1]

Shares

When the property is sold:

1 (*name 1*) will receive (*fraction or percentage*)[2] of the sale price, representing the return on (his)/(her) original contribution of £   towards the purchase price and purchase costs;

2 (*name 2*) will receive (*fraction or percentage*)[2] of the sale price, representing the return on (his)/(her) original contribution of £   towards the purchase price and purchase costs;

3 the amount required to redeem the mortgage will be paid from the remaining (*fraction or percentage*)[3] of the sale price ('the mortgage share');

4 if the amount required to redeem the mortgage exceeds the mortgage share, the excess will be paid by the co-owners (in equal shares) [OR] (as to   per cent by (*name 1*) and   per cent by (*name 2*)); [OR] (in the proportions that each of them has contributed towards the mortgage payments);[4]

5 subject to the above, the remaining balance of the mortgage share will be divided between the co-owners (in equal shares) [OR] as to   per cent for (*name 1*) and   per cent for (*name 2*)) [OR] (in the proportions that each of them has contributed towards the mortgage payments);[4]

6 the co-owners will pay the incidental costs of selling the property (in equal shares) [OR] as to   per cent by (*name 1*) and   per cent by (*name 2*)) [OR] (in the proportions that their respective shares of the rest of the net proceeds of sale bear to each other).

---

1 This is probably the most satisfactory formula for expressing fixed shares. In principle, it is the same as the formula in Precedent 11 at p 28 above. However, it is more flexible than Precedent 11 because it addresses the possibility that, when they purchase, the co-owners may have no definite plans as to the extent to which each of them will assume responsibility for the mortgage payments.

2 The numerator should represent the co-owner's contribution: the denominator should represent the purchase price plus the purchase costs.

3 The numerator should represent the mortgage advance: the denominator should represent the purchase price plus the purchase costs. The fractions or percentages in subclauses 1, 2 and 3 should come to 100 per cent of the purchase price and purchase costs.

4 The words 'in the proportions that each of them has contributed towards the mortgage payments' creates floating shares. In other words, those proportions will not be finally ascertained until the trust for sale comes to an end.

---

15 FLOATING SHARES: IN PROPORTION TO THE CONTRIBUTIONS MADE BY EACH CO-OWNER THROUGHOUT THE DURATION OF THE TRUST FOR SALE[1]

Shares

When the property is sold the net proceeds of sale[2] will be divided between the co-owners in proportion to (the extent to which the change in the value of the property is attributable to)[3] the contributions made by each of them towards the:

1 purchase price;
2 incidental costs of the purchase;
3 payment of mortgage interest;
4 payment of mortgage endowment policy premiums;
5 repayment of mortgage capital;
6 cost of repairs and improvements to the property;

7 payment of interest and repayment of capital on further advances and loans taken out for repairs and improvements to the property; (and

8 incidental costs of selling the property).[4]

---

1 For the distinction between fixed shares and floating shares, see p 11 above. For a discussion of some of the advantages and disadvantages of floating shares, see p 14 above.

2 For a definition of 'the net proceeds of sale', see Precedent 29(d) at p 50 below.

3 The words in brackets should be deleted if the shares are to be calculated by the addition of the contributions and the apportionment of the net proceeds of sale pro rata (see Precedent 16 below). The words in brackets must be included if the shares are to be calculated in accordance with the formulae set out in Precedents 18(a) (narrative form), and 18(b) (tabular form) at pp 35 and 38 below.

4 For a definition of 'the incidental costs of selling the property', see Precedent 29(c) at p 50 below. The sale costs should only be included here if the co-owners intend to pay the sale costs in the proportions that their respective shares bear to each other. If the co-owners intend to pay the sale costs in equal shares, or in some other fixed proportions, there should be included a separate clause to this effect (see Precedent 27 at p 48 below).

Other items could be included in this list, for example mortgage guarantee premiums, mortgage protection policy premiums, buildings insurance premiums, rent, rentcharge, ground rent, service charges, etc.

---

16 FLOATING SHARES: CALCULATION OF THE SHARES: ADDITION OF CONTRIBUTIONS AND APPORTIONMENT OF NET PROCEEDS OF SALE PRO RATA[1]

Calculation of shares

The share of the net proceeds of sale to which each co-owner is entitled will be calculated by:

1 adding together his or her contributions to produce 'the individual contribution'; and then

2 adding together (both)/(all) of the co-owners' individual contributions to produce 'the combined contributions'; and then

3 dividing the net proceeds of sale (plus the incidental costs of selling the property)[2] by the combined contributions to produce 'the dividend'; and finally

4 multiplying the individual contribution by the dividend to produce the share.

Warning. This method of calculating floating shares does not take into account the extent to which the change in the value of the property can be attributed to each co-owner's lump sum contributions and mortgage-related contributions. If the change in value is to be taken into account, Precedents 18(a) and 18(b) can be used instead (see p 35 to 41 below). Although this method of calculating the shares is far simpler than the formulae, it can, in certain circumstances, produce a perverse result. For an illustration, see the example in footnote 1 to Precedent 18(a) at p 37 below.

1 As there is more than one method of calculating floating shares, it is sensible to set out clearly the manner in which the shares will be calculated.

Example

Robin and Susie bought a bungalow for £165,000. The purchase costs came to £2,500. Robin paid £87,500 and Susie paid £18,000. They took out a mortgage for £62,000. They lived together for three years. Robin paid £15,000 towards the mortgage. Susie paid £5,000 towards the mortgage. They carried out improvements which cost £20,000. Susie paid £12,000 in cash towards the improvements but Robin paid nothing in cash towards the improvements. They obtained a loan of £8,000 for the improvements. Robin paid £1,500 on the loan and Susie paid £500. They sold the bungalow for £197,000. The amount required to redeem the mortgage was £60,000. The amount required to repay the loan was £7,500. The sale costs came to £5,000 and the net proceeds of sale were £124,500. Who got what?

Suggested solution

Robin and Susie's individual contributions were:

	Robin	Susie
Purchase price and costs	87,500	18,000
Mortgage payments	15,000	5,000
Improvements: cash	0	12,000
Loan payments	1,500	500
	£104,000	£35,500

The method of calculating Robin's share is as follows:

(a) his individual contribution is £104,000;
(b) the combined contributions are £139,500;
(c) the net proceeds of sale (£124,500) are divided by the combined contributions to produce a dividend of 0.89247;
(d) Robin's individual contribution is multiplied by the dividend to produce his share, which is £92,817.

Applying the same method, Susie's share is £31,683. Incidentally, had the formulae in Precedent 18 at pp 35–41 below been used on this occasion, Robin would have been better off by £74.

2 The sale costs should only be included if their payment is to be borne pro rata to the shares of the rest of the net proceeds of sale.

---

17 FLOATING SHARES: CALCULATION OF THE SHARES:[1] INTRODUCTORY CLAUSE TO THE FORMULAE[2]

Calculation of shares

The share of the net proceeds of sale to which each co-owner is entitled will be calculated in accordance with the provisions of Schedule (*number*).

---

1 It is assumed that this Clause would be immediately preceded by wording identical or similar to that contained in Precedent 15 at p 32 above.

2 The formulae contained in Precedent 18 (see below) are quite complicated. It may be considered preferable to set them out in a separate Schedule, rather than include them in the main body of the declaration of trust.

18 FLOATING SHARES: FORMULAE FOR CALCULATING FLOATING SHARES[1]

(a) Narrative form

<u>Schedule</u> (*number*)

1 The share of the net proceeds of sale to which each co-owner is entitled ('share') before the deduction of his or her share of the incidental costs of selling the property will be calculated by adding together his or her lump sum contributions and his or her mortgage-related contributions.

Lump sum contributions

2 Each co-owner's lump sum contributions ('lump sum') will be calculated by applying the following formula.

$$\frac{\text{Individual payments}}{\text{purchase price} + \text{improvements}} \times \text{sale price} = \text{lump sum}$$

WHERE:

2.1 *Individual payments* is the total of the individual co-owner's lump sum payments towards:

(a) the purchase price; and
(b) the incidental costs of purchasing the property; and
(c) repairs and improvements to the property.

2.2 *Purchase price* is the total of:

(a) (both)/(all) of the co-owners' lump sum payments towards the purchase price; and
(b) (both)/(all) of the co-owners' lump sum payments towards the incidental costs of purchasing the property; and
(c) the mortgage advance.

2.3 *Improvements* is the total of:

(a) (both)/(all) of the co-owners' lump sum payments towards repairs and improvements to the property; and
(b) all further mortgage advances and all loans, whether secured or unsecured, taken out for the purpose of carrying out repairs and improvements to the property.

2.4 *Sale price* is the gross sale price of the property before any deductions.

Mortgage-related contributions

3 Each co-owner's mortgage-related contributions ('mortgage related contribution') will be calculated by applying the following formulae.

   3.1 *First* [2(a)]

$$\frac{\text{loans}}{\text{purchase price} + \text{improvements}} \times \text{sale price} = \text{gross mortgage share}$$

   WHERE:

      3.1.1 *Loans* is the total of:

         (a) the mortgage advance; and
         (b) all further mortgage advances; and
         (c) all loans taken out for the purpose of carrying out repairs and improvements to the property; and
         (d) all improvement grants.

      3.1.2 *Purchase price* has the same meaning as it has in para 2.2 above.

      3.1.3 *Improvements* has the same meaning as it has in para 2.3 above.

      3.1.4 *Sale price* has the same meaning as it has in para 2.4 above.

      3.1.5 *Gross mortgage share* represents the extent to which the change in the value of the property can be attributed to the sums of money provided by way of mortgages, loans and grants.

   3.2 *Second*

$$\text{gross mortgage share} - \text{redemption} = \text{net mortgage share}$$

   WHERE:

      3.2.1 *Redemption* is the total amount required to redeem or repay:

         (a) the mortgage advance; and
         (b) all further mortgage advances; and
         (c) all loans taken out for the purpose of carrying out repairs and improvements to the property; and
         (d) all improvement grants.

   3.3 *Third* [2(b)]

$$\frac{\text{individual mortgage payments}}{\text{combined mortgage payments}} \times \text{net mortgage share} = \text{mortgage related contribution}$$

   WHERE:

      3.3.1 *Individual mortgage payments* is the total of each individual co-owner's contributions towards the repayment or payment of capital, interest and premiums on:

(a) the mortgage advance; and
(b) all mortgage-linked insurance policies; and
(c) all further mortgage advances; and
(d) all loans taken out for the purpose of carrying out repairs and improvements to the property; and
(e) all improvement grants.

3.3.2 *Combined mortgage payments* is the total of (both)/(all) of the co-owners' individual mortgage payments.

The share[2(c)]

4 Lump sum + mortgage related contribution = share

Sale costs

5 The incidental costs of selling the property will be paid by the co-owners (in equal shares) [OR] (in the proportions that each share bears to the other share or shares).

---

1 The formulae set out in this Precedent are identical to those set out in Precedent 18(b) below. The only difference is the style. Here they are described in narrative form; in Precedent 18(b) they appear in tabular form.

The formulae seek to identify and isolate the extent to which any change in the value of the property can be attributed to the lump sums provided by each co-owner and to the lump sum which they have borrowed on a mortgage. The change in value of the share purchased by the mortgage is then apportioned between the co-owners according to the sums which each has paid towards the mortgage.

In most cases, the application of these formulae will produce a more equitable result than the other method of calculating floating shares: namely the simple addition of the contributions, followed by an apportionment of the net proceeds of sale pro rata (Precedent 16 at p 33 above). The following example is an illustration.

Example
Tim and Claire bought a flat for £44,000. The purchase costs came to £1,000. Claire paid £4,000. Tim paid £1,000. They took out a mortgage for £40,000 and lived together for three and a half years. Tim paid £11,000 in mortgage payments and Claire paid £2,000 in mortgage payments. They sold the flat for £50,000. The amount required to redeem the mortgage was £39,000. The sale costs were £2,000 and the net proceeds of sale were £9,000. Who got what?

Addition of contributions: apportionment of net proceeds pro rata (wrong solution)
If Tim and Claire had executed a declaration of trust which contained the method of calculating floating shares set out in Precedent 16 (see p 33 above), the result would have been as follows.

Tim's contributions came to £12,000 overall – £1,000 towards the purchase and £11,000 towards the mortgage.

Claire's contributions came to £6,000 overall – £4,000 towards the purchase and £2,000 towards the mortgage.

The net proceeds of sale (£9,000) would be divided between them in the ratio 12:6.

Tim would get £6,000. Claire would get £3,000. Tim would receive twice as much as Claire. Even though the property has increased in value, Claire seems to have lost £1,000 on her original contribution of £4,000.

Suggested Solution: Applying the formulae

The result would have been totally different if these formulae had been applied, because they would have separated Tim's and Claire's lump sum contributions from their mortgage-related contributions.

The property went up in value, by roughly 11 per cent, from £45,000 (including purchase costs) to £50,000.

Tim's lump sum contribution of £1,000 increased by the same percentage to £1,111. Claire's lump sum contribution of £4,000 increased to £4,444.

The share of the property bought by the mortgage advance of £40,000 increased in value to £44,445. This is called the 'gross mortgage share'. By deducting from the gross mortgage share the amount required to redeem the mortgage (£39,000) we arrive at the 'net mortgage share' of £5,445. By virtue of his mortgage-related contributions, Tim is entitled to 11/13ths of the net mortgage share (£4,607). Claire is entitled to 2/13ths of the net mortgage share (£838). Tim's lump sum contribution (£1,111) and mortgage-related contribution (£4,607) are added to produce £5,718. Claire's lump sum contribution (£4,444) and mortgage-related contribution (£838) are added to produce £5,282. The sale costs (£2,000) are paid pro rata. Tim £1,040, Claire £960. Tim ends up with £4,678. Claire ends up with £4,322.

Warning. The application of these formulae could cause hardship if:

(a) a large share of the property is bought by the mortgage; and
(b) one co-owner contributes substantially more than the other towards the mortgage payments; and
(c) the property goes down in value.

2 To double-check the accuracy of the calculations at this stage:

(a) the co-owners' combined lump sum contributions plus the gross mortgage share should be the same as the sale price;
(b) the co-owners' combined mortgage-related contributions should be the same as the net mortgage share in para 3.2 above;
(c) the combined total of both or all shares should be the same as the net proceeds of sale plus the sale costs.

Note: A calculator is necessary. The formulae require exact figures. Approximate figures will not do.

(b) Tabular form[1]

Calculation of shares

The share of the net proceeds of sale to which each co-owner is entitled will be calculated by:

1 completing the record of contributions set out in the (first) Schedule; and then

2 applying the formulae set out in the (second) Schedule.

---

1 For the two Schedules containing the record of contributions and the formulae, see below. The formulae are the same as those expressed in narrative form in Precedent 18(a) above. They identify the extent to which each co-owner's lump sum contributions and mortgage-related contributions affect the value of the property.

FIRST SCHEDULE
RECORD OF CONTRIBUTIONS

PURCHASE		£	
NAME 1	Contribution to purchase price and costs		A
NAME 2	Contribution to purchase price and costs		B
Mortgage advance			C
Gross purchase price	[A + B + C]		D
IMPROVEMENTS			
NAME 1	Contributions		E
NAME 2	Contributions		F
Improvement grant(s) and further mortgage advance(s) and loan(s) taken out for improvements			G
Combined cost of improvements	[E + F + G]		H
MORTGAGE PAYMENTS			
NAME 1	Contributions		I
NAME 2	Contributions		J
Combined contributions	[I + J]		K
SALE			
Sale price (or, if one co-owner is selling his/her share in the property to the other, the agreed current market value of the whole property)			L
Mortgage redemption and repayment of any improvement grant and loan taken out for improvements			M
Sale costs: estate agency/legal fees/apportionments of outgoings			N
Net proceeds of sale	[L − (M + N)]		O

SECOND SCHEDULE

CALCULATION OF SHARES

STAGE ONE: In which the change in the value of the property is apportioned between the contributions towards the purchase and improvement of the property made by the co-owners individually and by virtue of the mortgage advance(s)			
NAME 1	$\dfrac{A + E}{D + H} \times L =$		P
NAME 2	$\dfrac{B + F}{D + H} \times L =$		Q
Mortgage(s)	$\dfrac{C + G}{D + H} \times L =$		R
Sale price	$[P + Q + R]$		L

STAGE TWO: In which the increase or reduction in the value of the property attributable to the amount(s) provided by way of the mortgage(s) is apportioned between the co-owners according to their respective contributions towards repayment of the mortgage(s)			
$R - M$			S
NAME 1	$\dfrac{I}{K} \times S =$		T
NAME 2	$\dfrac{J}{K} \times S =$		U

STAGE THREE: In which the co-owners' entitlements from stages one and two are added together			
NAME 1	$P + T$		V
NAME 2	$Q + U$		W
Net proceeds of sale + sale costs $[O + N]$			X

STAGE FOUR: In which the sale costs are apportioned between the co-owners in accordance with their entitlements in stage three			
NAME 1	$\dfrac{V}{X \times N}$		Y
NAME 2	$\dfrac{W}{X \times N}$		Z
Sale costs			N

STAGE FIVE: In which the co-owners' shares of the net proceeds of sale are ascertained			
NAME 1	V – Y		
NAME 2	W – Z		
Net proceeds of sale			**O**

19 FIXED SHARES OR FLOATING SHARES

(a) The average of two or more methods of calculating the shares[1]

Shares

When the property is sold:

1 (*name 1*) will receive the *average* of the sums to which (he)/(she) is entitled in Schedules (*number*) and (*number*) to this Declaration of Trust;
2 (*name 2*) will receive the *average* of the sums to which (he)/(she) is entitled in Schedules (*number*) and (*number*) to this Declaration of Trust.

---

1 If the average of two or more methods of calculating the shares is to be used, it is probably better to set out the different methods of calculation in separate Schedules. A single clause that attempted to describe various different methods would, almost certainly, be difficult to understand and would probably be very lengthy.

(b) Supplemental clause providing for the gradual equalisation of the shares[1]

Gradual Equalisation of Shares[2]

1 The co-owners intend that on the (seventh)[3] anniversary of the date (on which the purchase of the property was completed) [*OR*] (of this Declaration of Trust) their respective shares of the net proceeds of sale will become and remain equal, and to that intent the following provisions will apply.

2 In this Clause:

2.1 'the larger share' means the share of the co-owner who is entitled to the larger share of the net proceeds of sale;[4]
2.2 'the smaller share' means the share of the co-owner who is entitled to the smaller share of the net proceeds of sale; and
2.3 'the difference' means the difference between the larger share and the smaller share on the date when the property is sold or either share is realised.

3 For each complete year that has elapsed since the date (on which the purchase of the property was completed) [OR] (of this Declaration of Trust) the larger share will decrease by (1/14th)[5] of the difference and the smaller share will increase by (1/14th)[5] of the difference.

4 For the avoidance of doubt:

    4.1 no apportionment will be made in respect of any period of less than a year;[6]

    4.2 the calculations in this Clause will cease to have effect immediately after the (seventh)[3] anniversary of the date (on which the purchase of the property was completed) [OR] (of this Declaration of Trust); and

    4.3 if the co-owners separate, the calculations in this Clause will apply only in respect of each complete year that has elapsed since the date (on which the purchase of the property was completed) [OR] (of this Declaration of Trust) and the date on which the co-owners separated.[6]

---

1 This clause could apply equally to fixed shares and floating shares. It is recommended that this Clause should immediately follow the Clause setting out the respective shares.

2 The concept is quite simple. The co-owners 'split the difference' over a given period. Inheritance tax implications should be considered. There is certainly a transfer of value, but it is not entirely clear whether there is one transfer of value, or a series of transfers. The provisions of the Insolvency Act 1986, s 339, which relate to transactions at an undervalue, should also be considered.

3 Insert the appropriate anniversary. The concept of the gradual equalisation of assets in a common pool is ancient in origin. For example it appears in the laws of the 10th Century Welsh king, Hywel Dda, where a woman's 'agweddi' is half the pool after seven years' marriage (see Dafydd Jenkins *The Law of Hywel Dda* (trans) (1990, Gomer Press), at p 45 et seq.)

4 This Clause only envisages a gradual equalisation of the shares of two co-owners.

5 The denominator should be double the number of years. So, for a five-year period it would be 1/10th; for six years, 1/12th; for 10 years, 1/20th, etc. In most cases the fraction will be more intelligible than a percentage.

6 **Example**

David and Carol purchased a house and executed a declaration of trust on 20 January 1989. On 9 October 1991 they separated. On 16 March 1992 they sold the property. The net proceeds of sale came to £150,000, of which David was entitled to the 'larger share' of £110,000 and Carol was entitled to the 'smaller share' of £40,000. The declaration of trust provided that their respective shares would be equalised over a seven-year period. Who gets what?

The 'difference' between the larger share and the smaller share on the date when the property is sold is £70,000. David's share will decrease by 2/14ths of the difference and Carol's share will increase by 2/14ths of the difference. The numerator represents the two complete years from 20 January 1989 to 20 January 1991, during which time they were living together. No apportionment is made in respect of the period from 21 January 1991. So, David gets £100,000 and Carol gets £50,000.

D General Clauses

20 CONTINGENCIES: INTRODUCTORY CLAUSE[1]

Contingencies

- If one of the co-owners fails to pay his or her share of the mortgage payments, the provisions of Schedule (*number*) will apply.[2]
- If one of the co-owners wishes to sell the property and the other co-owner refuses to sell it, the provisions of Schedule (*number*) will apply.[3]
- If one of the co-owners dies and the other co-owner does not become solely and beneficially entitled to the property, the provisions of Schedule (*number*) will apply.[4]
- If one of the co-owners is declared bankrupt, the provisions of Schedule (*number*) will apply.[5]
- If one of the co-owners ceases permanently to reside in the property and the other co-owner continues to reside in it, the provisions of Schedule (*number*) will apply.[6]
- If one of the co-owners is unemployed or incapable of working, the provisions of Schedule (*number*) will apply.[7]
- If one of the co-owners is unemployed or incapable of working because she is pregnant, or he or she is looking after a child or children, the provisions of Schedule (*number*) will apply.[8]
- If one of the co-owners attends a full-time course of education which lasts for less than (one year), the provisions of Schedule (*number*) will apply.[9]
- If one of the co-owners attends a full-time course of education which lasts for more than (one year), the provisions of Schedule (*number*) will apply.[10]
- If the co-owners permit any other person to reside with them in the property, the provisions of Schedule (*number*) will apply.[11]
- If the co-owners separate within a period of (12 months) after purchasing the property, the provisions of Schedule (*number*) will apply.[12]
- If the co-owners are about to separate, or have recently separated, and both of them wish to keep the property, the provisions of Schedule (*number*) will apply.[13]

- If the co-owners carry out building works and contribute towards the cost of the building works disproportionately to their respective shares of the net proceeds of sale, the provisions of Schedule (*number*) will apply.[14]

- If one of the co-owners wishes to realise his or her share of the property, the provisions of Schedule (*number*) will apply.[15]

---

1 A declaration of trust may need to address a number of contingencies, uncertainties or risks. It is recommended that these are briefly introduced by a single sentence in the main body of the declaration, and that the substantive provisions are, in each case, incorporated in a separate Schedule at the end of the declaration.

    The contingencies included in these precedents are typical of many of the problems that arise, but are not exhaustive. They serve a variety of purposes.

    In some cases they are included primarily for information purposes, for example Precedent 37 (see p 59 below) and Precedent 33 (see p 54 below).

    Some of the contingencies provide that payments made by one co-owner on the other's behalf will be treated as a loan, and that their respective beneficial interests will not be affected. Examples include Precedents 34, 39 and 41 (see pp 55, 62 and 64 below).

    In the case of Precedent 40 the payments made by the other co-owner are treated as a gift. To a lesser degree, other precedents may contain a gift element, but generally such contingencies are designed to deal only with a temporary state of affairs.

    Where there is likely to be a long-term imbalance, the contingencies provide that fixed shares will be converted into floating shares. Illustrations can be found in Precedents 38 and 41(b) at pp 59 and 65 below.

    Some of the contingencies give a co-owner the opportunity to 'buy out' the other co-owner's share on favourable terms, but usually subject to a strict time limit. Examples include Precedents 36 and 44 (see pp 57 and 70 below).

    There are also contingencies which might best be described as dispute resolution contingencies. Illustrations are Precedents 42(a) and 42(b) (see p 67 below), which try to get to grips with the problem that could arise if both co-owners wish to keep the property.

Note: If more than one contingency Schedule is being used, care must be taken to ensure that they are not inconsistent with each other.

2 See Precedent 34 at p 55 below.
3 See Precedent 35 at p 56 below.
4 See Precedent 36 at p 57 below.
5 See Precedent 37 at p 59 below.
6 See Precedent 43 at p 68 below.
7 See Precedent 39 at p 62 below.
8 See Precedent 40 at p 63 below.
9 See Precedent 41(a) at p 64 below.
10 See Precedent 41(b) at p 65 below.
11 See Precedent 33 at p 54 below.
12 See Precedent 44 at p 70 below.
13 See Precedents 42(a) and (b) at p 67 below.
14 See Precedent 38 at p 59 below.
15 See Precedent 45 at p 72 below.

---

21 NET INCOME UNTIL SALE[1]

(a) General

Regardless of the manner in which the net proceeds of sale of the property are to be divided between them, the net income of the property until sale will be divided between the co-owners (in equal shares) [OR] (as to   per cent for (*name 1*) and as to   per cent for (*name 2*)).

---

1 Note that in the case of a husband and wife who are living together, special rules relate to the apportionment of income arising from property held in their joint names. These rules are contained in the Income and Corporation Taxes Act 1988, ss 282A and 282B, which were inserted by the Finance Act 1988, with effect from the year 1990/91.

(b) Payments from lodgers

Regardless of the manner in which the net proceeds of sale of the property are to be divided between them, any payment made to one or both of the co-owners by anyone who normally resides with them as a contribution towards his or her living and accommodation expenses will be divided between the co-owners (in equal shares) [OR] (as to   per cent for (*name 1*) and as to   per cent for (*name 2*)).

(c) Payments from grown-up children

Regardless of the manner in which the net proceeds of sale of the property are to be divided between the co-owners, any payments received by (*name 2*) from any of (his)/(her) children who normally reside in the property as a contribution towards his or her living and accommodation expenses will belong to (*name 2*) [OR] (the co-owners in equal shares).

22 CIRCUMSTANCES IN WHICH AN APPLICATION CAN BE MADE TO THE COURT FOR AN ORDER TO SELL THE PROPERTY

(a) Separation[1]

Either co-owner can apply to the court for an order that the property be sold if the co-owners have lived apart for a continuous period of at least (three) months immediately preceding the presentation of the application.

---

1 If this Clause is being used in conjunction with any of the contingency schedules, there must be no inconsistency between the time limits.

(b) A co-owner's death[1]

After the end of a period of (six) months from the date of the death of a co-owner, his or her personal representatives, or any person who is entitled under the deceased co-owner's will or the law relating to intestacy to his or her beneficial interest in the property, can apply to the court for an order that the property be sold.

---

1 If this Clause is used in conjunction with the contingency schedule in Precedent 36 (see p 57 below) there must be no inconsistency between the timespans.

   It may be preferable to specify a period commencing on the death rather than on the date on which a grant of representation is first taken out, because the issue of the grant could be delayed for various reasons.

---

23 CONTRIBUTIONS TOWARDS REPAIRS AND IMPROVEMENTS NOT TO AFFECT THE CO-OWNERS' FIXED SHARES[1]

No contribution in money or money's worth which either co-owner may make towards repairs and improvements to the property will affect the size of their respective shares of the net proceeds of sale.

---

1 If a definition of 'repairs and improvements' is considered necessary, see Precedent 29(g) at p 51 below. Compare the Matrimonial Proceedings and Property Act 1970, s 37.

---

24 COVENANTS

(a) Prohibited acts

Neither co-owner will do or attempt to do any of the following things without the other co-owner's consent, and if they are living apart that consent must be in writing:

1 carry out or take out a loan for the purpose of carrying out any structural alterations or major repairs or improvements to the property;

2 grant any tenancy or licence or allow anyone else to occupy the property;

3 transfer his or her beneficial interest in the property other than by Will or Codicil;

4 charge or incumber the property or any part of it or any interest in it.

(b) Positive acts

Each co-owner will:

1 *Obligations*

Always comply with the obligations imposed on the co-owners jointly and individually in:

1.1 the registers kept at the Land Registry;
1.2 this Declaration of Trust;
1.3 the mortgage;
1.4 any insurance policy that is linked to the mortgage;
1.5 any insurance policy that affects the building or its contents;
1.6 any order affecting the property that has been issued by a body acting on statutory authority;
1.7 the Lease;
1.8 the Memorandum and Articles of Association of the Management Company.

2 *Payments*

Promptly pay his or her share of the mortgage payments, insurance premiums, and all other outgoings on the property.

3 *Repair*

Keep and contribute towards the cost of keeping the property in reasonable repair, condition and decoration.

4 *Insure*

Keep and contribute towards the cost of keeping the property adequately insured under comprehensive cover to its full re-instatement value.

5 *Keep accounts*

Keep proper accounts, receipts and statements recording all the contributions made by each and both of the co-owners towards the mortgage payments and the costs of all repairs and improvements to the property.

6 *Execute further assurances*

Complete, sign and execute any form, document and deed which may be required in order to transfer the legal estate and beneficial interest in the property or otherwise to implement the provisions of this Declaration of Trust.

7 *Allow access*

Let any valuer have access to the property and any information about the property which may be relevant in assessing its open market value.

8 *Indemnity*

Indemnify the other co-owner from and against the consequences of the failure of the co-owner giving this indemnity to comply with any of the obligations imposed on him or her.

25 LEGAL ADVICE[1]

Each of the co-owners has received independent legal advice on the provisions and implications of this Declaration of Trust.

---

1 See, generally, 'Independent Legal Advice' at p 106 below.
  Note that:

  'the effect of acting in different interests generally is, first, that the solicitor acting with perfect propriety may suddenly find that he is in the position of having a duty to one client, the effect of which if carried out will be contrary to the interest of the other client, and secondly, that the solicitor does so at his peril and with the consequent risk of proceedings for negligence being brought against him by one client or the other' (*Cordery on Solicitors* (Butterworths, 6th Edn) at p 202).

---

26 COSTS OF THIS DECLARATION

(*Name 1*) will pay all the legal costs relating to the preparation and execution of this Declaration of Trust.

[*OR*]

The co-owners will pay the legal costs relating to the preparation and execution of this Declaration of Trust (in equal shares).

[*OR*]

Each of the co-owners will pay the costs incurred by him or her in obtaining independent legal advice on the provisions and implications of this Declaration of Trust.

27 SALE COSTS[1]

The co-owners will pay the incidental costs of selling the property (in equal shares) [*OR*] (in the proportions that their respective shares of the rest of the net proceeds of sale of the property bear to each other).

1 It is important that the co-owners clearly agree in advance how the incidental costs of selling the property will be borne between them. These costs usually include estate agents' commission as well as legal fees, and are sometimes substantial.

    There is no need to include this Clause if the method of calculating the co-owners' shares already takes the sale costs into account.

28 COSTS OF TRANSFER OF BENEFICIAL INTEREST

Unless the co-owners agree otherwise, if one of them transfers all his or her legal estate and beneficial interest in the property to the other (or the other's nominee), the valuation fees, legal fees and other costs incurred by the transferor will be paid by the transferor, and the valuation fees, legal fees and other costs incurred by the transferee will be paid by the transferee.

29 DEFINITIONS

(a) Sale price

'The sale price' means:

1 the price for which the property is sold; and
2 the price paid by the buyer of the property for any chattels jointly owned by the co-owners, whether or not a separate price is paid for those chattels.

(b) Amount required to redeem the mortgage[1]

'The amount required to redeem the mortgage' means the sums of money required by the lenders to enable the co-owners to repay all mortgages, charges and loans to which the property is subject (other than a charge created by one of the co-owners affecting his or her beneficial interest alone) and to enable the co-owners to be completely released and discharged from the performance of all their obligations under such mortgages, charges and loans, and includes:

1 all legal and administrative fees incurred or charged by any lender in connection with the repayment; and
2 any financial penalty imposed by any lender for early repayment.

---

1 In the case of an endowment mortgage or insurance-linked mortgage it may be considered desirable to add the words 'less the surrender values of all insurance policies linked to the mortgage, whether or not those policies have been assigned to or deposited with the lenders'.

(c) Incidental costs of selling the property[1]

'The incidental costs of selling the property' means the total sum of money (including VAT) to be paid in respect of:

1 estate agent's commission; and
2 legal costs and disbursements; and
3 apportionments of rates, taxes, insurance, and other outgoings on the property; and
4 any other costs incurred is connection with the sale or transfer of the property or any interest in it.

1 Note that in the 'short form' complete precedents, 'the incidental costs of selling the property' has been abbreviated to 'the sale costs'.

(d) Net proceeds of sale[1]

'The net proceeds of sale' means the sale price,[2] less:

1 the amount required to redeem the mortgage;[3] and
2 the incidental costs of selling the property.[4]

1 Note that there is a statutory definition of 'the net proceeds of sale' (Law of Property Act 1925, s 35).
2 For a definition of 'the sale price', see Precedent 29(a) above.
3 For a definition of 'the amount required to redeem the mortgage', see Precedent 29(b) above.
4 For a definition of 'the incidental costs of selling the property', see Precedent 29(c) above.

(e) Open market value

'The open market value' means the best price for the property that the co-owners could reasonably be expected to obtain if they sold the property on the date of the valuation, assuming that:

1 the property is being sold with vacant possession; and
2 there is no discount in respect of the joint ownership of the property; and
3 a buyer, who is not connected with (either)/(any) of the co-owners, is ready, willing and able to complete the purchase of the property immediately for cash; and
4 all carpets, curtains, fixtures and fittings which are jointly owned by the co-owners are included in the sale.

(f) Mortgage payments

'The mortgage payments' means the sums of money paid or payable from time to time to the lender(s) in respect of all mortgages, charges and loans to which the property is subject, and includes:

1 the payment of interest; and
2 the repayment of capital; and
3 the payment of insurance premiums; and
4 the payment of penalties imposed by the lender(s); and
5 the payment of interest and the repayment of capital on all loans taken out, with or without security, for the purpose of carrying out repairs and improvements to the property.

(g) Repairs and improvements[1]

'Repairs and improvements' means major repairs necessary to maintain the fabric of the property, and any of the following measures undertaken with a view to improving its fitness for occupation:

1 installation of a fixed bath, shower, wash basin, sink or lavatory, and any necessary associated plumbing;
2 damp proofing measures;
3 provision or improvement of ventilation and natural lighting;
4 provision of electric lighting and sockets;
5 provision or improvement of drainage facilities;
6 improvements to the structural condition of the property;
7 improvements to the facilities for storing, preparing and cooking food;
8 provision of heating, including central heating;
9 provision of storage facilities for fuel and refuse;
10 improvements to the insulation of the property; and
11 any other major repairs analogous to those listed above.[2]

---

1 It is submitted that the definition of 'repairs and improvements' will depend on the age and condition of the property, and perhaps also the socio-economic backgrounds of the co-owners. For an alternative definition, see the definition of 'building works' in Precedent 38 at p 59 below.
2 This definition repeats, almost verbatim, the definition of repairs and improvements in the Income Support (General) Regulations 1987, SI 1987/1967, Sch 3, para 8(3).
   When a couple buy a property with the intention of carrying out substantial repairs and improvements, it may be preferable to express their shares of the net proceeds of sale as floating, rather than fixed. For the distinction between fixed shares and floating shares, see p 11 above.

(h) Co-owners

'The co-owners' means (*name 1*) and (*name 2*) and the trustees for the time being of the property.

30 THE NATURE OF THIS DECLARATION

This Declaration of Trust:

1 is a deed[1] and is executed as a deed[2] by the (co-owners) [OR] (parties to it);
2 can be varied by a subsequent Declaration of Trust executed by all the persons who are able to vary the original trusts;[3]
3 will be legally binding on the (co-owners) [OR] (parties to it) unless and until it is varied or set aside by an order of the court;[4]
4 contains the entire understanding of the (co-owners) [OR] (parties to it) and supersedes any previous agreements, representations and promises made by them in respect of the property.[5]

---

1 The Law of Property Act 1925, s 53(1)(b) requires that 'a declaration of trust respecting any land or any interest therein must be manifested and proved by some writing signed by some person who is able to declare such trust or by his will'. Although the declaration must be in writing, it is not essential that it be executed as a deed, unless there are covenants in it.
2 Law of Property (Miscellaneous Provisions) Act 1989, s 1.
3 For a form of deed of variation, see Precedent 49 at p 91 below.
4 For example, the court could set the declaration of trust aside on the grounds of fraud or mistake (*City of London Building Society v Flegg* [1988] AC 54; *Wilson v Wilson* [1969] 1 WLR 1470). The beneficial interests may also be affected by orders under, eg the Insolvency Act 1986, the Children Act 1989, the Inheritance (Provision for Family and Dependants) Act 1975.
5 *Lloyds Bank Plc v Rosset* [1990] 1 All ER 1111 at 1118.

---

31 EXECUTION IN DUPLICATE[1]

This Declaration of Trust has been executed in (duplicate)/(triplicate)/(quadruplicate) so that each (co-owner) [OR] (person who has a beneficial interest in the property) may possess a copy of it, and (both)/(all) copies will be regarded as one deed, and each copy will be as efficacious as the other(s).

---

1 For the effect of multiple execution of deeds see, generally, Co Litt 229a, and *Burchell v Clark* (1876) 2 CPD 88 at 96.

---

32 ATTESTATION CLAUSE[1]

SIGNED as a Deed by *(name 1)* in the presence of:

SIGNED as a Deed by *(name 2)* in the presence of:

1 It is usual, but not essential, for a declaration of trust to be executed as a deed. For provisions relating to deeds and their execution, see the Law of Property (Miscellaneous Provisions) Act 1989, s 1.

E Contingencies

33 IF THE CO-OWNERS PERMIT ANY OTHER PERSON TO RESIDE WITH THEM IN THE PROPERTY[1]

SCHEDULE (*number*)

1 This Schedule applies if:

    1.1 the co-owners permit any other person to reside with them in the property; and

    1.2 there is no alternative agreement between the co-owners.

2 In this Schedule:

    2.1 'the licensee' means any person (aged 18 or over) who normally resides with the co-owners, whether or not he or she is related to or dependent on either of them;[2] and

    2.2 'the licence' means the terms and conditions on which the co-owners permit the licensee to occupy the property.

3 The co-owners permit the licensee to occupy the property as a bare licensee.[3]

4 The licensee will have no right to exclusive possession of the property or any part of it.[4]

5 The licensee will not acquire any tenancy or beneficial interest in the property despite:

    5.1 any payment the licensee makes to either or both of the co-owners as a contribution towards his or her living and accommodation expenses; and

    5.2 any repairs or improvements to the property which the licensee carries out with or without the consent of the co-owners.

6 The licence can be terminated by the licensee at any time.[5]

7 The licence can be revoked by either of the co-owners at any time.[6]

8 The licence is personal to the licensee and cannot be transferred by him or her to any other person.

9 The co-owners will take whatever steps are necessary to ensure that the licensee clearly understands the terms and conditions on which he or she is permitted to occupy the property.

1 The co-owners may permit other occupants to reside with them in a variety of circumstances: for example lodgers, the grown-up child of one of the co-owners or the boyfriend or girlfriend of a co-owner. This Schedule provides that, in the absence of any contrary agreement between the co-owners, the other occupant will be a bare licensee. In many cases where the occupation of premises is shared on an informal basis, particularly if the parties are related, the non-owner will have a bare licence. If, however, an intention to create legal relations can be found together with some form of consideration, there may be a contractual licence.
2 Although, in general, a bare licence can be revoked at any time, the licence of a child (even an adult child) to remain in the home will only be revocable in exceptional circumstances (*Egan v Egan* [1975] Ch 218).
3 Anyone sharing residential accommodation with the consent of the owners is, at the very least, a bare licensee. The owners' consent to the sharing of accommodation prevents the licensee from being a trespasser.
4 Without exclusive possession there cannot be a tenancy. A lodger will always be a licensee and never a tenant. 'The occupier is a lodger if the landlord provides attendance or services which require the landlord or his servants to exercise unrestricted access to and use of the premises. A lodger is entitled to live in the premises but cannot call the place his own' (*Street v Mountford* [1985] AC 809 at 818, per Lord Templeman).
5 *Australian Blue Metal v Hughes* [1963] AC 74 at 98.
6 The licence can be revoked by either co-owner at will and without notice (*Crane v Morris* [1965] 1 WLR 1104 at 1108). The licence can also be revoked by one co-owner without reference to the other (*Annen v Rattee* (1984) 273 EG 503, CA).

34 IF A CO-OWNER FAILS TO PAY HIS OR HER SHARE OF THE MORTGAGE PAYMENTS[1]

SCHEDULE (*number*)

1 This Schedule applies if:

1.1 there is no alternative agreement between the co-owners; and

1.2 one of the co-owners ('the debtor') is unable or unwilling or otherwise fails to pay his or her share of the mortgage payments when it is due; and

1.3 the other co-owner ('the creditor') pays all or part of the debtor's share of the mortgage payments on the debtor's behalf.(; and

1.4 the provisions of Schedule(s)   do not apply).[2]

2 The payment made by the creditor on the debtor's behalf ('the loan') will be treated as a loan from the creditor to the debtor.

3 The loan is made on the condition that:

3.1 it must be repaid as soon as possible; and

3.2 if it has not been repaid within (three) months from the date on which it was made, the loan, or so much of it as remains outstanding, will bear interest at a rate of (one) per cent a year above the rate of interest payable from time to time in respect of the mortgage (before)/(after) the deduction of basic rate income tax.

1 'Where . . . a fund is being distributed, a party cannot take anything out of the fund until he has made good what he owes to the fund' (*Re Rhodesia Goldfields Ltd* [1910] 1 Ch 239 at 247, per Swinfen Eady J). Anyone who discharges another's secured obligation, wholly or in part, is entitled to be repaid, out of the security, the amount of the sum or sums paid by him (*Pitt v Pitt* (1823) Turn & R 180; *Outram v Hyde* [1875] 24 WR 268; *Cowcher v Cowcher* [1972] 1 All ER 943 at 951).

2 For example if a co-owner is unemployed or incapable of working (see Precedent 39 at pp 62 and 63 below), if a co-owner is unemployed or incapable of working because of pregnancy or childcare (see Precedent 40 at p 63 below), or if a co-owner attends a full-time course of education (see Precedent 41 at p 64 below).

35 IF ONE CO-OWNER WISHES TO SELL THE PROPERTY AND THE OTHER CO-OWNER REFUSES TO SELL IT[1]

SCHEDULE (*number*)

1 This Schedule applies if:

    1.1 there is no alternative agreement between the co-owners; and

    1.2 one of the co-owners ('the applicant') wishes to sell the property; and

    1.3 the other co-owner ('the objector') refuses to sell it.[2]

2 The applicant will give written notice to the objector of the applicant's wish to sell the property.

3 The date on which the objector receives that notice is 'the application date'.

4 After the end of a period of (12) weeks beginning on the application date the applicant can apply to the court for an order that the property be sold if:[3]

    4.1 the objector has not contractually agreed to purchase the applicant's estate and interest in the property; and

    4.2 the objector refuses to sell the property.

1 This precedent could be used in conjunction with Precedent 45 (see p 72 below). If both precedents are used, it is essential to ensure that the dates on which an application can be made to the court coincide.

2 The prime duty of trustees for sale is to sell the property. They have power to postpone the sale. For the power to take precedence over the duty, the trustees must be unanimous. See, generally, M P Thompson *Co-Ownership* (Sweet & Maxwell, 1988) at Chapter 3.

3 The application should be made under the Law of Property Act 1925, s 30.

36 IF ONE CO-OWNER DIES AND THE OTHER DOES NOT BECOME SOLELY AND BENEFICIALLY ENTITLED TO THE PROPERTY

SCHEDULE (*number*)

1 This Schedule applies if:

    1.1 one of the co-owners ('the deceased') dies; and

    1.2 the other co-owner ('the survivor') does not become solely and beneficially entitled to the property.[1]

2 This Schedule applies subject to and without prejudice to all rights that the survivor may have under the deceased's will[2] and generally in law.[3]

3 The survivor will be primarily liable for:

    3.1 the payment of the mortgage;

    3.2 the payment of all outgoings on the property;

    3.3 keeping the property adequately insured; and

    3.4 keeping the property in reasonable repair and condition.

4 In this Schedule:

    4.1 'the death' means the date on which the deceased died;

    4.2 'the share' means the deceased's beneficial interest in the property; and

    4.3 'the estate' may mean either the deceased's personal representative(s) or the person(s) entitled to the share under the deceased's will or the law relating to intestacy.[4]

5 If the survivor is asked to do so, he or she will, as soon as practicable after the death, appoint the estate to be a new trustee of the property and will register the new trustee as a joint proprietor of the property, and the costs of effecting such appointment and registration will be paid by the estate.[5]

6 When the property or the share is sold the estate will be credited with a lump sum payment by way of reimbursement of all (if any) mortgage payments it has made in respect of the property since the death.

7 Part 1 of this Schedule applies during the period of (six) months beginning with the death ('the concessionary period').[6]

8 Part 2 of this Schedule applies after the end of the concessionary period.

Part 1

9 During the concessionary period the survivor can reside in the property rent-free.

10 During the concessionary period the value of the share can be discounted

by   per cent, by virtue of the fact that the property is jointly owned.[7]

11 During the concessionary period the survivor or the survivor's nominee can purchase the share for its value immediately after the death.[8]

Part 2

12 After the concessionary period the estate can apply to the court for an order that the property be sold.[9]

13 After the concessionary period the value of the share will not be discounted even though the property is jointly owned.[10]

14 After the concessionary period the survivor will pay an occupation rent to the estate.[11]

15 The occupation rent will be such proportion of the fair rent as the value of the share bears to the value of the whole of the net proceeds of sale of the property.

16 The fair rent is the rent which would be assessed by the Rent Officer for an unfurnished letting of the whole of the property to a protected tenant.[12]

---

1 This Schedule would not apply if the co-owners were beneficial joint tenants, or if the deceased had, by will, made an absolute gift of his or her share to the survivor.
2 For example a life or lesser interest, or an option to purchase.
3 For example under the Inheritance (Provision for Family and Dependants) Act 1975.
4 The definition of 'the estate' is inevitably vague. Much will depend on the circumstances of each individual case.
5 For the recommended procedures where registered land is held on a trust for sale and it is necessary to appoint a new trustee, see Ruoff and Roper *Registered Conveyancing* (Sweet & Maxwell, 1991) at para 32–13.
6 The concessionary period is designed to safeguard the survivor's rights of occupation for a reasonable time, and to encourage the survivor to purchase the deceased's share.
7 In *Wight and Another v CIR Lands Tribunal* (1982) 264 EG 935 it was held that, because it was unlikely that a purchaser would be able to obtain an order for sale under the Law of Property Act 1925, s 30, the discount in the value of a half share for capital transfer tax purposes should be 15 per cent.
8 The words 'immediately after the death' should cover the effect of the payment of any mortgage-linked insurance policy proceeds, and the valuation discount which applies during the concessionary period.
9 The application would be made under the Law of Property Act 1925, s 30. See, generally, M P Thompson *Co-Ownership* (Sweet & Maxwell, 1988) at Chapter 3.
10 See footnote 7 above.
11 For 'occupation rent' see, generally: *Leake v Bruzzi* [1974] 1 WLR 1528; *Suttill v Graham* [1977] 1 WLR 819; and *Dennis v McDonald* (1982) FLR 398.
12 See the dicta of Sir John Arnold P in *Dennis v McDonald* (1982) FLR 409.

37 IF A CO-OWNER IS DECLARED BANKRUPT[1]

SCHEDULE (*number*)

1 This Schedule applies if one of the co-owners ('the bankrupt') is declared bankrupt.

2 The provisions of this Schedule are:

2.1 not a matter for agreement or negotiation between the co-owners;
2.2 an abbreviated summary of the law;
2.3 included in this Declaration of Trust for information purposes only.

3 The bankrupt's beneficial interest in the property will automatically vest in his or her trustee in bankruptcy ('the trustee');[2]

4 The trustee has a statutory duty to get in, realise and distribute the bankrupt's estate[3] and in the exercise of that duty the trustee may apply to the court for an order that the property be sold.[4]

5 The bankrupt's rights of occupation will depend on whether a child under 18 was living with the bankrupt at:

5.1 the time when the bankruptcy petition was presented; and
5.2 the commencement of the bankruptcy.[5]

6 If the bankrupt has entered into a transaction at an undervalue with anyone else in respect of his or her share of the property, the trustee may apply to the court for an order restoring the position to what it would have been if the bankrupt had not entered into that transaction.[6]

---

1 Note para 2. This Schedule is purely for information purposes.
2 Insolvency Act 1986, s 306.
3 Ibid, s 305(2) and Ch IV.
4 An order under the Law of Property Act 1925, s 30.
5 Insolvency Act 1986, ss 336 and 337. See *Re Gorman (A Bankrupt)*, *ex parte Trustee of the Bankrupt v The Bankrupt* [1990] 1 WLR 616.
6 Insolvency Act 1986, s 339. For the 'relevant time' limits, see ibid, s 341.

---

38 IF THE CO-OWNERS EXTEND, ALTER, IMPROVE OR REPAIR THE PROPERTY

(Conversion from fixed shares to floating shares)[1]

SCHEDULE (*number*)

1 This Schedule applies if the co-owners:

1.1 carry out building works (as defined below); and

1.2 contribute towards the cost of the building works disproportionately to their respective shares of the net proceeds of sale; and

1.3 fail to execute a further Declaration of Trust to reflect the change in circumstances.

2 This Schedule also applies if the co-owners:

2.1 carry out building works; and

2.2 take out a loan or further mortgage for that purpose; and

2.3 repay or are in the process of repaying that loan or further mortgage disproportionately to the shares in which they had been making the mortgage payments before the building works commenced; and

2.4 fail to execute a further Declaration of Trust to reflect the change in circumstances.

3 In this Schedule 'building works' means any works of a major nature which enhance or are intended to enhance the value of the property, and includes, but is not restricted to:

3.1 the building of an extension to the property;

3.2 major alterations to the exterior or interior of the property;

3.3 the conversion of the property into separate flats or units;

3.4 major works undertaken with a view to improving the fitness of the property for occupation;

3.5 the purchase of additional land to be enjoyed with the property;

3.6 the construction of a garage or outbuildings;

3.7 major works affecting the landscape of the garden;

3.8 major works to the boundaries;

3.9 major works connected with the access to or exit from the property;

3.10 all works analogous to those listed above.

4 Immediately before the building works commence the property will be valued or will be treated as having been valued ('the unimproved value').

5 The unimproved value will be assessed:

5.1 by the co-owners themselves at such figure as they agree; or

5.2 by a professionally qualified property valuer instructed by the co-owners; or

5.3 if the co-owners fail to agree the unimproved value or on instructing a valuer, by a valuer appointed by the President of the Royal Institution of Chartered Surveyors.

6 Immediately before the building works commence there will be a deemed sale of the property by the co-owners as if:

6.1 it were being sold at the unimproved value; and

6.2 each co-owner were able to realise his or her share ('the fixed share')

of the net proceeds of sale calculated in accordance with the provisions of Clause (*number*) of this Declaration of Trust.

7 Immediately after the deemed sale of the property there will be a deemed re-acquisition of it by the co-owners as if:

7.1 they were acquiring it at the unimproved value; and

7.2 the fixed share of each co-owner were his or her cash contribution towards the acquisition price.

8 Immediately after the deemed re-acquisition of the property the provisions of Clause (*number*) of this Declaration of Trust relating to the calculation of the co-owners' shares of the net proceeds of sale will cease to have effect and the following provisions will apply.

9 After the deemed re-acquisition of the property the co-owners will hold the property and its net proceeds of sale in trust for themselves as beneficial tenants in common in shares which are proportionate to the contributions made by each of them towards the deemed re-acquisition of the property and the payments made by each of them after the deemed re-acquisition towards:

9.1 the building works;

9.2 any subsequent building works;

9.3 mortgage interest;

9.4 mortgage capital;

9.5 mortgage-linked insurance premiums;

9.6 interest and capital on loans taken out for the purpose of carrying out the building works and any subsequent building works; and

9.7 the incidental costs of selling the property.

10 (Formulae for calculating floating shares).

---

1 For the distinction between fixed shares and floating shares and a discussion of their advantages and disadvantages, see p 11 above.

Example

Karen and Simon decided to 'improve' their house. In its unimproved state it is worth £88,000. The amount required to redeem their mortgage is £48,000. When they bought the house they executed a declaration of trust which stated that Karen would receive 75 per cent of the net proceeds of sale, and Simon would receive 25 per cent.

The building works take exactly a year to complete. During that time Simon pays £21,000 towards the works and £1,000 towards the mortgage payments. During that time Karen pays £5,000 towards the works and £3,000 towards the mortgage payments.

As soon as the building works have been completed, Karen and Simon decide to move house. They sell the house for £128,000. The amount required to redeem their mortgage is still £48,000. The net proceeds of sale come to £80,000. Who gets what?

If their declaration of trust had not incorporated this Schedule, Karen would still be entitled to 75 per cent of the net proceeds, and Simon 25 per cent. On that basis Karen would receive £60,000 and Simon would receive £20,000.

The effect of this Schedule is to create a deemed sale and re-acquisition of the property when the building works begin, and to convert Karen's and Simon's shares from fixed shares to floating shares.

Since the deemed re-acquisition, Karen's contributions have been £30,000 (her original 75 per cent fixed share treated as her downpayment on the re-acquisition) plus £5,000 (towards the building works) plus £3,000 (her mortgage payments). So, her total contribution has been £38,000.

Since the deemed re-acquisition, Simon's contributions have been £10,000 (his original 25 per cent fixed share treated as his downpayment on the re-acquisition) plus £21,000 (towards the building works) plus £1,000 (his share of the mortgage). So, his total contribution has been £32,000.

The net proceeds of sale (£80,000) are divided between Karen and Simon in the proportions 38:32. Karen receives £43,429 and Simon receives £36,571. The incidental costs of selling the property are paid by them in the same proportions.

2 See Precedents 15 to 18 at pp 32 to 35 above.

---

39 IF A CO-OWNER IS UNEMPLOYED OR INCAPABLE OF WORKING[1]

SCHEDULE (*number*)

1 This Schedule applies if:

  1.1 the co-owners are living together;[2] and

  1.2 one of the co-owners ('the unemployed co-owner') is unemployed or incapable of working; and

  1.3 because of a reduction in his or her income the unemployed co-owner has difficulty in maintaining his or her share of the mortgage payments; and

  1.4 the co-owners do not execute a further Declaration of Trust to reflect the change in circumstances; and

  1.5 the provisions of Schedule (*number*) do not apply.[3]

2 The unemployed co-owner will do all he or she can to contribute towards the mortgage payments from whatever resources are available to him or her.[4]

3 Subject to the above, the other co-owner will be responsible for all the mortgage payments from the date on which the unemployed co-owner ceased to be employed or his or her incapacity to work began ('the commencement date').[5]

4 The mortgage payments made by the other co-owner on behalf of the unemployed co-owner:

  4.1 during the period of (six) months[6] starting on the commencement date will not affect the beneficial interests of either co-owner in the property;

  4.2 after the end of the period of (six) months starting on the commencement date will be treated as a loan from the other co-owner to the unemployed co-owner.[7]

5 The loan is made on the basis that:

    5.1 it must be repaid as soon as possible; and

    5.2 if it has not been repaid before the property is sold it, or so much of it as remains outstanding, will be repaid to the other co-owner out of the unemployed co-owner's share of the net proceeds of sale.

---

1 '. . . the judge must look at the contributions of each to the "family" finances and determine as best he may what contribution each was making towards the purchase of the house. This is not to be carried out as a strictly mathematical exercise; for instance, if the man was ill for a time and out of work so that the woman temporarily contributed more, that temporary state of affairs should not increase her share, nor should her share be decreased if she was temporarily unable to work whilst having a baby. The contributions must be viewed broadly by the judge to guide him to the parties' unexpressed, and probably unconsidered, intentions as to the beneficial ownership of the house' (*Bernard v Josephs* (1983) FLR 178 at 188, per Griffiths LJ).

2 If the parties were not living together the temporary support obligation contained in para 4.1 of this Schedule might be considered inappropriate.

3 For example Precedents 40 and 41 below.

4 For example savings, or any redundancy payment.

5 Alternatively, the commencement date could be the date on which the unemployed co-owner is no longer able to keep up his or her agreed share of the mortgage payments.

6 The timespan which the co-owners consider appropriate in the circumstances should be inserted here. Note, that in the passage from *Bernard v Josephs* (above), Griffiths LJ merely envisaged a 'temporary state of affairs' which should not affect the beneficial interests.

7 If the co-owners wish to penalise 'fault', a further paragraph should be added to the effect that: 'Despite the provisions of paragraph 4 of this Schedule all mortgage payments made by the other co-owner on behalf of the unemployed co-owner will be treated as a loan (a) from the commencement date itself if the unemployed co-owner lost employment through misconduct or voluntarily left employment without good cause; or (b) from the date on which the unemployed co-owner, without good cause, refused or failed to take a reasonable opportunity to secure employment'.

---

40 IF A CO-OWNER IS UNEMPLOYED OR INCAPABLE OF WORKING BECAUSE SHE IS PREGNANT OR HE OR SHE IS LOOKING AFTER A CHILD OR CHILDREN[1]

SCHEDULE (*number*)

1 This Schedule applies if:

    1.1 the co-owners are living together;[2] and

    1.2 (*name 2*) is unemployed or incapable of working because she is pregnant; and

    1.3 either of the co-owners is unemployed or incapable of working because he or she is looking after his, her or their child or children; and

    1.4 that co-owner who is unemployed or incapable of working has difficulty in maintaining his or her share of the mortgage payments because of a reduction in his or her income; and

1.5 the co-owners fail to execute a further Declaration of Trust to reflect the change in circumstances.

2 The co-owner who is unemployed or incapable of working will do all he or she can to contribute towards the mortgage payments from whatever resources are available.[3]

3 Subject to the above, the other co-owner will be responsible for all the mortgage payments, and the mortgage payments that he or she makes will not affect the beneficial interests of either co-owner in the property.

---

1 Note the dicta of Griffiths LJ in *Bernard v Josephs* (1983) 4 FLR 178 at 188 (see Precedent 39, footnote 1 at p 63 above). In his view the woman's share should not be decreased 'if she was temporarily unable to work whilst having a baby' (ibid, at p 188B). The word 'temporarily' is significant. The implication is that if the state of affairs is anything other than 'temporary', the beneficial interests should be affected.

2 The support obligation might be considered inappropriate if the co-owners are not living together.

3 For example, statutory maternity pay or savings.

---

41 IF A CO-OWNER ATTENDS A FULL-TIME COURSE OF EDUCATION

(a) Mortgage payments made by the other co-owner to be treated as a loan[1]

SCHEDULE (*number*)

1 This Schedule applies if:

1.1 one of the co-owners ('the student') attends a full-time course of education ('the course'); and

1.2 the course does not last for more than (one year); and

1.3 the student has difficulty in maintaining his or her share of the mortgage payments because of a reduction in his or her income; and

1.4 the co-owners do not execute a further Declaration of Trust to reflect the change in circumstances.

2 The student will do all that he or she can to contribute towards the mortgage payments from whatever resources are available.[2]

3 Subject to the above, the other co-owner will be responsible for the mortgage payments from the date on which the student begins the course.

4 The mortgage payments made by the other co-owner on the student's behalf will be treated as a loan to the student from the other co-owner.

5 The loan is made on the basis that:

5.1 it is interest free; and

5.2 the student will repay the loan as soon as he or she can; and

5.3 if it has not been repaid before the property is sold, the loan, or so much of it as remains outstanding, will be repaid to the other co-owner out of the student's share of the net proceeds of sale.

---

1 This precedent is intended to cover 'a temporary state of affairs' which should not materially affect the beneficial interests of either co-owner (*Bernard v Josephs* (1983) FLR 178 at 188). It assumes that the course is of comparatively short duration and will last no longer than, say, one academic year. If the course is of a longer duration, perhaps the beneficial interests should be affected: in which case Precedent 41(b) (see below) may be preferred, or used in addition, to this precedent. This precedent establishes that the payments made on the student's behalf by the other co-owner are to be treated as a loan, and not a gift.

Query: If the student is not living in the property during term time, should the other co-owner be paying the student an 'occupation rent'? (*Dennis v McDonald* (1982) FLR 398).

2 For example from savings, scholarship income, or a grant.

(b) Conversion of fixed shares into floating shares[1]

SCHEDULE (*number*)

1 This Schedule applies if:

1.1 one of the co-owners ('the student') attends a full-time course of education ('the course'); and

1.2 the course lasts or is expected to last for more than (one year); and

1.3 while the student is on the course the other co-owner pays a larger share of the mortgage payments than he or she had originally agreed to pay (in Clause   of this Declaration of Trust); and

1.4 the co-owners do not execute a further Declaration of Trust to reflect the change in circumstances.

2 Immediately before the student begins the course:

2.1 the property will be valued or treated as having been valued ('the pre-course value'); and

2.2 a statement of the amount required to redeem the mortgage will be obtained or treated as having been obtained.

3 Immediately before the student begins the course there will be a deemed sale of the property as if:

3.1 it were being sold by the co-owners at the pre-course value; and

3.2 each co-owner could then realise his or her fixed share of the net proceeds of sale ('the fixed share') calculated in accordance with the provisions of Clause   of this Declaration of Trust.

4 Immediately after this deemed sale of the property there will be a deemed re-acquisition of it by the co-owners as if:

4.1 they were acquiring it at the pre-course value; and

4.2 each co-owner's fixed share were his or her cash contribution towards the acquisition price.

5 Immediately after the deemed re-acquisition of the property the provisions of Clause   of this Declaration of Trust relating to the calculation of the fixed share of each co-owner will cease to have effect and the following provisions will apply instead.

6 After the deemed re-acquisition of the property the co-owners will hold the property and its net proceeds of sale in trust for themselves as beneficial tenants in common in shares which are proportionate to the contributions made by each of them towards the deemed re-acquisition of the property and the payments made by each of them after the deemed re-acquisition towards:

6.1 mortgage interest;

6.2 mortgage capital;

6.3 mortgage-linked insurance premiums;

6.4 repairs and improvements to the property;

6.5 interest and capital on loans taken out for the purpose of carrying out repairs and improvements to the property; and

6.6 the incidental costs of selling the property.

7 The share of the net proceeds of sale to which each co-owner will be entitled will be calculated in accordance with the provisions of Schedule *(number)*.[2]

---

1 For the distinction between fixed shares and floating shares, see p 11 above. For a discussion of the relative advantages and disadvantages of each type of shareholding, see pp 12 to 15 above.

This precedent is intended to cover the situation where one of the co-owners embarks on a comparatively lengthy course of further education, ie one which will last for more than, say, a year. In this case the beneficial interests of the co-owners are affected. By contrast, Precedent 41(a) (above) is designed to deal with a more temporary state of affairs, where the course lasts for no longer than, say, a year, and the beneficial interests are not materially affected.

Example

In July 1988, Steve and Vicky bought a terraced house. They contributed more or less the same amount towards the purchase price, and agreed to share the mortgage payments equally. They executed a declaration of trust stating that they were beneficial tenants in common in equal shares. In October 1990, Steve began a three-year course leading to a degree in computer studies. At that time the house was worth £45,000, and the amount required to redeem their mortgage was £30,000. While Steve was away studying, Vicky remained in the house and made all the mortgage payments herself. Christmas 1991 was not a happy time for them. Each, quite rightly, suspected that the other had found a new partner. So, they decided to go their own separate ways.

In June 1992, the house was sold for £40,000. The amount required to redeem the mortgage was still £30,000. The net proceeds of sale came to £10,000. Who got what?

If they followed the 50:50 shareout in their declaration of trust, Vicky and Steve would have received £5,000 each.

However, the effect of the incorporation of this Schedule into their declaration of trust meant that their fixed shares (50:50) were converted into floating shares when Steve began his computer studies course.

Vicky paid the mortgage on her own for 20 months, while Steve paid nothing. The total mortgage payments she made came to £5,500. So, her 'floating share' was worth a basic £13,000, which represented her cash contribution to the deemed re-acquisition of the property in October 1990 (£7,500) plus the £5,500 which she contributed towards the mortgage payments. Steve's 'floating share' remained stationary at £7,500, being his cash contribution to the deemed re-acquisition.

The net proceeds of sale (£10,000) were divided between them in the ratio 13,000:7,500. Vicky was entitled to £6,341, and Steve was entitled to £3,659. The incidental costs of selling the property came to £1,250. These were paid in the same ratios: Vicky paid £793 and Steve £457.

2 For the formulae for calculating floating shares, see Precedents 15 to 18 at pp 32 to 35 above.

---

42 IF BOTH CO-OWNERS WISH TO KEEP THE PROPERTY

(a) One co-owner to have prior rights

SCHEDULE (*number*)

1 This Schedule applies if:

    1.1 the co-owners are about to separate or have recently separated;[1] and

    1.2 both of them wish to keep the property; and

    1.3 neither of them is willing to relinquish the property to the other; and

    1.4 each of them is able to purchase the other's share.

2 (*Name 2*) will have the right to remain in the property and to purchase (*name 1's*) share in it (because) (*state reasons, if considered appropriate*).

3 This Schedule will not apply if:

    3.1 the co-owners have been living apart for a continuous period of at least (two) months; and

    3.2 (*name 1*) has been living in the property during the whole of that period.

---

1 The words 'or have recently separated' are intended to cover the possibility of constructive desertion.

(b) Rules for determining who has prior rights

SCHEDULE (*number*)

1 This Schedule applies if:

    1.1 The co-owners are about to separate or have recently separated; and

1.2 both of them wish to keep the property; and

1.3 neither of them is willing to relinquish the property to the other; and

1.4 each of them is able to purchase the other's share.

2 The co-owner who has the superior right to remain in the property and to purchase the other's share in it will be determined in accordance with the following order of priority, and the co-owner who is first described in this list will be preferred to the other co-owner:

2.1 the co-owner with whom a child under the age of 18 will live after the co-owners have separated;

2.2 if the preceding category applies equally to both of the co-owners, the co-owner with whom the greater number of children under 18 will live after the co-owners have separated;

2.3 if both of the preceding categories apply equally to both of the co-owners, the co-owner with whom the children whose school is nearest to the property will live after the co-owners have separated;

2.4 the co-owner whose only or principal place of business is at the property;

2.5 the co-owner whose only or principal place of business or employment is nearer to the property;

2.6 the co-owner who is entitled to the larger share of the net proceeds of sale of the property.

3 This Schedule will not apply if:

3.1 the co-owners have been living apart for a continuous period of at least (two) months; and

3.2 the co-owner who does not have the superior right to remain in the property has been living in the property during the whole of that period.

43 IF A CO-OWNER MOVES OUT BEFORE THE PROPERTY IS SOLD[1]

SCHEDULE (*number*)

1 *Applicability*

This Schedule applies if:

1.1 one of the co-owners ('the non-resident') ceases permanently to reside in the property;[2] and

1.2 the other co-owner ('the occupier') continues to reside in the property; and

1.3 there is no alternative agreement between the co-owners. [; and

1.4 the provisions of Schedule (*number*) do not apply.][3]

2 *Crystallisation of shares*

The co-owners' respective shares of the net proceeds of sale of the property will be quantified and will crystallise on the date on which the non-resident leaves the property with the intention of never resuming residence in it with the occupier ('the separation date').[4]

3 *The settlement date*

In this Schedule 'the settlement date' means the date on which the non-resident:

3.1 receives his or her share of the net proceeds of sale of the property together with the additions but subject to the deductions mentioned below; or

3.2 receives such sum as he or she has agreed to accept in full and final settlement in consideration of the transfer of his or her legal estate and beneficial interest in the property; or

3.3 pays to the occupier such sum as the occupier has agreed to accept in full and final settlement in consideration of the transfer of the occupier's legal estate and beneficial interest in the property to the non-resident or to such other person(s) as the non-resident directs.

4 *Election*

If the settlement date is more than (six) months after the separation date the non-resident can elect to have the value of his or her share on the settlement date substituted for its value on the separation date.[5]

5 *Occupier's post-separation contributions*

Before the net proceeds of sale are divided, the occupier will be credited with a lump sum payment equal to all the payments that he or she has made during the period between the separation date and the settlement date towards:

5.1 the mortgage; and
5.2 repairs and improvements to the property.

6 *Non-resident's post-separation contributions*

Before the net proceeds of sale are divided, the non-resident will be credited with a lump sum payment equal to all the payments (if any) that he or she has made during the period between the separation date and the settlement date towards:

6.1 the mortgage; and
6.2 repairs and improvements to the property.

7 *Occupation rent*

7.1 Before the net proceeds of sale are divided, the non-resident will be credited with a lump sum payment representing an occupation rent in respect of the occupier's occupation of the property during the period from the separation date to the settlement date or during such shorter period as the non-resident agrees;

7.2 the occupation rent will be such proportion of the fair rent as the value of the non-resident's share bears to the value of the whole of the net proceeds of sale on the separation date;

7.3 the fair rent is the rent which would be assessed by the Rent Officer for an unfurnished letting of the whole of the property to a protected tenant.[6]

---

1 See, generally: Stephen Parker *Cohabitees* (Longman, 1991) 3rd Edn, at pp 152 to 154; M P Thompson *Co-Ownership* (Sweet & Maxwell, 1988) at pp 50 to 52; Jacqueline Priest *Families Outside Marriage* (Family Law, 1993) at pp 21 to 25; and Peter Sparkes 'The Quantification of Beneficial Interests: Problems arising from Contributions to Deposits, Mortgage Advances and Mortgage Instalments' Oxford Journal of Legal Studies, Vol 11, No 1 (Spring 1991), at pp 60 to 61.

2 For a discussion of the meanings of expressions such as 'ceases permanently to reside', see *Re Coxen* [1948] 2 All ER 492 at 500.

3 For example Precedent 44 (below).

4 Note that in *Hall v Hall* [1982] FLR 379, the Court of Appeal held that the equity was to be valued when the parties separated. This decision was not followed by the same court in *Turton v Turton* [1988] 1 FLR 23 at 34A, where Kerr LJ stated that:

> 'unless there is some express declaration or agreement to the effect that the parties' respective beneficial shares are to be valued at the time of their separation if and when this should occur, there could never be any sufficient ground for attributing any such intention to them merely by implication from the circumstances. In the result, therefore, the parties' beneficial interests would always have to be regarded in the normal way under a trust for sale, with the effect that they would until such time as the property is sold, and that they will then attach to the proceeds of sale'.

5 It may be sensible to include a clause to this effect in order to cover fluctuations in value during inflationary and deflationary periods.

6 For consideration of the proper way in which an 'occupation rent' should be assessed, see *Dennis v McDonald* (1982) FLR 398.

---

44 IF THE CO-OWNERS SEPARATE SHORTLY AFTER THEY PURCHASE THE PROPERTY[1]

SCHEDULE *(number)*

1 This Schedule applies if:

1.1 the co-owners separate within a period of (12) months from the date (on which they completed the purchase of the property) [OR] (of this Declaration of Trust); and

1.2 it is possible to procure the release of the non-resident (as defined below) from his or her obligations under the mortgage; and

1.3 there is no alternative agreement between the co-owners.

2 In this Schedule:

2.1 'the occupier' means the co-owner who continues to occupy the property;

2.2 'the non-resident' means the co-owner who has ceased to reside in the property;

2.3 'the non-resident's share' means all the legal estate and beneficial interest of the non-resident in the property freed and discharged from his or her obligations under the mortgage;

2.4 'the separation date' means the date on which the non-resident left the property with the intention of never resuming residence in it with the occupier, being a date within a period of (12) months from the date (of completion of the purchase of the property) [OR] (of this Declaration of Trust).

3 Within a period of (three) months beginning on the separation date the occupier can purchase the non-resident's share for the amount that the non-resident paid towards the purchase price of the property (and the incidental costs of purchasing it),[2] disregarding the amounts which the non-resident has paid towards:

3.1 the mortgage interest;

3.2 the mortgage capital;

3.3 mortgage-linked insurance premiums;

3.4 repairs and improvements to the property. (; and

3.5 the incidental costs of purchasing the property.)[2]

4 If at the end of a period of (three) months beginning on the separation date, the occupier has not purchased the non-resident's share for the amount stated above or for such lesser amount as the non-resident has agreed, the non-resident can apply to the court for an order that the property be sold.

5 The non-resident can elect that the provisions of this Schedule will not apply, but only if:

5.1 their application would result in an unconscionable gain for the occupier; and

5.2 the circumstances are such that the occupier has effectively ousted the non-resident from the property.[3]

---

1 This Schedule is designed to cover the practical problems arising if the co-owners separate within, say, 12 months of completing the purchase of the property. The party remaining in occupation is given an opportunity to buy out the share of the partner who has left the property for the leaver's original cash contribution towards the purchase price, or such lesser sum as the leaver agrees.

2 The incidental costs of the purchase must be included either in the amount for which the occupier is able to purchase the leaver's share, or as one of the payments made by the leaver which can be disregarded. Other disregards might include the price paid towards any fitted carpets and curtains.

3 This clause is intended to avoid inequity in a case of constructive desertion. Its

application is not necessarily limited to a period of inflationary property prices. The leaver might have been paying the lion's share of the mortgage payments; or could have paid a substantial amount towards repairs and improvements to the property.

---

45 IF A CO-OWNER WISHES TO REALISE HIS OR HER SHAREPROPERTY[1]

SCHEDULE (*number*)

1 This Schedule applies if:

    1.1 one of the co-owners ('the seller') wishes to realise his or her beneficial interest in the property ('the share'); and

    1.2 there is no alternative agreement between the co-owners.

2 At his or her own expense the seller will obtain the following information ('the relevant information'):

    2.1 a valuation of the open market value of the property prepared by a professionally qualified property valuer who is familiar with the locality of the property;

    2.2 an up-to-date statement of the amount required to redeem the mortgage and every other charge to which the property is subject;

    2.3 an up-to-date statement of the surrender value of all mortgage-linked insurance policies; and

    2.4 all other information which may be relevant to the valuation of the co-owners' respective shares.

3 The seller will give to the other co-owner ('the buyer'):

    3.1 the relevant information; and

    3.2 a written offer to sell the share ('the offer').

4 The date on which the buyer receives the relevant information and the offer is 'the offer date'.

5 The offer will state:

    5.1 the price at which the seller is willing to sell the share to the buyer or the buyer's nominee;

    5.2 the date on which the seller wishes to complete the transaction, being a date at least (eight) weeks after the offer date; and

    5.3 all the other terms and conditions (if any) on which the seller is willing to sell the share.

6 At his or her own expense the buyer can obtain any further information which may be relevant to the valuation of the co-owners' respective shares.

7 Within a period of (four) weeks beginning on the offer date the buyer can either:

    7.1 accept the offer in writing and communicate such acceptance to the seller; or

    7.2 give to the seller a written counter-offer ('the counter-offer').

8 The counter-offer will state:

    8.1 all the terms and conditions (including the price and completion date) on which the buyer or the buyer's nominee is willing to buy the share; or

    8.2 all the terms and conditions (including the price and completion date) on which the buyer is willing to sell the buyer's share in the property to the seller or the seller's nominee.

9 All negotiations between the co-owners should be concluded within a period of (eight) weeks beginning on the offer date.

10 After the end of a period of (12) weeks beginning on the offer date either co-owner can apply to the court for an order that the property be sold if:

    10.1 neither co-owner has agreed to buy the other's share; and

    10.2 the other co-owner refuses to sell the property.[2]

---

1 With some minor adaptations to reflect their respective bargaining positions, this Schedule could be applied *mutatis mutandis* if one co-owner wishes to 'buy out' the other.

2 The application would be made under the Law of Property Act 1925, s 30. See, generally, M P Thompson *Co-Ownership* (Sweet & Maxwell, 1988) at p 53 *et seq*.

Forms

46 DECLARATION OF TRUST BY CO-OWNERS

(a) Fixed shares

(i) Short form

THIS DECLARATION OF TRUST is made on (*date*)
BETWEEN 'the co-owners' (1) (*name 1*) of (*address*) ('*name 1*') and (2) (*name 2*) also of (*address*) ('*name 2*').

IT IS AGREED AND DECLARED that:

1 The co-owners:

   1.1 are the proprietors of (*address*) title to which is registered at the Land Registry under title number (*number*) ('the property');
   1.2 purchased the property on (*completion date*);
   1.3 purchased the property for £ (*purchase price*);
   1.4 paid incidental purchase costs of £ (*costs*);
   1.5 obtained an advance of £   from and mortgaged the property to (*lender*) ('the mortgage');
   1.6 are beneficial tenants in common.

2 *(Name 1)*:

   2.1 paid £   towards the purchase price;
   2.2 paid £   towards the incidental purchase costs;
   2.3 will pay   per cent of the mortgage payments;
   2.4 will receive   per cent of the sale price,[1] less:
      (a)   per cent of the amount required to redeem the mortgage;[2] and
      (b)   per cent of the incidental costs of selling the property.

3 *(Name 2)*:

   3.1 paid £   towards the purchase price;
   3.2 paid £   towards the incidental purchase costs;
   3.3 will pay   per cent of the mortgage payments;
   3.4 will receive   per cent of the sale price[3], less:

    (a)   per cent of the amount required to redeem the mortgage;[4]
    and
    (b)   per cent of the incidental costs of selling the property.

SIGNED as a Deed by (*name 1*) in the presence of:

SIGNED as a Deed by (*name 2*) in the presence of:

---

1 Presumably $\dfrac{2.1 + 2.2 + (2.3 \times 1.5)}{1.3 + 1.4}$ expressed as a percentage.

2 Presumably the same percentage as in 2.3.

3 Presumably $\dfrac{3.1 + 3.2 + (3.3 \times 1.5)}{1.3 + 1.4}$ expressed as a percentage.

4 Presumably the same percentage as in 3.3.

(ii) Long form

THIS DECLARATION OF TRUST is made on (*date*)
BETWEEN 'the co-owners' (1) (*name 1*) of (*address*) ('*name 1*') and (2) (*name 2*) also of (*address*) ('*name 2*').

IT IS AGREED AND DECLARED that:

1 Recitals

  1.1 The co-owners are the proprietors of (*address*) title to which is registered at the Land Registry under title number (*number*) ('the property').

  1.2 The co-owners purchased the property on (*completion date*).

  1.3 The co-owners purchased the property for £   ('the purchase price').

  1.4 The incidental costs of the purchase totalled £   ('the purchase costs').

  1.5 (*Name 1*) paid £   towards the purchase price and the purchase costs.

  1.6 (*Name 2*) paid £   towards the purchase price and the purchase costs.

  1.7 The co-owners obtained an advance of £   from and have mortgaged the property to (*lender*) ('the mortgage').

  1.8 (*Name 1*) will pay   per cent of the mortgage payments.

  1.9 (*Name 2*) will pay   per cent of the mortgage payments.

 1.10 The co-owners will pay the incidental costs of selling the property in equal shares ('the sale costs').

 1.11 The co-owners will pay the costs incurred in connection with the preparation and execution of this Declaration in equal shares.

 1.12 In the absence of any agreement to the contrary, if one of the co-owners transfers all his or her legal estate and equitable interest in the property to the other co-owner, the legal costs incurred by the transferor will be paid by the transferor and the legal costs incurred by the transferee will be paid by the transferee.

2 Trusts

The co-owners:

2.1 hold the property on trust to sell it;

2.2 have power to postpone the sale;

2.3 have powers to deal with the property which are equal to those of a sole beneficial owner;

2.4 hold the property and its net proceeds of sale and its net income until sale in trust for themselves as beneficial tenants in common.

3 Shares

When the property is sold:

3.1 *(Name 1)* will receive   per cent of the sale price, less:

    (a)   per cent of the amount required to redeem the mortgage; and

    (b) 50 per cent of the sale costs;

3.2 *(Name 2)* will receive   per cent of the sale price less:

    (a)   per cent of the amount required to redeem the mortgage; and

    (b) 50 per cent of the sale costs.

3.3 If the deductions from one co-owner's share exceed the value of the percentage of the sale price to which he or she is entitled the excess will be paid out of the other co-owner's share.

4 Contingencies

4.1 If one co-owner fails to pay his or her share of the mortgage payments when it is due, the provisions of Schedule 1 will apply.

4.2 If one or both of the co-owners pay(s) for extensions, alterations, repairs or improvements to the property, the provisions of Schedule 2 will apply.

4.3 If one co-owner is unemployed or incapable of working, the provisions of Schedule 3 will apply.

4.4 If anyone else normally resides with the co-owners, the provisions of Schedule 4 will apply.

5 The nature of this declaration

This Declaration of Trust:

5.1 is a deed and is executed as a deed by the co-owners;

5.2 can be varied by a subsequent Declaration of Trust executed by both of the co-owners or those who are able to vary the trusts contained in it;

5.3 can be set aside or varied by the court.

SCHEDULE 1

(If a co-owner fails to pay his or her share of the mortgage payments when it is due.[1])

SCHEDULE 2

(If the co-owners pay for extensions, alterations, repairs or improvements to the property.[2])

SCHEDULE 3

(If a co-owner is unemployed or incapable of working.[3])

SCHEDULE 4

(If anyone else normally resides in the property with the co-owners.[4])

SIGNED as a Deed by (*name 1*) in the presence of:

SIGNED as a Deed by (*name 2*) in the presence of:

---

1 See Precedent 34 at p 55 above.
2 See Precedent 38 at p 59 above.
3 See Precedent 39 at p 62 above.
4 See Precedent 33 at p 54 above.

(iii) One co-owner alone to be responsible for the mortgage payments:

THIS DECLARATION OF TRUST is made on (*date*)
BETWEEN 'the co-owners' (1) (*name 1*) of (*address*) ('*name 1*') and (2) (*name 2*) also of (*address*) ('*name 2*').

IT IS AGREED AND DECLARED that:

1 Recitals

1.1 The co-owners are the proprietors of (*address*) ('the property').
1.2 Title to the property is registered under title number (*number*).
1.3 The property is mortgaged to (*lender*) ('the mortgage').
1.4 The co-owners purchased the property on (*date*).
1.5 The purchase price was £   .
1.6 The incidental costs of the purchase came to £   .
1.7 (*Name 1*) contributed £   towards the purchase price and purchase costs.

1.8   (*Name 2*) contributed £   towards the purchase price and pur-
      chase costs.
1.9   The mortgage advance was £
1.10 Although the mortgage is in the co-owners' joint names (*name 1*)
      will be primarily responsible for the mortgage payments.

2 Trusts

The co-owners declare that they:

2.1 hold the property on trust to sell it;
2.2 have power to postpone the sale;
2.3 have powers to deal with the property which are equal to those of a
     sole beneficial owner;
2.4 hold the property and its net proceeds of sale and its net income until
     sale in trust for themselves as beneficial tenants in common.

3 Shares

When the property is sold:

3.1 (*name 1*) will receive   per cent of the sale price, less:

   (a) 100 per cent of the amount required to redeem the mortgage; and
   (b) 50 per cent of the incidental costs of selling the property;

3.2 (*name 2*) will receive   per cent of the sale price, less:

   (a) 0 per cent of the amount required to redeem the mortgage; and
   (b) 50 per cent of the incidental costs of selling the property;

3.3 if the amounts to be deducted from (*name 1's*) share of the sale price
     exceed the value of that share, then the excess will be paid from
     (*name 2's*) share.

4 Definitions

4.1 'The sale price' means:

   (a) the price for which the property is sold; and
   (b) the price paid by the buyer of the property for any chattels jointly
        owned by the co-owners, whether or not a separate price is paid
        for those chattels.

4.2 'The amount required to redeem the mortgage' means the sum of
     money required by the lender to enable the co-owners to repay the
     mortgage and be completely released and discharged from all obliga-
     tions under it.

4.3 'The incidental costs of selling the property' means the total sum of
     money (including VAT) to be paid in respect of:

(a) estate agents' commission;
(b) legal costs and disbursements;
(c) apportionments of rates, taxes, insurance, and other outgoings on the property.

SIGNED as a Deed by (*name 1*) in the presence of:

SIGNED as a Deed by (*name 2*) in the presence of:

(b) Floating shares

(i) Tabular form

THIS DECLARATION OF TRUST is made on (*date*)
BETWEEN 'the co-owners' (1) (*name 1*) of (*address*) ('*name 1*') and (2) (*name 2*) also of (*address*) ('*name 2*').

IT IS AGREED AND DECLARED that:

1 Recitals

1.1 The co-owners are the proprietors of (*address*) ('the property').
1.2 Title to the property is registered at the Land Registry under title number (*number*).
1.3 The co-owners purchased the property on (*completion date*).
1.4 The purchase price was £   ('the purchase price').
1.5 The purchase costs came to £   ('the purchase costs').
1.6 (*Name 1*) paid £   towards the purchase price and the purchase costs.
1.7 (*Name 2*) paid £   towards the purchase price and the purchase costs.
1.8 The co-owners obtained an advance of £   from and have mortgaged the property to (*lender*).
1.9 The co-owners intend to contribute towards the mortgage payments in the proportions that their respective incomes bear to each other, or in such other proportions as they may from time to time agree.

2 Trusts

The co-owners:

2.1 hold the property on trust to sell it;
2.2 have power to postpone the sale;
2.3 have powers to deal with the property equal to those of a sole beneficial owner;
2.4 hold the property and its net proceeds of sale and its net income until sale in trust for themselves as beneficial tenants in common.

3 Shares

When the property is sold the net proceeds of sale will be divided between the co-owners in proportion to the extent to which the change in value of the property can be attributed to the contributions made by each of them towards the:

3.1 purchase price;
3.2 purchase costs;
3.3 mortgage payments;
3.4 cost of repairs and improvements to the property; and
3.5 the incidental costs of selling the property will be borne pro rata.

4 Calculation of shares

The share of the net proceeds of sale to which each co-owner is entitled will be calculated by:

4.1 completing the record of contributions set out in the First Schedule; and then
4.2 applying the formulae set out in the Second Schedule.

FIRST SCHEDULE (Record of contributions).[1]

SECOND SCHEDULE (The formulae).[2]

SIGNED as a Deed by (*name 1*) in the presence of:

SIGNED as a Deed by (*name 2*) in the presence of:

---

1 See Precedent 18(b) at p 38 above.
2 Ibid.

(ii) Long form

THIS DECLARATION OF TRUST is made on (*date*)
BETWEEN 'the co-owners' (1) (*name 1*) of (*address*) ('*name 1*') and (2) (*name 2*) also of (*address*) ('*name 2*').

IT IS AGREED AND DECLARED as follows:

1 Recitals

1.1 The co-owners are the proprietors of (*address*) title to which is registered at the Land Registry under title number (*number*) ('the property').
1.2 The co-owners purchased the property on (*completion date*).
1.3 The co-owners purchased the property for £   ('the purchase price').
1.4 The incidental costs of the purchase totalled £   ('the purchase costs').

1.5   (*Name 1*) paid £   towards the purchase price and the purchase costs.

1.6   (*Name 2*) paid £   towards the purchase price and the purchase costs.

1.7   The co-owners obtained an advance of £   from and have mortgaged the property to (*lender*) ('the mortgage').

1.8   The co-owners intend to contribute to the mortgage payments (whether they are repayments of capital or payments of interest or insurance premiums) in the proportions that their incomes bear to each other or in such other proportions as they may from time to time agree.

1.9   Each of the co-owners has received independent legal advice on the provisions and implications of this Declaration.

1.10 The legal costs incurred in connection with the preparation and execution of this Declaration (including the costs of obtaining independent legal advice) will be paid by the co-owners in equal shares.

2 Trusts

The co-owners:

2.1 hold the property on trust to sell it;

2.2 have power to postpone the sale;

2.3 have powers to deal with the property equal to those of a sole beneficial owner;

2.4 hold the property and its net proceeds of sale and its net income until sale in trust for themselves as beneficial tenants in common.

3 Shares

When the property is sold its net proceeds of sale will be divided between the co-owners in proportion to the contributions made by each of them towards the:

3.1 purchase price;

3.2 purchase costs;

3.3 mortgage payments;

3.4 cost of repairs and improvements to the property; and

3.5 other payments (if any) analogous to those above.

4 Calculation of shares

The share of the net proceeds of sale to which each co-owner is entitled will be calculated by:

4.1 adding together his or her contributions to produce 'the individual contribution'; and then

4.2 adding together both of the co-owners' individual contributions to produce 'the combined contributions'; and then

4.3 dividing the net proceeds of sale plus the incidental costs of selling the property by the combined contributions to produce 'the dividend'; and finally

4.4 multiplying the individual contribution by the dividend to produce the share.

5 Sale and transfer costs

5.1 When the property is sold the incidental costs of selling it will be paid by the co-owners in the proportions that their respective shares bear to each other.

5.2 In the absence of any agreement to the contrary, if one of the co-owners transfers all his or her legal estate and equitable interest in the property to the other co-owner or to a third party at the direction of the other co-owner, the valuation fees, legal fees and other costs incurred by the transferor will be paid by the transferor, and the valuation fees, legal fees and other costs incurred by the transferee will be paid by the transferee.

6 Contingencies

6.1 If one of the co-owners dies and the other does not become solely and beneficially entitled to the property, the provisions of Schedule 1 will apply.

6.2 If one of the co-owners wishes to sell the property and the other refuses to sell it, the provisions of Schedule 2 will apply.

6.3 If the co-owners decide to separate and both of them wish to keep the property, the provisions of Schedule 3 will apply.

6.4 If one of the co-owners moves out of the property before it is sold, the provisions of Schedule 4 will apply.

7 This declaration

This Declaration of Trust:

7.1 contains the whole agreement between the co-owners and supersedes any earlier agreements, representations or promises made by either co-owner in respect of the property;

7.2 can be varied by a subsequent Declaration of Trust executed by all the persons who are able to vary the original trusts;

7.3 has been executed in duplicate so that each of the co-owners may possess a copy of it, and both copies will be regarded as one deed, and each copy will be as efficacious as the other.

SCHEDULE 1.[1]

SCHEDULE 2.[2]

SCHEDULE 3.[3]

SCHEDULE 4.[4]

SIGNED as a Deed by (*name 1*) in the presence of:

SIGNED as a Deed by (*name 2*) in the presence of:

---

1 See Precedent 36 at p 57 above.
2 See Precedent 35 at p 56 above.
3 See Precedent 42 at p 67 above.
4 See Precedent 43 at p 68 above.

---

47 THE PERSON WHO 'MOVES IN'

(a) Deed of surrender of any potential right to claim a beneficial interest in the property[1]

THIS DEED made on (*date*)
BETWEEN (1) (*name 1*) of (*address*) ('*name 1*') and (2) (*name 2*) also of (*address*) ('*name 2*') WITNESSES that:

1 Recitals

1.1 (*Name 1*) is the registered proprietor of (*address*) ('the property').
1.2 (*Name 2*) has lived in the property with (*name 1*) since (*date*).

2 Surrender

In consideration of (*name 1*) continuing to provide (him)/(her) with accommodation (*name 2*) releases, renounces and surrenders to (*name 1*) all if any rights that (he)/(she) may have at any time to claim a beneficial interest in the property, regardless of any contributions (he)/(she) may make towards:

2.1 (his)/(her) living and accommodation expenses; and
2.2 the payment of any mortgage on the property; and
2.3 any repairs and improvements to the property.

3 Reservation of right

Nothing in this Deed deprives (*name 1*) of the right at any time during (his)/(her) life or by Will to transfer all or any part of (his)/(her) legal estate and beneficial interest in the property to (*name 2*).

4 Procedural safeguards

(*Name 2*) acknowledges that (he)/(she) understands the nature and effect of this Deed and is entering into it:

4.1 freely and voluntarily;

4.2 without any form of pressure or coercion from (*name 1*) or anyone else; and

4.3 after receiving independent legal advice on its provisions and implications.

SIGNED as a Deed by (*name 1*) in the presence of:

SIGNED as a Deed by (*name 2*) in the presence of:

---

1 Stamp duty of 50p is payable as the deed amounts to a 'surrender of any kind whatsoever not chargeable with duty as a conveyance on sale' (Stamp Act 1891, Sch 1).

(b) Declaration of trust by sole owner acknowledging that the partner has acquired a beneficial interest

THIS DECLARATION OF TRUST is made on (*date*)
BETWEEN 'the parties' (1) (*name 1*) of (*address*) ('*name 1*') and (2) (*name 2*) also of (*address*) ('*name 2*').

IT IS AGREED AND DECLARED that:

1 Recitals

1.1 (*Name 1*) is the sole proprietor of (*address*) ('the property').

1.2 Title to the property is registered at the Land Registry under title number (*number*).

1.3 The property is mortgaged to (*lender*) ('the mortgage').

1.4 (*Name 2*) moved into the property on (*date*) and has lived there with (*name 1*) ever since.

1.5 (*Name 2*) has been contributing towards the mortgage payments (and has paid for repairs and improvements to the property).

1.6 The parties intend to continue living together for an indefinite length of time.

2 Acknowledgment, declaration and covenants

(*Name 1*):

2.1 acknowledges that (*name 2*) has acquired a beneficial interest in the property by virtue of (his)/(her) contributions towards the mortgage payments (and repairs and improvements);

2.2 declares that (he)/(she) holds the property and its net proceeds of sale and its net income until sale in trust for (himself)/(herself) and (*name 2*) as beneficial tenants in common;

2.3 will apply to the Land Registry for a restriction to be entered in the register in order to protect (*name 2's*) beneficial interest in the property; and

2.4 will do all (he)/(she) can to transfer the property and the mortgage into the parties' joint names, if (*name 2*) wishes.

3 Valuation of prior share

When (*name 2*) moved into the property:

3.1 its open market value was £   ;

3.2 the amount required to redeem the mortgage was £   ; and

3.3 the equity to which (*name 1*) was then entitled was £   ('the prior share').

4 Calculation of shares

When the property is sold:

4.1 (*name 1*) will receive (*fraction or percentage*) of the sale price representing the return on the prior share;

4.2 the remainder of the net proceeds of sale will be divided between the parties in equal shares;

4.3 if the incidental costs of selling the property and the amount required to redeem the mortgage exceed the remainder of the net proceeds of sale, the excess will be paid from (*name 1's*) share of the sale price representing the return on the prior share.

5 Contingency

Unless the parties agree otherwise, if they separate or are about to separate:

5.1 (*name 1*) will have the right to remain in the property and to purchase (*name 2's*) share in it;

5.2 (*name 1*) will complete the purchase of (*name 2's*) share within a period of (eight) weeks beginning on the date on which (he)/(she) moves out of the property;

5.3 if at the end of that period of (eight) weeks (*name 1*) has not completed the purchase of (*name 2's*) share, (*name 2*) can apply to the court for an order that the property be sold;

5.4 (*name 1*) will pay the valuation fees, legal fees and other costs which (he)/(she) incurs; and

5.5 (*name 2*) will pay the valuation fees, legal fees and other costs which (he)/(she) incurs.

SIGNED as a Deed by (*name 1*) in the presence of:

SIGNED as a Deed by (*name 2*) in the presence of:

48 DECLARATION OF TRUST BY SOLE OWNER

(a) Another person has contributed to the purchase price[1]

THIS DECLARATION OF TRUST is made on (*date*)
BETWEEN (1) (*name 1*) of (*address*) ('*name 1*') and (2) (*name 2*) of (*address*) ('*name 2*').

IT IS AGREED AND DECLARED that:

1 (*Name 1*):

    1.1 is the proprietor of (*address*) title to which is registered at the Land Registry under title number (*number*) ('the property');

    1.2 purchased the property on (*completion date*);

    1.3 purchased the property for £   ('the purchase price');

    1.4 paid £   towards the purchase price;

    1.5 paid £   towards the incidental purchase costs which amounted in total to £   ('the purchase costs');

    1.6 obtained an advance of £   from and mortgaged the property to (*lender*) ('the mortgage').

2 (*Name 2*):[2]

    2.1 paid £   towards the purchase price (and the purchase costs);

    2.2 made that payment with the intention of acquiring a beneficial interest in the property;[3]

    2.3 is not a registered proprietor of the property.

3 (*Name 1*):

    3.1 acknowledges that the payment made by (*name 2*) towards the purchase price (and the purchase costs) was neither a gift nor a loan to (him)/(her);[4]

    3.2 declares that (he)/(she) holds the property and its net proceeds of sale in trust for (himself)/(herself) and (*name 2*) as beneficial tenants in common;

    3.3 will apply to the Land Registry for the entry of the appropriate restriction in order to protect the beneficial interest of (*name 2*).[5]

4 When the property is sold:

    4.1 (*name 1*) will receive   per cent of the sale price from which will be deducted:

        (a) the amount required to redeem the mortgage; and

        (b) the incidental costs of selling the property;

4.2   (*name 2*) will receive   per cent of the sale price.[6]

SIGNED as a Deed by (*name 1*) in the presence of:

SIGNED as a Deed by (*name 2*) in the presence of:

---

1 'A resulting trust arises where a person acquires a legal estate but has not provided the consideration or the whole of the consideration for its acquisition, unless a contrary intention is proved' (*Cowcher v Cowcher* [1972] 1 All ER 943 at 949e, per Bagnall J).

2 If necessary, the parties' relationship could be stated at this point. For example: '(*name 2*): is the (mother)/(father) of (*name 1*)'.

3 *Sekhon v Alissa* [1989] 2 FLR 94.

4 'The next question is whether the mother's contribution was to be an unsecured loan or to give her a beneficial interest. In my judgment the law presumes a resulting trust in her favour and that presumption has to be rebutted by evidence that she intended a personal loan without acquiring any interest in the property' (*Sekhon v Alissa* [1989] 2 FLR 94 at 99D, per Hoffmann J).

5 An interest behind a trust for sale is a minor interest (Land Registration Act 1925, s 3(xv)(a)). Although it is clear that the 1925 legislation was intended to impose a trust for sale in all cases of beneficial co-ownership, this is one of the circumstances which it did not expressly cover. See, generally, Law Commission Working Paper No 94, 'Trusts of Land' (1986), at para 6.5. 'It is essential to ensure by the entry of a restriction that capital moneys will be paid and applied in accordance with law and the lawful requirements of the owners of the minor interests' (Ruoff and Roper *Registered Conveyancing* (Sweet & Maxwell) 4th Edn at p 122.

6 Presumably $\dfrac{name\ 2's\ contribution}{purchase\ price\ +\ purchase\ costs}$ expressed as a percentage.

(b) Elderly person buys his or her council house with financial assistance from his or her children

THIS DECLARATION OF TRUST is made on (*date*)
BETWEEN (1) (*name 1*) of (*address*) ('*name 1*') and (2) (*name 2*) of (*address*) ('*name 2*').

IT IS AGREED AND DECLARED that:

1 Recitals

1.1   (*Name 1*) is the sole proprietor of (*address*) title to which is registered at the Land Registry under title number (*number*) ('the property').

1.2   The property formerly belonged to (*Borough/City/County/District*) Council ('the Council').

1.3   (*Name 1*) purchased the property from the Council on (*date*) ('completion date').

1.4   On completion date the value of the property was £

1.5   The value of the property was discounted by £   ('the discount') because (*name 1*) had occupied the property as a Council tenant for (*number*) years.

1.6   In the transfer to (him)/(her) it was stated that (*name 1*) had paid the Council £   for the property ('the purchase price').

1.7   The incidental costs of purchasing the property came to £ ('the purchase costs').

1.8   (*Name 1*) paid £   towards the purchase price and the purchase costs.

1.9   (*Name 2*), who is (*name 1's*) (son)/(daughter), paid £   towards the purchase price and the purchase costs.

1.10 (*Name 2*) contributed to the purchase partly as an investment and partly to enable (*name 1*) to live in (his)/(her) own home.

1.11 (*Name 2*) intends that (*name 1*) should continue to live in the property for as long as (he)/(she) wishes, rent-free.

1.12 (*Name 2*) acknowledges that the discount should primarily enure for the benefit of (*name 1*).

1.13 (*Name 1*) acknowledges that (he)/(she) would have been unable to purchase the property without financial assistance from (*name 2*).

2 Trusts

(*Name 1*) declares that (he)/(she) holds the net proceeds of sale of the property in trust for (himself)/(herself) and (*name 2*) as beneficial tenants in common.

3 Shares

When the property is sold:

3.1   (*name 1*) will receive   per cent of the sale price, representing the return on the discount and (his)/(her) contribution towards the purchase price and the purchase costs, *less* (50) per cent of the incidental costs of selling the property ('*name 1's* share');

3.2   (*name 2*) will receive   per cent of the sale price, representing the return on (his)/(her) contribution towards the purchase price and the purchase costs, *less* (50) per cent of the incidental costs of selling the property ('*name 2's* share');

3.3   if all or any part of the discount has to be repaid to the Council, it will be paid from (*name 1's*) share;

3.4   if (*name 2's*) share is less than (his)/(her) original contribution towards the purchase price and the purchase costs, the shortfall will be paid from (*name 1's*) share.

4 Gradual diminution of (*name 1's*) share

4.1   In consideration of the fact that (he)/(she) would have been unable to purchase the property without financial assistance from (*name 2*), and in consideration of the assurance from (*name 2*) that (he)/(she) can continue to live in the property rent-free for as long as (he)/(she) wishes, (*name 1*) agrees that the value of (his)/(her) share will gradually decrease and that the value of (*name 2's*) share will proportionately increase, and to that intent the following provisions will apply.

4.2 When the property is sold or when either party realises (his)/(her) (his or her) share in it ('the disposal') (*name 1's*) share will be reduced by (10) per cent for each complete year that has elapsed between the (1st) anniversary of completion date and the disposal.

4.3 The amount by which (*name 1's*) share is reduced will be added to (*name 2's*) share.

4.4 For the avoidance of doubt:

(a) there will be no reduction of (*name 1's*) share before the (1st) anniversary of completion date because of the provisions relating to the repayment of the discount to the Council; and

(b) there will be no reduction of (*name 1's*) share in respect of any period of less than a complete year.

5 Terms of continued occupation

(*Name 2*) agrees that (*name 1*) can continue to live in the property rent-free for as long as (he)/(she) wishes on the terms that (*name 1*):

5.1 pays all the outgoings on the property;

5.2 keeps it in reasonable repair and condition;

5.3 keeps it insured to its full reinstatement value; and

5.4 complies with all the covenants and conditions to which it is subject.

SIGNED as a Deed by (*name 1*) in the presence of:

SIGNED as a Deed by (*name 2*) in the presence of:

---

1 The purchase of a Council House by a tenant with financial assistance from his or her children is, potentially, fraught with difficulties and raises important policy issues. The former tenant and his or her children should receive independent legal advice. Among the questions to be asked are as follows.

(a) Who is to have the benefit of the discount?

(b) Who will be liable for the repayment of the discount if there is a disposal of the property within the relevant period?

(c) To what extent should the children be allowed to benefit at the expense of their parent and, indirectly, the ratepayer and taxpayer?

(d) How can the children be protected from losing out on the transaction?

(e) What is the underlying purpose of the children's involvement?

(f) What are the parties' intentions regarding the former tenant's continued occupation of the property?

(g) Does the former tenant have other children who might reasonably be expected to benefit from his or her estate?

(h) To what extent is securing entitlement to or increasing the amount of any income-related benefits a 'significant operative purpose' behind any value-shifting exercise? See, generally, the Income Support (General) Regulations 1987, SI 1987/1967, reg 51, and the Commissioner's decision in *R (SB) 40/85*.

49 VARIATION OF A DECLARATION OF TRUST[1]

THIS VARIATION is made on (*date*)
BETWEEN 'the co-owners'[2] (1) (*name 1*) of (*address*) ('*name 1*') and (2) (*name 2*) (also) of (*address*) ('*name 2*').

IT IS AGREED AND DECLARED that:

1 Recitals

    1.1 This deed is supplemental[3] to the Declaration of Trust ('the Declaration') made between the co-owners on (*date*).

    1.2 The co-owners wish to vary the Declaration as follows.

2 Revocation

The co-owners revoke Clause(s) (*number(s)*) [AND/OR] Schedule(s) (*number(s)*) of the Declaration.

3 Shares

From now onwards the co-owners will hold the property (as defined in the Declaration)[4] and its net proceeds of sale in trust for themselves as beneficial tenants in common in the following shares:

(*set out the shares*)

4 Confirmation

The co-owners confirm the Declaration in all other respects.

SIGNED as a Deed by (*name 1*) in the presence of:

SIGNED as a Deed by (*name 2*) in the presence of:

---

1 'If all the beneficiaries are *sui iuris* they can join together with the trustees and declare different trusts which supersede those contained in the original declaration. These new trusts operate *proprio vigore* by virtue of a self-contained instrument, namely the deed of arrangement or variation. The original declaration will have lost any force or relevance' (*Re Holmden's Settlement Trusts* [1968] AC 685 at 713C, per Lord Wilberforce).

2 This precedent assumes that the original co-owners are the parties able to vary the trusts. If the variation is being made by, say, the personal representatives of one of the co-owners, the wording should be adapted accordingly.

3 Law of Property Act 1925, s 58: 'any instrument . . . expressed to be supplemental to a previous instrument, shall, as far as may be, be read and have effect as if the supplemental instrument contained a full recital of the previous instrument'. It would be sensible to endorse a memorandum of the variation on the original declaration of trust.

4 The words in brackets 'as defined in the Declaration' are not, strictly speaking, necessary. See footnote 3 above.

CHAPTER 2: COHABITATION CONTRACTS

INDEX

Forms

PART 1: INTRODUCTORY TEXT

Introduction[1]

A cohabitation contract is an agreement between an unmarried couple[2] who are living together or intending to live together.[3] In some jurisdictions it is essential that the contract be in writing, although in other jurisdictions the courts have been prepared to uphold oral contracts 'implied-in-fact'.[4] At one extreme, a cohabitation contract may contain simple, basic provisions dealing with one or two aspects of the parties' property and finances;[5] at the other extreme, it can be a comprehensive code which attempts to regulate every minute detail of day-to-day living.[6]

Cohabitation contracts have commanded an increasing amount of attention and publicity over the last 20 years,[7] but their actual incidence in England and Wales is still extremely uncommon. In practice, there is probably a greater public demand for antenuptial agreements (or marriage contracts),[8] by which a couple who are intending to marry seek to 'opt out' of our current system of matrimonial law, in the hope that they can remain subject to the legal provisions which would have applied had they stayed as cohabiting partners or legal strangers.[9] By contrast, an unmarried couple who enter into a cohabitation agreement 'contract in' to a relationship which will henceforth be governed, wholly or partly, by the law of contract and will, therefore, be subject to the common law and equitable remedies available for breach.[10]

---

1 See, generally, Chris Barton *Cohabitation Contracts* (Gower, 1985).

2 The couple need not be respectively male and female. Conceivably, there could be other parties to the contract. The New South Wales De Facto Relationships Act 1984, s 44(1) defines a cohabitation contract as 'an agreement between a man and a woman, whether or not there are other parties to the agreement . . .'

3 There may be a difference in the legal status of an agreement made between parties who are already living together, and an agreement between a couple intending to live together. If the parties are already cohabiting, the contract cannot be considered as promoting sexual immorality. Compare *Walker v Perkins* [1764] 1 Wm Bl 517, where a contract entered into before cohabitation was held to be void; and *Annandale v Harris* (1727) 2 P Wms 432, where a contract entered into on the breakdown of the relationship was held to be valid.

4 The unwritten agreements seem to have commanded more attention in the USA. In the celebrated case *Marvin v Marvin* 18 Cal 3d 660 (Cal 1976), the court upheld an oral contract as 'implied-in-fact' by virtue of the couple's cohabitation. By contrast, New

York State rejects contracts 'implied-in-fact' and will only accept express, written agreements (*Morone v Morone* 50 NY 2d 481 (NY 1980)).

5 For an example, see Precedent 83 at p 156 below.

6 See, generally, Lenore J Weitzman *The Marriage Contract: Spouses, Lovers, and the Law* (The Free Press, NY, 1981). A good illustration can be found at p 320: 'Absent truly extraordinary circumstances, we agree to spend at least one evening a week enjoying each other – alone together. An evening begins at 7 pm'.

7 Possibly the terminus a quo in England and Wales was the article by P Gray, 'A New Lease of Life' (1973) 123 NLJ 591, which contained a precedent antenuptial agreement.

8 See The Law Society's Family Law Committee's Memorandum 'Maintenance and Capital Provision on Divorce' (May 1991). See also Chapter 5, Precedent 4 at p 235 below and generally.

9 The typical antenuptial agreement is made by an older couple, one or both of whom has been married before. See, generally, Alexander Lindey, 'Lindey on Separation Agreements and Antenuptial Contracts' (May 1991, Cumulative Supplement) (Matthew Bender & Co Inc, NY).

10 For the remedies see, generally, Treitel *The Law of Contract* (Sweet & Maxwell) 8th Edn at Chapter 21.

Cohabitation Contracts and Declarations of Trust

It is important to distinguish between a cohabitation contract and a declaration of trust. A series of judicial pronouncements, which began as a gentle reminder[1] and has become progressively more vehement in tone,[2] has made it virtually mandatory that any legal practitioner who acts for a couple buying a residential property should ensure that they declare their respective beneficial interests in the property by means of an express declaration of trust. There is nothing mandatory about a cohabitation contract, even though it covers much the same ground as a declaration of trust. Indeed, it is questionable whether a cohabitation contract is valid and enforceable. While this apparent paradox exists, practitioners may prefer to deal with the beneficial ownership of land in a separate declaration of trust, and cover any other aspects of the couple's relationship and finances in a separate cohabitation contract.

1 *Cowcher v Cowcher* [1972] 1 All ER 943 at 959, per Bagnall J.

2 *Bernard v Josephs* (1983) FLR 178 at 187F, per Griffiths LJ; *Walker v Hall* (1984) FLR 126 at 129E, per Dillon LJ; *Taylor and Harman v Warners* (unreported) 21 July 1987 (but see the article by Ross Crail in *The Law Society's Gazette*, 29 June 1988, at p 26, where Warner J found the solicitors guilty of negligence; *Springette v Defoe* (1992) *The Independent*, March 24.

Validity and Enforceability

The validity of a cohabitation contract is a matter of substantive law. Its enforceability is a matter of procedural law.[1]

Until the question of validity has been clarified by Parliament or the court, a cohabitation contract could fail for two reasons:[2]

1 because it is sexually immoral;[3] and
2 because it is likely to prejudice the status of marriage.[4]

It is improbable that any court nowadays would strike down a typical cohabitation contract on either of these grounds.[5]

Even if a cohabitation contract were valid, it could be unenforceable for a variety of reasons, for example because of:

1 an absence of intention to create legal relations;[6]
2 an absence of consideration;[7]
3 uncertainty;[8]
4 duress or coercion;[9] or
5 inequality of bargaining power.[10]

Entering into a formal, written agreement should have the effect of rebutting the presumption that the parties do not intend their domestic arrangements to be legally binding.[11] The lack of consideration can be overcome by executing the contract as a deed.[12] The problem of uncertainty, whether it is caused by ambiguity, vagueness or incompleteness, is essentially a problem for the draftsman. It seems likely, therefore, that in future the main difficulties of enforceability will be undue pressure, inequality of bargaining power and, perhaps, misrepresentation.[13] It is for these reasons that some of the jurisdictions that recognise cohabitation contracts insist that each of the parties must have been separately advised by a legal practitioner[14] and that both parties must have made full disclosure of their assets, liabilities and family backgrounds.[15]

---

1 Cheshire and Fifoot *Law of Contract* (Sweet & Maxwell) 8th Edn, which states at p 171:

> '(English Law) has allowed an intermediate position where a contract, though valid, may yet be "unenforceable" by an action at law unless and until certain technical requirements are satisfied The "unenforceable contract" is clearly a creature of procedural rather than of substantive law'.

2 A third reason would be where a cohabitation contract seeks to oust the jurisdiction of the court.

3 'The law will not enforce an immoral promise, such as a promise between a man and a woman to live together without being married or to pay a sum of money or to give some other consideration in return for immoral association' (*Fender v St John-Mildmay* [1938] AC 1 at 42, per Lord Wright).

4 *Lowe v Peers* (1768) 4 Burr 2225, [1558–1774] All ER Rep 364; *Spiers v Hunt* [1908] 1 KB 720; *Fender v St John-Mildmay* above, at 44.

5 Both of these public policy grounds converge where one party to the contract is still married to someone else. In at least one American case the court denied relief where the plaintiff was the married party, concluding that if it enforced the agreement it would be encouraging the breakdown of a marriage and supporting an immoral, adulterous association (*McCall v Frampton*, 99 Misc 2d 159, 415 NYS 2d 752 (NY 1979)).

6 *Balfour v Balfour* [1919] 2 KB 571.

7 *Bret v JS* (1600) Cro Eliz 756.

8 *Layton v Martin* [1986] 2 FLR 227 at 239: 'The offer is no more than a statement of intention cast in general terms . . . The more general and less precise the language of the

so-called contract, the more difficult it will be to infer (the intention to create a legally binding contract)', per Scott J.

9 *Zamet v Hyman* [1961] 1 WLR 1442.

10 In recent years a number of states in the USA have abandoned the 'fair and reasonable' test and have adopted an 'unconscionability' test. Basically, the contract will be enforceable provided that it was not unconscionable when it was made.

11 *Merritt v Merritt* [1970] 1 WLR 1211.

12 See generally, G H Treitel *The Law of Contract* (Sweet & Maxwell) 8th Edn at Chapter 3.

13 Note *Posner v Posner* 257 So 2d 530 (Fla, 1972). When entering into an antenuptial agreement Mr Posner had misrepresented the extent of his assets by failing to disclose his entitlement under a trust. The Florida Supreme Court held that full disclosure is essential if an agreement is to be upheld.

14 For example the De Facto Relationships Act 1984 (New South Wales), s 47.

15 In the USA a number of cases have involved non-disclosure or incomplete disclosure before entry into an antenuptial agreement (qv *Posner* above). The indication is that cohabitation contracts might be construed in the same way: Alexander Lindey *Lindey on Separation Agreements and Antenuptial Contracts* (Matthew Bender & Co Inc, NY, 1991) at Chapter 95.1.

Comparative Law

Cohabitation contracts – or, perhaps more accurately, the recognition of cohabitation contracts – originated in the USA. There were some decisions on them before the 1970s, but they were relatively few and went largely unnoticed.[1] The seminal case of *Marvin v Marvin*[2] was heard in California in 1976. In the course of his judgment Tobriner J said:[3]

'The fact that a man and woman live together without marriage, and engage in a sexual relationship, does not in itself invalidate agreements between them relating to their earnings, property or expenses. Neither is such an agreement invalid merely because the parties may have contemplated the creation or continuation of a nonmarital relationship when they entered into it. Agreements between nonmarital partners fail only to the extent that they rest upon a consideration of meretricious sexual services'.

This decision had considerable impact, and now more than half of the United States have indicated a willingness to recognise and enforce agreements between cohabitees. Only two States – Georgia[4] and Illinois[5] – have expressly refused to recognise such agreements.

Almost immediately, the *Marvin* doctrine crossed the 49th parallel into Canada where several provinces made statutory provision for the recognition of cohabitation contracts.[6] Usually the provision consisted of a section or two in a general Act relating to family law or family property.[7]

Meanwhile, in Australia the New South Wales Law Reform Commission published a 'Report on De Facto Relationships' in 1983, and this was followed by the De Facto Relationships Act 1984, which came into force on 1 July 1985. According to this Act,[8] a de facto relationship is 'the relationship between de facto partners, being the relationship of living or having lived together as husband and wife on a bona fide domestic basis although not married to each other'. This definition obviously excludes gay and lesbian partnerships and multiple relationships. The Act has been criticised for drawing a distinction between married and unmarried couples in the fields of property and maintenance.[9] Entitlement to maintenance between former de facto partners is more restricted than that between spouses; and the distribution of property is based solely on compensation for contributions, with no further adjustment for post-separation financial inequalities.

The impact of the De Facto Relationships Act 1984 has been disappointing. Very few cases have come to court, and it is reported that in Sydney 'the drafting of cohabitation and separation agreements is an infrequent practice even in specialised family law firms'.[10] The other States and Territories have been slow to follow the lead given by New South Wales.[11]

---

1 See, generally, Walter O Weyrauch and Sanford N Katz, *American Family Law in Transition* (BNA Books, Washington DC, 1983).

2 The facts, very briefly, were these. In June 1964 Michelle Triola met Lee Marvin, the filmstar. In October 1964 they entered into an oral agreement that while they lived together they would combine their efforts and earnings and would share equally all property accumulated as a result of their efforts whether individual or combined. They also agreed to hold themselves out to the general public as husband and wife. They lived together until May 1970, when their cohabitation ended at his insistence. He continued to support her financially for about 18 months.

3 There were several *Marvin* trials. The decision of Tobriner J in the Supreme Court of California was in *Marvin v Marvin* (I) (1976).

4 *Rehak v Mathis* 238 SE 2d 81 (Ga 1977).

5 *Hewitt v Hewitt* 394 NE 2d 1204 (Ill 1979), although in *Spafford v Couts* 118 Ill App 566 (1983), the court suggested that contracts not based entirely on living together, and not resembling marriage claims, may be enforced.

6 Prince Edward Island appears to have been the first province to legislate on cohabitation agreements (Family Law Reform Act, SPEI 1978).

7 See, generally, Winifred H Holland *Unmarried Couples: Legal Aspects of Cohabitation* (1982, The Carswell Company Limited) at p 143 et seq.

8 De Facto Relationships Act 1984, s 3(1). The opposite of 'de facto' is 'de iure'. Spouses are 'de iure partners'.

9 See, generally, HA Finlay and RJ Bailey-Harris *Family Law in Australia* (Butterworths, 1989) at Chapter 9. See also 'Support', footnote 2, at p 104 below.

10 Ibid at para 937, quoting J Wade, 'Discretionary Property Scheme for De Facto Spouses – The Experiment in New South Wales' (1987) 2 ALFJ 75.

11 In Western Australia, cohabitation and separation agreements between de facto partners can be registered in the Family Court under the Family Court Act 1975 (WA), s 70(2).

Recent Recommendations

On 7 March 1988 the Committee of Ministers of the Council of Europe recommended that the governments of member states should take the necessary measures:

' (i) to ensure that contracts relating to property between persons living together as an unmarried couple, or which regulate matters concerning their property either during their relationship or when their relationship has ceased, should not be considered to be invalid solely because they have been concluded under these conditions; and

(ii) to apply the same principle to testamentary dispositions'.[1]

In May 1991 the Law Society's Family Law Committee published a Memorandum on 'Maintenance and Capital Provision on Divorce' which considers, in depth, the question of 'marriage contracts' (or antenuptial agreements), as distinct from cohabitation contracts. The Committee recommended the following.[2]

'(i) Legislation should be introduced to make marriage contracts enforceable.

(ii) This should provide for a number of procedural safeguards including a requirement that each party take independent legal advice before signing a contract.

(iii) Provision should also be made in a contract for a system of regular reviews and a list of events which should trigger a review/revocation of the contract.'

On 11 June 1991, Teresa Gorman, the Conservative Member of Parliament for Billericay, presented a 'ten-minute rule Bill'[3] in the House of Commons.[4] The Cohabitation (Contract Enforcement) Bill states that:[5]

'1 Any two persons who are not married to each other, and who cohabit or intend to do so, may enter into a cohabitation contract to regulate the financial arrangements between them and to define their respective rights in and ownership of property, including land, whether held at that time or acquired thereafter.

2 (1) The general law of contract shall apply to any such cohabitation contract provided that the contract is in writing and signed by each party in the presence of an attesting witness.

(2) There shall be a rebuttable presumption that persons entering into a cohabitation contract have the intention to create legal relations.

(3) A cohabitation contract shall be enforceable notwithstanding the absence of consideration.

3 A cohabitation contract shall not be rendered invalid by reason only that part is adjudged invalid or unenforceable.

4 (1) Except as provided for by subsection (2) below, a cohabitation contract shall terminate on the marriage of the parties, or of either of them to another person, but without prejudice to any rights which existed before termination of the contract.

(2) A cohabitation contract shall not terminate on the marriage of the parties to each other provided that it contains –

(a) a statement that the parties intend that it shall continue after their marriage to each other; and

(b) a certificate in a form prescribed by the Lord Chancellor that before entering into the contract each party received independent legal advice.

5 (1) This Act may be cited as the Cohabitation (Contract Enforcement) Act 1991.

(2) This Act extends to England and Wales only.'

On 6 May 1992 the Scottish Law Commission published its 'Report on Family Law'.[6] Part XVI of the Report deals with cohabitation, and is based on the results of a Discussion Paper, 'The Effects of Cohabitation in Private Law', which was circulated in May 1990.[7] The Scottish Law Commission received suggestions from a number of consultees that, if cohabitation were to have certain legal consequences, cohabitees should be able to 'opt out' of them. The Commission thought it unnecessary to include any specific provisions on 'opting out' in its Draft Bill, in view of the nature and limited extent of its proposals.[8] As far as cohabitation contracts are concerned, it made this recommendation:[9]

'A contract between cohabitants or prospective cohabitants relating to property or financial matters should not be void or unenforceable solely because it was concluded by parties in, or about to enter, this type of relationship'.

None of the recommendations discussed above has yet been implemented or enacted.

---

1 R(88)3. Strasbourg 1988. ISBN 92–871–1606–7.
2 The Law Society's Family Law Committee Memorandum (May 1991) at p 28.
3 For 'ten-minute rule Bills' generally, see J A G Griffith and Michael Ryle *Parliament: Functions, Practice and Procedures* (Sweet & Maxwell, 1989) at pp 390 to 392; Erskine May *Parliamentary Practice* (Butterworths) 21st Edn at pp 463, 464.
4 *Hansard*, 6th Series, Vol 192, p 791.
5 HCB 1990/91, 175. ISBN 0–10–317591–1.
6 Scot Law Com No 135.
7 Scot Law Com Discussion Paper No 86.
8 Scot Law Com No 135, para 16.47.
9 Ibid, para 16.46.

Support

Neither partner in a cohabitation relationship has a duty to support the other,[1] and neither partner has a right to claim maintenance from the other.[2] It could be argued that the social security legislation on income-related benefits is an exception to this general rule, but even this provides no enforceable support obligation between cohabitees.[3] Any support obligation between the partners can only arise out of an agreement.[4] By contrast, each parent has a duty to maintain his or her child.[5]

---

1 Compare marriage. For a discussion of the common law duty to maintain and a consideration of its relevance nowadays, see S M Cretney and J M Masson *Principles of Family Law* (Sweet & Maxwell, 1990) 5th Edn at p 323 *et seq*. See also *Windeler v Whitehall* [1990] 2 FLR 505: 'If this were California, this would be a claim for palimony, but it is England and it is not' (at p 506, per Millet J).
2 In New South Wales a de facto partner may be awarded maintenance if the court is satisfied that the applicant is unable to support himself or herself because (a) he or she has the care and control of a child under 12 or a physically or mentally handicapped child under 16; or (b) his or her earning capacity has been adversely affected by the

circumstances of the relationship (De Facto Relationships Act 1984, s 27). An order for periodic maintenance will cease when the child reaches 12 or 16, as the case may be; or, where the applicant's earning capacity has been adversely affected, three years after the date of the order, or four years after the date on which the partners last ceased to live together, whichever is the shorter (ibid, s 30).

3 Social Security Act 1986, ss 20(11) and 22(5). *Cf* Pat Clayton *The Cohabitation Guide* (Wildwood House, London, 1981) at p 76: 'the law does not require cohabitants to maintain each other, but the Supplementary Benefits Commission does'.

4 The US courts have tended to avoid periodical payments and have preferred to award lump sum payments analogous to any other contract recovery (Alexander Lindey *Lindey on Separation Agreements and Antenuptial Contracts* (Matthew Bender & Co Inc, NY, 1991), at Chapter 95–39.

5 Child Support Act 1991, s 1(1).

Disclosure of Material Facts

As a general rule, a person who is about to enter into a contract is under no duty to disclose material facts known to him and unknown to the other party. An exception to this rule is a contract 'uberrimae fidei' (of the utmost good faith).[1] Uberrima fides is a prerequisite for the validity of contracts between those who stand in a special relationship to one another: solicitor and client; insurer and insured; guardian and ward. It also applies to 'family arrangements', where there should be the fullest disclosure of all material facts known to each party, even though no enquiry about them may have been made. It is unclear whether a cohabitation contract would be classified as a family arrangement and, thus, subject to the rigorous requirements of uberrima fides. The indications are that it would probably not.[2]

One of the leading American authorities on domestic contracts, Alexander Lindey, suggests that 'in order to protect the validity and enforceability of any (cohabitation) agreement, complete disclosures of all material facts should be made. At a minimum, the disclosures should include the property, assets and expectancies of the respective parties, and their intentions and expectations regarding the relationship'.[3] As far as purely financial disclosure is concerned, he cites a decision in West Virginia where it was held that 'it is not necessary that both parties execute a detailed, written financial statement such as is required by a bank before making a loan'.[4] General knowledge of the other's financial situation is sufficient.[5] As far as expectancies are concerned, the 'reasonableness' of a contract is determined from the date on which it was executed, rather than the date on which it is enforced,[6] so the parties would not be expected to disclose rights that have not been created at the time when the contract is signed.[7]

1 See, generally, G H Treitel *The Law of Contract* (Sweet & Maxwell) 8th Edn at pp 349 to 362.

2 See *Wales v Wadham* [1977] 1 WLR 199 at 218.

3 Alexander Lindey *Lindey on Separation Agreements and Antenuptial Contracts* (Matthew Bender & Co Inc, NY, 1991) at Chapter 95–1.

4 *Pajak v Pajak* 385 SE 2d 384 (W Va 1989).
5 Lindey (above), at Chapter 90–08.
6 Ibid, at Chapter 90–07.
7 *Gula v Gula*, 380 Pa Super 249 551 A 2d 324 (1988).

Independent Legal Advice

Lindey states that 'the careful practitioner will urge that the parties obtain separate counsel, not only to avoid conflict of interest problems, but also to insure the survival of the instrument against allegations of misrepresentation, fraud, or overreaching'.[1]

In the De Facto Relationships Act 1984, the New South Wales legislature has provided strict procedural safeguards for the execution of a cohabitation agreement which, if not observed, could result in the court making 'such order as it could have made if there were no cohabitation agreement . . . between the partners'.[2] One of these safeguards is:[3]

> 'that each partner was, before the time at which the agreement was signed by him or her, as the case may be, furnished with a certificate in or to the effect of a prescribed form by a solicitor which states that, before that time, the solicitor advised that partner, independently of the other partner, as to the following matters:-
>   (i) the effect of the agreement on the rights of the partners to apply for an order (of the court);
>   (ii) whether or not, at that time, it was to the advantage, financially or otherwise, of that partner to enter into the agreement;
> (iii) whether or not, at that time, it was prudent for that partner to enter into the agreement;
>   (iv) whether or not, at that time, and in the light of such circumstances as were, at that time, reasonably foreseeable, the provisions of the agreement were fair and reasonable; and
>   (v) that the certificates referred to . . . are endorsed on or otherwise accompany the agreement.'[4]

The advice given by the College of Law to practitioners in England and Wales is as follows.[5]

> 'It is likely that the cohabitants will ask one solicitor to draw up the contract. As there is a potential conflict of interests the solicitor should not accept instructions from both parties. However, the solicitor can accept instructions from one party. If the parties are established clients, the solicitor can act for one if the other agrees, which is likely as, at this stage, the relationship is amicable. The other party should be advised to seek independent advice'.

1 Lindey, above, at Chapter 95–1.
2 De Facto Relationships Act 1984, s 47(d).
3 Ibid, s 47(1)(d) and (e).
4 For a form of certificate, see Precedent 47 at p 133 below.
5 The College of Law Lectures 'The Unmarried Family' (1990) at p 4.

Contents of a Cohabitation Contract

There are three main 'types' of cohabitation contract.

1 Sharing everything (Precedent 84(a) at p 156 below).
2 Keeping everything separate (Precedent 84(b) at p 159 below).
3 Where one partner is dependent on the other (Precedent 84(c) at p 162 below).

Frequently, a contract is a hybrid of these types.

In his book *Cohabitation Contracts*[1], Chris Barton identified a number of topics which should, perhaps, be addressed by partners at the start of their relationship,[1] and which could be included in a cohabitation contract. In identifying these topics he acknowledged the pioneering work of Lenore J Weitzman in *The Marriage Contract*[2], from whom Barton's list and the following list are largely drawn. The topics include the following.

1 *Statement of the purpose of the contract* (Precedent 58(d) at p 139 below).
2 *The extent to which the parties intend to create legal relations* (Precedents 43, 58(b) and 58(c) at pp 131, 138 and 139 below).
3 *Personal details about the parties* (for example their ages, their family backgrounds, their jobs, and financial disclosures) (Precedents 33(a), 33(b) and 59 at pp 127 and 140 below).
4 *Aims and expectations of the parties* (Precedent 3 at p 113 below).
5 *Duration of the contract* (for example indefinite or fixed–term) (Precedent 28 at p 124 below).
6 *Careers and employment* (whether one party's career has priority over the other party's career) (Precedent 12 at p 117 below).
7 *Income and earnings* (whether they are to be pooled or kept separate) (Precedents 42(a) and 42(b) at p 131 below).
8 *Bank accounts, building society accounts, credit card accounts* (Precedents 5(a), 5(b), 23(a) and 23(b) at pp 114 and 122 below).
9 *Living expenses* (for example who pays what) (Precedents 49 and 52 at pp 134 and 136 below).
10 *Home ownership* (Precedents 29 and 55 at pp 125 and 137 below).
11 *Household goods* (in particular those already owned by either or both of the parties, how they are to be treated) (Precedent 84 at p 167 below).
12 *After-acquired property* (ie property acquired while the couple are living together, whether it is to be treated as community property) (Precedents 2(a) and (b) at p 113 below).
13 *Gifts received from third parties and gifts between the partners themselves* (Precedents 35 and 36 at p 128 below).
14 *Debts* (Precedent 24 at p 122 below).
15 *Insurance Policies* (life insurance, medical insurance (Precedents 48 and 51 at pp 133 and 136 below).
16 *Living arrangements* (including, perhaps, the parties' policy towards guests) (Precedent 37 at p 128 below).

17 *Household tasks* (how they are going to be allocated) (Precedent 40 at p 129 below).

18 *Surname* (whether the partners will keep their own surnames, whether one will assume the other's surname, what surname the partners' children will have) (Precedent 73 at p 147 below).

19 *Sexual relations* (Precedent 71 at p 145 below).

20 *Family planning* (Precedent 8 at p 115 below).

21 *Confidentiality* (Precedents 17 and 53 at pp 119 and 136 below).

22 *Personal behaviour* (for example smoking, hobbies, privacy).

23 *Relations with family and friends.*

24 *Children* (their general intentions, child-care) (Precedents 13 and 14 at p 118 below).

25 *Religion* (Precedent 63 at p 142 below).

26 *Health* (for example whether the parties have private health insurance) (Precedent 51 at p 136 below).

27 *Illness and incapacity* (whether the partners would have any standing with the hospital or medical authorities) (Precedent 41 at p 130 below).

28 *Pension arrangements* (Precedent 54 at p 137 below).

29 *Succession rights and wills* (Precedents 30, 62 and 82 at pp 125, 141 and 154 below).

30 *Breaches of the contract* (remedies, specified damages or arbitration) (Precedent 64 at p 142 below).

31 *Dispute resolution* (mediation or conciliation) (Precedents 27(a), (b) and (c) at pp 123 and 124 below).

32 *Review of the contract* (ad hoc or regular) (Precedents 66 and 67 at p 143 below).

33 *Termination of the relationship or the contract* (when, how, what arrangements should there be for the children and for the division of property?) (Precedents 74, 75, 76 and 77 at pp 147 to 152 below).

34 *Marriage* (whether it will affect the terms of the contract) (Precedents 50 and 77 at pp 135 and 152 below).

This list is by no means exhaustive. In addition, a number of general or miscellaneous clauses should be inserted in the contract. Among them:

35 *provisions relating to variations and amendments* (Precedent 79 at p 153 below);

36 *a statement to the effect that each party has received independent legal advice about the contract* (Precedents 1, 47 and 58(h) at pp 113, 133 and 140);

37 *consideration* (Precedents 18 and 19 at p 120 below);

38 *the costs of the contract* (who is going to pay them?) (Precedent 21 at p 121 below);

39 *further assurances* (Precedent 34 at p 128 below);

40 *proper law* (which law will govern the contract?) (Precedent 57 at p 138 below);

41 *severance* (Precedent 70 at p 145 below);

42 *a statement that the contract represents the whole agreement and entire under-standing between the parties* (Precedent 81 at p 154 below).

---

1 Chris Barton *Cohabitation Contracts* (Gower, 1985) at Chapter 5.
2 Lenore J Weitzman *The Marriage Contract: Spouses, Lovers and the Law* (The Free Press, NY, 1981).

PART 2: CHECKLIST – POINTS TO CONSIDER WHEN ADVISING ON AND DRAFTING A COHABITATION CONTRACT

The initial interview

Despite the observations on independent legal advice in the preceding text (see p 106 above), it is submitted – on no authority, other than mere practicality – that a practitioner could, and in many cases should, see both parties together for a preliminary interview.

In the course of that interview it is suggested that the practitioner could do the following.

1 Clearly explain to the couple that, if as a result of their discussions they decide to go ahead with a cohabitation contract, the practitioner will be able to act for only one of them, and will recommend the other to obtain independent legal advice.[1]
2 Advise the couple generally on the common law, equitable, and statutory rights and obligations of cohabiting partners.[2]
3 If necessary, explain how these rights and obligations differ from those which apply to an engaged or married couple.[3]
4 Discover whether their needs could be met more readily and effectively by other deeds and documents instead of, or in addition to, a cohabitation contract.[4]
5 Inform the couple of the present status of a cohabitation contract in English law.[5]
6 Discuss the remedies that are available for breach of contract.[6]
7 Establish whether, in the light of the advice given, there is consensus that they both wish to enter into a cohabitation contract.
8 Clarify the extent to which they wish the contract to be legally binding on them.[7]
9 Establish exactly which partner the practitioner will represent henceforth.
10 Give the other party the name, address and telephone number of at least one legal practitioner who can give competent, independent advice.
11 Extract from the client all the information required to prepare a preliminary draft contract.[8]
12 Find out which partner will pay the practitioner's costs.[9]

Drafting

The usual drafting rules[10] apply to a cohabitation contract with, perhaps, the following modifications and caveats.

1 It may be necessary to state a lot of facts and intentions, with the result that the recitals may be lengthier than in most documents.
2 The parties will be setting down the ground rules for a relationship which may be entirely unique to them: it is not a marriage, and it may be difficult simply to compartmentalise this relationship into a pre-existing formula.[11]
3 Four copies of the draft should be prepared (for the draftsman, the client, the client's partner, and the remaining copy for the partner's legal adviser).

Submitting the Draft to the Client

When discussing the draft contract with the client, either in correspondence or at a further meeting, the practitioner should:

1 inform the client once again about his or her rights and obligations in the absence of the contract;
2 state how those rights and obligations are or may be affected by the draft contract;
3 advise the client whether the draft is fair and reasonable in the circumstances;
4 advise the client whether or not it is in his or her best interests, financially or otherwise, to enter into the contract;
5 establish that nothing has been erroneously omitted or admitted, and that the draft reflects the whole agreement between the parties;
6 re-iterate the advice given before, that the client's partner should seek independent legal advice;
7 warn the client that under no circumstances should he or she:

(a) try to 'explain' the draft contract to his or her partner;
(b) make any verbal promises that are not expressly included in the draft contract; and
(c) pressurise his or her partner into agreeing the draft and signing the contract.

---

1 See p 106 above and, in particular, the advice given by The College of Law in 'The Unmarried Family' (1990) at p 4.
2 This could involve discussing a wide range of topics, and will largely depend on the client's personal circumstances. It might include: joint ownership of a home; joint ownership of personal property, such as bank accounts and household goods; business interests; children; parental responsibility; child support; support for the former partner in the event that the relationship breaks down; social security; succession; rights under

the Inheritance (Provision for Family and Dependants) Act 1975; pension nominations; succession to a tenancy; inheritance tax; etc.

3 For the statutory provisions peculiar to engaged couples, see the Law Reform (Miscellaneous Provisions) Act 1970, ss 1 to 3. If the couple intend to marry each other, they will probably require an antenuptial agreement instead of a cohabitation contract. See, generally, page 229 below. See also Chapter 5, Precedent 4 at p 235 below

4 For example a declaration of trust, a settlement, a will, a pension scheme nomination, a power of attorney or enduring power of attorney, a maintenance agreement or a parental responsibility agreement.

5 See, generally, 'Validity and Enforceability', at p 99 above.

6 See, generally, Precedent 64 at p 131 below.

7 See Precedents 43 and 58 at pp 131 and 138 to 140 below.

8 This will involve taking down full details of the parties' names, address, financial assets and liabilities, general family background, children, rights of ownership, debts, aims and expectations, etc.

9 See Precedent 21 at p 121 below.

10 See, generally, J M Aitken *Piesse: The Elements of Drafting* (The Law Book Company Limited) 8th Edn; and Mark Adler *Clarity for Lawyers* (The Law Society, 1990).

11 Graphically stated by Professor John H Sinclair in *Handbook of Conveyancing Practice in Scotland* (Butterworths/Law Society of Scotland) 2nd Edn at p 41, as follows: 'Solicitors who use standard forms uncritically and repetitively may remember the argument that it doesn't require a lawyer to press the start button on a word processor or photocopier'.

PART 3: PRECEDENTS

Clauses

1 ACKNOWLEDGMENT OF ADVICE RECEIVED[1]

Each party acknowledges that he or she has been separately advised by a qualified lawyer and is aware of the rights and obligations of cohabitees generally and the manner in which those rights and obligations are or may be affected by this Contract.

---

1 For the need to be independently advised, see p 106. See also Precedents 58(h), 47 and 4 at pp 140, 133 and 114 below.

---

2 AFTER-ACQUIRED PROPERTY

(a) Separate

Any property that is subsequently owned by one party alone (whether created by its owner, or acquired by purchase, gift, inheritance or otherwise), and any income derived from it, and any increase in its value, will remain the separate property of the party who owns it.

(b) Shared

Any property that is subsequently acquired by either party (whether by purchase, gift, inheritance or otherwise), and any income derived from it, and any increase in its value will belong to both parties equally, unless they expressly agree otherwise in writing.

3 AIMS AND EXPECTATIONS[1]

The parties' aims and expectations are:

1 to build and maintain a relationship which is based on mutual friendship, love, loyalty, respect and trust; and

2 to support each other not only financially but also emotionally.

---

1 Lenore J Weitzman *The Marriage Contract: Spouses, Lovers, and the Law* (The Free Press, NY, 1981) at p 421, states that out of the contracts surveyed in her empirical study, 87 per cent began with an express statement of the couple's aims and expectations. Very rarely was child-bearing or child-rearing mentioned in this context.

Amendments (*see* Precedent 79 at p 153 below).

Arbitration (*see* Precedent 27 at p 123 below).

4 ATTESTATION CLAUSE INCORPORATING LEGAL ADVISER'S CERTIFICATE[1]

SIGNED as a Deed[2] by (*name 1*) in my presence after I had given (him)/(her) independent legal advice on the effects and implications of this Contract:

---

1 See footnote to Precedent 47 at p 133 below.
2 Execution as a deed may overcome any difficulties arising from the lack of consideration.

---

5 BANK ACCOUNTS

(a) Separate[1]

1 Each party will maintain separate bank or building society accounts and the money in each such account will remain his or her separate property.

2 The parties do not intend to open any joint account.

---

1 Note *Paul v Constance* [1977] 1 WLR 527, CA: in the context of their relationship the words used by the defendant to indicate that the money held in a deposit account in his sole name was as much the plaintiff's as his own were sufficient to constitute a declaration of trust.

(b) Shared[1]

1 The parties will (open and) maintain an account in their joint names ('the joint account') at (*name and address of bank or building society branch*).

2 The joint account and any interest credited to it will, at all times, belong

to the parties in equal shares, regardless of the actual sums which either of them may have paid into or withdrawn from the joint account.

3 Each party may draw cheques on and withdraw cash from the joint account (up to a limit of £   , but any cheque or withdrawal exceeding that sum must be signed or made by both parties).

4 If either party purchases goods or makes an investment in his or her sole name out of funds held in the joint account then, in the absence of any contrary agreement between the parties, the goods or the investment will belong to the person making the purchase or investment.[1]

1 See, generally, Stephen Parker *Cohabitees* (Longman), 3rd Edn at pp 163 to 165.
2 *Re Bishop* [1965] Ch 450; *Jones v Maynard* [1951] Ch 572. See, generally, M P Thompson *Co-Ownership* (Sweet & Maxwell, 1988) at pp 28 to 31.

6 BENEFICIAL INTERESTS: SEPARATE

Neither party will acquire, or seek to acquire, or claim to have acquired a beneficial interest in any present or future property owned solely by the other party.

7 BINDING EFFECT OF CONTRACT

This Contract is legally binding on the parties and their respective executors and administrators, estates and assigns.

8 BIRTH CONTROL[1]

(*Name*) will be primarily responsible for birth control arrangements.

1 Lenore J Weitzman *The Marriage Contract: Spouses, Lovers and the Law* (The Free Press, NY, 1981) at pp 440 and 441, states that responsibility for birth control was discussed in 86 per cent of the cohabitation contracts surveyed in her empirical study. Over half of the arrangements made the female either solely responsible or responsible until an effective male contraceptive is available.
    Whilst the allocation of responsibility for birth control would probably not render the contract illegal on public policy grounds, it is submitted that the inclusion in the contract of any contingency plans for an unwanted pregnancy might be contra bonos mores.

Breach of contract (*see* Precedent 64 at p 142 below).

9 BUSINESS INTERESTS: SEPARATE

1 The present and future business interests of (*name*) and any income derived from them, and any increase in their value are, will be and will remain (his)/(her) separate property.

2 (*Name's*) 'business interests' include (but are not restricted to (*set out details*)).
[OR] (any asset, interest, share, rights and obligations in any business, trade, profession or vocation, or any firm, partnership, company or organisation in which (he)/(she) may be engaged, employed or concerned or to which (he)/(she) may render services now or in the future.

3 (*Name*) warrants that (his)/(her) business interests are currently worth approximately £

10 CANCELLATION OF COHABITATION CONTRACT

THIS AGREEMENT made on (*date*)
BETWEEN (1) (*name 1*) of (*address*) and (2) (*name 2*) of (*address*).
WITNESSES that the parties now cancel and rescind in all respects and for all purposes the Cohabitation Contract made by them on (*date*) on which this Agreement is endorsed.

SIGNED as a Deed by (*name 1*) in the presence of:

SIGNED as a Deed by (*name 2*) in the presence of:

Captions (*see* Precedent 38 at p 129 below).

11 CARS

(a) Separate

1 The car that each party owns now and any vehicle that may be acquired to replace it is and will remain the separate property of that party.

2 Each party is solely responsible for the costs of acquiring, insuring, maintaining and running his or her car.

3 Each party will permit and effect proper insurance cover to enable the other party to drive his or her car.

(b) Shared

1 The (*description of car*) registration number (*number*) that the parties own at present ('the car') belongs to the parties in equal shares, regardless of whose name actually appears on the vehicle registration document, and regardless of the contributions made by either party towards its acquisition.

2 Unless the parties agree otherwise in writing, any vehicle which is subsequently acquired to replace the car will also belong to the parties in equal shares, regardless of whose name actually appears on the vehicle registration document, and regardless of the contributions made by either party towards its acquisition.

(c) One party to provide a car for the other

1 Until the termination of this Contract (*name 1*) will provide (*name 2*) with a car for (his)/(her) own use and enjoyment.

2 (*Name 1*) will pay all the running expenses of the car, including vehicle excise duty, insurance, maintenance, repairs, (membership of the AA/RAC) and petrol.

3 The car will be replaced every (3) years with another car, and each replacement will be no more than (1 year) old when it is acquired, and will have an engine capacity of not less than (1600) cc.

4 (*Name 1*) will retain ownership of the car.

5 On the termination of this Contract (*name 2*) will deliver up possession of the car to (*name 1*).

12 CAREERS[1]

The parties consider that (*name 1's*) career is of greater social and economic importance to them than (*name 2's*) career and (*name 2*) agrees that if (*name 1*) is required to move elsewhere to further (his)/(her) career (*name 2*) will transfer (his)/(her) own job to the new location.

---

1 Lenore J Weitzman *The Marriage Contract: Spouses, Lovers and the Law* (The Free Press, NY, 1981) discusses this subject under the heading 'Domicile', at p 432. She notes that a significant minority of couples still subscribe to the traditional view that the choice of domicile rests with the male.

Cheques (*see* Precedent 5 at p 114 above).

13 CHILD CARE

(a) Allocation of responsibility

The parties intend to share the responsibility of looking after their children and so far as practicable will take turns in staying home from work whenever a child is unwell or the children are on holiday.

See also Precedent 14 (below), to which this clause could, if considered appropriate, be added as a sub-clause.

(b) Support of carer

If one party temporarily stops working in order to stay at home to look after the children, the other party will pay him or her (one half) of his or her disposable income until the youngest child is placed in a nursery or primary school.

See Precedent 14 (below), to which this clause could, if considered appropriate, be added as a sub-clause.

14 CHILDREN: STATEMENT OF INTENTIONS

The parties have been advised and understand that any provision in this Contract which affects their child or children may be unenforceable in law or varied by the Court.[1] Nevertheless, if the parties have a child or children, they intend:

1 jointly to register the child's birth;[2]

2 that the child's surname will be (*surname*);[3]

3 that the child's forename(s) will be chosen by the parties jointly;[3]

4 by means of a Parental Responsibility Agreement to provide for (*name 1*) to have parental responsibility for the child;[4]

5 that any major decision about the child's health and welfare, education and upbringing will be made by the parties jointly;

6 to contribute financially towards the child's upbringing for as long as is necessary on the basis of their respective abilities to pay;[5] and

7 that if they separate, the parent with whom the child is living will use his or her best endeavours to ensure that the child maintains contact with the parent with whom he or she is no longer living.

1 Children Act 1989, ss 1 and 2. See, generally, Chris Barton *Cohabitation Contracts* (Gower, 1985) at pp 47 to 48. See also Precedent 63 at p 142 below, on the religious upbringing of children.
2 Births and Deaths Registration Act 1953, ss 10 and 10A (as amended).
3 The right to determine the child's name is vested in the parent who has parental responsibility. For the position where the child's father and mother were not married to each other at the time of the child's birth, see Children Act 1989, 2(2).
4 Children Act 1989, s 4. For the prescribed form of parental responsibility agreement, see Chapter 3, Precedent 5 at p 180 below.
5 See, generally, Children Act 1989, Sch 1, and Child Support Act 1991.
6 For 'contact orders' see Children Act 1989, s 8(1).

15 COMMENCEMENT

THIS COHABITATION CONTRACT is made on (*date*)
BETWEEN 'the parties': (1) (*name 1*) of (*address*) ('*name 1*') and (2) (*name 2*) (also) of (*address*) ('*name 2*').

IT IS AGREED that:

16 COMMENCEMENT DATE

This Contract will come into force on (*date*).

Conciliation (*see* Precedent 27 at p 123 below).

17 CONFIDENTIALITY[1]

Each party promises never to use, disclose or divulge to the detriment or disadvantage of the other any confidential information about the other's private life, family life or business affairs which may have come to his or her knowledge during the course of their relationship.

1 In *Argyll v Argyll* [1965] Ch 302, it was held that communications between husband and wife during their marriage are protected against disclosure to third parties. There is no English authority on comparable protection for unmarried couples, although in *Stephens v Avery* [1988] Ch 449, an injunction was granted restraining the disclosure of details about a lesbian relationship.

18 CONSIDERATION: SPECIFIC[1]

In consideration of *(name 2)* giving up (his)/(her) present job in order to live with *(name 1)*, *(name 1)* will *(set out details)*.

---

1 According to Alexander Lindey *Lindey on Separation Agreements and Antenuptial Contracts* (Matthew Bender & Co Inc, NY, 1991), at Chapter 95–35, the prevailing approach of the US courts towards cohabitation contracts 'involves examining the details of the alleged agreement to discern the actual consideration exchanged, rather than stopping at the mere labeling of the arrangement as meretricious because the parties were cohabiting'. For example *Mullen v Suchko*, 279 Pa Super 499, 421 A 2d 310 (1980), where the man asked the woman to leave a job she had held for 33 years in order to live and travel with him. There was no mention of any sexual obligations. The court held that the agreement was enforceable because her job surrender and agreement to live and travel with him were 'traded' for his agreement to support her. There was an identifiable valid consideration which stood apart from any probable sexual relationship. It is submitted that English courts would probably adopt a similar approach. For example *Parker v Clark* [1960] 1 WLR 286.

19 CONSIDERATION: GENERAL[1]

This Contract is made in consideration of the mutual promises (and releases) it contains and for other good and valuable consideration the sufficiency of which each of the parties acknowledges.

---

1 As a general rule a promise is not binding as a contract in English law unless it is either made in a deed or supported by some consideration. See, generally, G H Treitel *The Law of Contract* (Sweet & Maxwell) 8th Edn at Chapter 3, and Chris Barton *Cohabitation Contracts* (Gower, 1985) at p 48. It is recommended that, in order to overcome the potential difficulties over lack of consideration, a cohabitation contract should be executed as a deed.

20 COOLING-OFF CLAUSE

(a) Counselling

If either party is seriously thinking of ending the relationship, both parties will attend at least (2) counselling session(s) before making any final decision.

(b) Trial separation

If either party is seriously thinking of ending the relationship, both parties will spend at least (7) days apart before making any final decision.

21 COSTS

(a) Shared equally

The legal costs relating to the preparation (negotiation) and execution of this Contract (including the combined total of the costs incurred by each of the parties in obtaining independent advice) will be paid by the parties in equal shares.

(b) One party to pay all the costs

(*Name 1*) will pay all the legal costs relating to the preparation (negotiation) and execution of this Contract (including the costs incurred by (*name 2*) in obtaining independent advice and assistance).

(c) One party to pay for independent advice

1 (*Name 1*) will pay the legal costs relating to the preparation (negotiation) and execution of this Contract.
2 (*Name 2*) will pay the costs incurred by (him)/(her) in obtaining independent legal advice on the provisions and implications of this Contract.

Counselling (*see* Precedent 20 above).

22 COVENANTS RELATING TO RESIDENTIAL PROPERTY[1]

Each party promises:

1 at all times to comply with the covenants and conditions affecting (*address*) ('the property');

2 at all times to keep the property in good repair and condition and insured to its full reinstatement value;

3 not to create or attempt to create any mortgage or charge over the property or any part of it or any interest in it without the other's consent; and

4 not to create or attempt to create any tenancy, licence, agreement or any other right affecting the property without the other's consent.

---

1 It may be sensible to include these covenants in a cohabitation contract if they are not already incorporated in, for example, a declaration of trust.

23 CREDIT CARDS

(a) Separate

Each party will maintain separate credit accounts and neither party will use the other's credit.

(b) Shared[1]

1 (*Name 1*) will nominate (*name 2*) to use a credit card on (his)/(her) (*credit company*) account number (*account number*).

2 Between the parties themselves (*name 2*) will be responsible for the payment for all purchases made by (him)/(her) on the account and for any interest attributable to those purchases.

3 (*Name 2*) promises at all times to use the card with care and consideration and to indemnify (*name 1*) against any loss incurred as a result of (his)/(her) use, misuse or abuse of the card.

---

1 Usually a principal cardholder can nominate one other person to be an authorised user of a credit card. The authorised user generally has to sign an acknowledgment accepting and agreeing to be bound by the conditions of use imposed by the bank or credit company. The card itself is usually the company's property. The principal cardholder is usually liable for repayment. It may be worthwhile checking each individual agreement and the terms and conditions of use.

---

24 DEBTS[1]

1 Each of the parties will remain personally liable for any current and future debts incurred in his or her sole name.

2 The payment by one party of any part of the other's personal debts will in no way render the payer liable for or obliged to make any further payment in respect of those debts.

---

1 Lenore J Weitzman *The Marriage Contract: Spouses, Lovers and the Law* (The Free Press, NY, 1981) comments that 56 per cent of the cohabitation contracts which she surveyed referred to debts. However, not one cohabiting couple made precontract debts a community obligation, and 42 per cent of cohabitees (compared with 22 per cent of engaged or married couples) made postcontract debts a separate obligation. She concludes that 'cohabitors were more likely to keep separate both their economic resources and their economic obligations' (at p 428).

25 DECLARATION OF TRUST[1]

The rights and interests of the parties in the property known as (*address*) and its net proceeds of sale are set out in a Declaration of Trust dated (*date*) and are not in any way varied or affected by this Contract.

1 It may be considered preferable to deal with the beneficial interests in jointly owned property in a completely separate declaration of trust rather than to include, possibly lengthy, additional clauses in the cohabitation contract. The execution of a declaration of trust by an unmarried couple who jointly own property is now virtually a mandatory requirement. The execution of a cohabitation contract is certainly not mandatory and, indeed, its legal status is uncertain at present (see p 99).

26 DEED[1]

This Contract is a deed and is executed by the parties as a deed.

1 One of the grounds on which it is argued that a cohabitation contract may be unenforceable at law is lack of consideration. This problem can be overcome by executing the cohabitation contract as a deed. To take effect as a deed the instrument must make it clear on its face that it is intended to be a deed (whether by describing itself as a deed or expressing itself to be executed as a deed) and it must be validly executed as a deed by the parties to it (Law of Property (Miscellaneous Provisions) Act 1989, s 1(2)).

27 DISPUTE RESOLUTION

(a) Arbitration[1]

(If any attempt at conciliation or mediation is unsuccessful)[2] any difference, disagreement or dispute arising out of or in connection with this Contract will be referred to an Arbitrator nominated at the request of either party by the (President) of the (Area) District Law Society.

1 Lenore J Weitzman *The Marriage Contract* (above) at pp 437 to 439, states that 'more than half of the couples agreed on procedures to deal with persistent disagreements. The three most frequently mentioned contingency plans were: (1) setting aside time to discuss differences; (2) seeking professional counselling or other third party assistance; and (3) abiding by the decision of the arbitrator'. For 'cooling-off' clauses, see Precedent 20 at p 120 above.
2 For clauses referring the dispute to a conciliator or mediator, see **(b)** and **(c)** below.

(b) Conciliation[1]

Any difference, disagreement or dispute arising out of or in connection with this Contract will be referred in the first instance to (the Family Conciliation Service) without prejudice to the right of either party to apply subsequently to the Court for adjudication.

---

1 For conciliation generally, see Thelma Fisher *Family Conciliation within the UK* (Family Law, 1992). The advantages of conciliation/mediation over arbitration/litigation are that the process is non-adversarial; the parties are allowed to resolve their own difficulties themselves; the location may be more convenient; and the process should be quicker, cheaper and less stressful. In addition, any question over the legality of a cohabitation contract would not be an issue.

(c) Named mediator[1]

1 Any difference, disagreement or dispute which arises out of or in connection with this Contract will be referred in the first instance to (*name*) who will act as a mediator.

2 If (*name*) is unwilling or unable to act as mediator the problem will be referred to (*name B*) instead.

---

1 In certain circumstances, for example where the parties are members of a particular religious group or where they are gay or lesbian, a named mediator may be preferred to, for example, the Family Conciliation Service. Selecting a personal friend might place that friend in a difficult position. It is probably wiser to choose someone who is known to and respected by both parties but who is not a close, personal friend of either. As a courtesy to the proposed mediator, and to avoid any potential problems about acceptance of that role, the parties should obtain the consent of the proposed mediator before making such an appointment. For the advantages of mediation/conciliation over arbitration or litigation, see footnote to (b) above.

Dissolution (*see* Precedents 75 and 76 at p 148 below).

28 DURATION

(a) Indefinite[1]

The parties plan to live together indefinitely.

---

1 Lenore J Weitzman *The Marriage Contract* (above), at p 424, observes that in 48 (81 per cent) of the 59 contracts she surveyed the duration of the contract was discussed. Half were open-ended, describing a relationship of indefinite duration. The other half limited the contract to a specified number of years. The average duration was three years.

(b) Fixed term[1]

Unless it terminates earlier in accordance with the provisions of Clause (*number*), this Contract will terminate on (*date*).

1 See footnote to **(a)** above.

29 DWELLING

(a) Joint tenancy[1]

The parties own (*address*) as beneficial joint tenants, regardless of the actual contributions made by either party towards its acquisition.

1 See, generally, Chapter 1 'Declarations of Trust'.

(b) Tenancy in common[1]

The parties own (*address*) as beneficial tenants in common as to   per cent of the net proceeds of sale for (*name 1*) and as to   per cent for (*name 2*), regardless of the actual contributions made by either party towards its acquisition.

1 See, generally, Chapter 1 'Declarations of Trust'.

(c) One party is sole owner

(*Name 1*) owns (*address*) and (*name 2*) acknowledges that (he)/(she) has not acquired, will not acquire and will not claim to have acquired any beneficial interest in that property.

30 ESTATE RIGHTS[1]

1 Neither party is under any obligation to make financial provision for or to confer any other benefit on the surviving party on death.

2 Neither party has agreed, promised or represented to the other that he or she will execute a will or sign any other instrument which will make financial provision for or confer any other benefit on the surviving party.[2]

3 Each party releases, renounces and surrenders to the other party and the

other party's estate any right which he or she may have as a cohabitee to apply to the court for an order under section 2 of the Inheritance (Provision for Family and Dependants) Act 1975 or any statutory modification or re-enactment of it.[3]

4 Nothing in this Contract constitutes a renunciation of the right of the surviving party (if entitled) to obtain a grant of representation to the estate of the deceased party or a disclaimer by the surviving party of any financial provision, benefit or right conferred by the deceased party in his or her will or arising otherwise as a result of his or her death.

---

1 See Chapter 4, Introductory Text. See also Precedent 82, footnotes, at p 154 below.
2 See *Synge v Synge* [1894] 1 QB 466, CA, where the man made an antenuptial promise in writing to leave the woman a life interest, and the woman was entitled to enforce the promise. See also *Re Basham (Deceased)* [1987] 1 WLR 1498 – deceased giving assurances as to a stepdaughter's future rights to his estate.
3 See footnote 1 to Precedent 62 at p 142 below.

---

31 EXECUTION OF THIS CONTRACT[1]

This Contract has been executed in duplicate and each copy will be deemed an original and will constitute one and the same agreement between the parties.

---

1 For multiple execution of deeds, see generally, Co Litt 229a; *Burchell v Clark* [1876] 2 CPD 88 at 96, CA.

Expectations (*see* Precedent 3 at p 113 above).

Family planning (*see* Precedent 8 at p 115 above).

32 FIDUCIARY DUTY[1]

Each party promises to show the utmost good faith and to deal fairly with the other in implementing the provisions of this Contract.

---

1 As a general rule a person who is about to enter into a contract is under no duty to disclose material facts known to him but not known to the other party. An exception to the general rule is a contract 'uberimmae fidei'. A 'family arrangement' is a contract 'uberimmae fidei', but it is not clear whether a cohabitation contract would be classified

as a 'family arrangement'. The possible effect of a clause of this nature is to classify the contract as one of the utmost good faith. See, generally, G H Treitel *The Law of Contract* (Sweet & Maxwell) 8th Edn at pp 349 to 362.

33 FINANCIAL DISCLOSURE

(a) By one party only[1]

1 (*Name 1*) has disclosed to (*name 2*) details of the income, earning capacity, property and other financial resources, and the financial needs, obligations and responsibilities which (he)/(she) has now and is likely to have in the foreseeable future.

2 (*Name 1*) has neither asked for, nor received, nor wishes to receive similar information from (*name 2*).

1 As a general rule, a person who is about to enter into a contract is under no duty to disclose material facts known to him but not known to the other party. A contract 'uberrimae fidei' is an exception to such general rule. It is not clear whether a cohabitation contract would be classified as a contract 'uberrimae fidei', akin to a family arrangement. In *Wales v Wadham* [1977] 1 WLR 199 at 218, it was held that although there might be cases where there was a duty to make full and frank disclosure before there was a duty to do so by affidavit, when the jurisdiction of the court had been invoked, no such duty arose in this case because the parties had made a bargain at arm's length. On contracts 'uberrimae fidei' see, generally, G H Treitel *The Law of Contract* (Sweet & Maxwell) 8th Edn at pp 349 to 362. See also, generally, 'Disclosure of Material Facts', at p 105 above.

(b) By both cohabitees[1]

1 (*Name 1*) estimates that (his)/(her) net capital resources are currently worth about £   and that (his)/(her) net annual income from all sources is approximately £   .

2 (*Name 2*) estimates that (his)/(her) net capital resources are currently worth about £   and that (his)/(her) net annual income from all sources is approximately £   .

3 Both parties acknowledge that each of them has been given the opportunity to examine the other's financial records.

1 See, generally, 'Disclosure of Material Facts' at p 105 above.

34 FURTHER ASSURANCES[1]

When required to do so, each party will complete, sign and execute any deed, document or form which may be needed in order to implement the provisions of this Contract.

---

1 On covenants for further assurance see, generally, Odgers' *Construction of Deeds and Statutes* (Sweet & Maxwell) 5th Edn at pp 172 and 173.

Future property (*see* Precedent 2 at p 113 above).

35 GIFTS BETWEEN COHABITEES

(a) Presumption that the gift is absolute[1]

Any gift from one party to the other will be presumed to be an absolute gift unless it is expressly given on the condition that it will be returned to the giver on the termination of the parties' relationship.

---

1 For the law relating to gifts generally, see *Halsbury's Laws of England* (Butterworths) 4th Edn, Vol 20. For gifts between couples who are engaged to be married, see Law Reform (Miscellaneous Provisions) Act 1970, s 3.

(b) Reservation of rights

Nothing in this Contract regarding the separate property and assets of the parties deprives either party of the right to give to or receive from the other property and assets of any description by way of gift, transfer or legacy.

36 GIFTS RECEIVED: SEPARATE

Any gift, inheritance or unexpected good fortune received by either party will be and will remain the separate property of that party.

37 GUESTS

Neither party will, without first obtaining the other party's consent, invite any friend, relative or guest to stay (for longer than (*24 hours*)).

38 HEADINGS[1]

The headings in this Contract have been inserted for convenience and reference and must not be interpreted as defining, limiting or extending the substance and scope of the provisions above which they appear.

1 Headings first appeared in statutes in Clauses Consolidation Acts 1845. 'Headnotes cannot control the plain meaning of the words of the enactment, though they may in some cases be looked upon in the light of the preambles if there is any ambiguity in the meaning of the sections on which they throw light' (*R v Hare* [1934] 1 KB 354 at 355, per Avory J). Paragraph headings have appeared in deeds and documents comparatively recently. It is assumed that the same rules of construction would apply to headings in deeds and headings in statutes.

39 HOUSEKEEPING ALLOWANCE: FIXED SUM

1 For as long as the parties are living together (*name 1*) will pay to (*name 2*) a housekeeping allowance of £ a (week)/(month).

2 The allowance will be adjusted at least once a year in line with the Retail Prices Index.

3 Any property purchased by (*name 2*) from any surplus or accumulations of the allowance will belong to (*name 2*) absolutely.[1]

1 Compare the Married Women's Property Act 1964, s 1. In the case of a married couple any property acquired from the housekeeping allowance belongs to the husband and wife in equal shares in the absence of any agreement between them to the contrary. In the absence of any contrary agreement between cohabitees, any surplus from the housekeeping allowance would probably revert to the payer on the basis of a presumed resulting trust. Section 26 of the Family Law (Scotland) Act 1985 contains a similar presumption that parties to a marriage share equally in money and property derived from a housekeeping allowance. The Scottish Law Commission in its 1992 *Report on Family Law* has recommended that this presumption should be applied to cohabitees (Scot Law Com No 135, at paras 16.12 and 16.13).

40 HOUSEWORK[1]

The parties will share the housework equally.

[OR]

The parties will take turns in doing the housework.

[OR]

1 (*Name 1*) will be primarily responsible for the following household tasks:[2]

2 (*Name 2*) will be primarily responsible for the following household tasks:[2]

---

1 Chris Barton *Cohabitation Contracts* (Gower, 1985) at p 56, lists the division of household tasks as a possible item for inclusion in a cohabitation contract. As far as English law is concerned it is possible that the court would apply the maxim 'de minimis non curat lex', which could have adverse effects on the validity of the contract as a whole. If such a clause is to be included, consider also including a clause about severance (see Precedent 70 at p 145 below). Lenore J Weitzman *The Marriage Contract: Spouses, Lovers and the Law* (The Free Press, NY, 1981), at p 433, notes that only in one contract was the female partner given overall responsibility for all the housework; 26 per cent of couples chose to share the housework equally and a further 26 per cent chose to take turns. At p 444 Weitzman states that in a number of contracts a fixed penalty was imposed on any party who failed to perform his or her specific chores.

2 List the household tasks: eg shopping, cooking, laundry, ironing, gardening, mowing the lawn, washing the dishes, cleaning, repairs and decorations to the house, car maintenance, cleaning the car, etc.

---

41 ILLNESS OR INCAPACITY

(a) Attorneyship[1]

Each party will as soon as practicable execute an instrument appointing the other party to be his or her attorney for the purpose of the Enduring Powers of Attorney Act 1985.

---

1 If either party should become seriously ill or incapacitated the other party could be treated by various authorities as a 'legal stranger'. If the cohabitee has been appointed as an attorney, he or she will have authority to act on behalf of the incapacitated party. If the parties separate, an enduring power of attorney ('EPA') can easily be revoked. If, however, the EPA has been registered in the Court of Protection, revocation must be confirmed by the court (Enduring Powers of Attorney Act 1985, s 8(3)). See, generally, Stephen Cretney *Enduring Powers of Attorney* (Jordans, 1991) 3rd Edn, and *Encyclopaedia of Forms and Precedents* (Butterworths) 5th Edn, Vol 31.

(b) Next of kin[1]

So far as it is legally possible to do so each party will nominate and appoint the other to be his or her 'next of kin' or 'nearest relative'[2] (for contact, emergency, visiting, advocacy and representation purposes).

---

1 One of the functions of a cohabitation contract is, in many cases, to enlarge the extremely limited common law and statutory rights of the cohabitee. In a time of crisis a cohabitee could be treated as a 'legal stranger'. See, generally, Pat Clayton *The Cohabitation Guide* (Wildwood House, London, 1981) pp 22 to 25.

2 Under the Mental Health Act 1983, s 26(6), a cohabitee may, in certain circumstances, be treated as a spouse if he or she has been living with the patient for a period of not less than six months.

(c) Support[1]

For as long as the parties are living together each will be responsible for supporting the other.

1 See footnotes to Precedent 72a) at p 146 below and, generally, 'Support', at p 104 above.

42 INCOME

(a) Separate

Each party's income from all sources and all accumulations of that income will be and will remain his or her separate property and will not be subject to division between the parties on the termination of their relationship.

(b) Shared

The parties will pool and commingle their respective incomes from all sources (and will share equally all accumulations of and property acquired from their pooled incomes, regardless of the actual income earned or received by either party).

Inheritance (*see* Precedents 30 and 36 at pp 125 and 128 above).

43 INTENTION TO CREATE LEGAL RELATIONS

1 (Part I) [*OR*] (Clauses   to   inclusive) of this Contract contain(s) agreements that will be legally binding on the parties and their personal representatives and estates.

2 (Part II) [*OR*] (Clauses   to   inclusive) of this Contract contain(s) agreements to which the parties are bound in honour only and which give rise to no legal rights and for the breach of which no legal action will lie.

3 (Part III) [*OR*] (Clauses   to   inclusive) of this Contract contain(s) provisions of general application.

44 INTERPRETATION OF THIS CONTRACT[1]

No provision in this Contract will be construed against one party merely because it was drafted or inserted by his or her legal adviser.

---

1 This clause is designed to negate the effect of the 'contra proferentem' rule of construction, whereby the wording of a document is construed more strongly against the party putting it forward. This rule of construction is applied in cases of ambiguity, where other rules of construction fail.

---

45 JOINT PROPERTY

(a) Joint tenancy[1]

Any property or asset acquired jointly by the parties while they are living together will belong to them as beneficial joint tenants, regardless of their respective contributions towards its acquisition, unless they provide otherwise in writing[2] and clearly identify their respective shares or interests in the property or asset in question.

---

1 This clause relates to any jointly acquired assets, and could include investments, a dwelling and personal chattels.
2 This clause envisages that all joint property will be held as beneficial joint tenants unless the contrary is provided in a separate declaration of trust in writing. In the case of pure personalty, an oral declaration suffices, but is hardly satisfactory.

(b) Tenancy in common[1]

Any property or asset acquired jointly by the parties while they are living together will belong to them as beneficial tenants in common in shares corresponding to the actual contributions made by each of them towards the acquisition of the property or asset, unless they provide otherwise in writing.

---

1 See footnotes to **(a)** above.

---

46 JOINT USE: SEPARATE OWNERSHIP

The use by one party of any property which belongs to the other party will not give rise to the joint ownership of that property.

47 LEGAL ADVISER'S CERTIFICATE[1]

I (*legal adviser's name*) of (*professional address*), (a solicitor of the Supreme Court) [OR] (a Fellow of the Institute of Legal Executives) [OR] (*as the case may be*), CERTIFY that before (he)/(she) signed this Contract I advised (*name 1*) independently of (*name 2*) on:

1 (his)/(her) rights and responsibilities in the absence of this Contract; and
2 the manner in which those rights and responsibilities are or may be affected by this Contract; and
3 whether or not it was prudent or advantageous, financially or otherwise, to enter into this Contract; and
4 whether or not at that time and in the light of such circumstances as were then reasonably foreseeable the provisions of this Contract were fair and reasonable.

Dated:

Signed:

---

1 This certificate is based on the wording of the De Facto Relationships Act 1984 (New South Wales), s 47(d), which requires that the certificates be endorsed on, or annexed to, or should otherwise accompany the agreement. (ibid, s 47(e)).

For a briefer certificate incorporated as part of the attestation clause, see Precedent 4 at p 114 above.

---

48 LIFE INSURANCE: AGREEMENT TO TAKE OUT AND MAINTAIN A POLICY[1]

(*Name 1*) will take out a policy of insurance on (his)/(her) life in the sum of £   for the benefit of (*name 2*) and for as long as (he)/(she) has an obligation to do so under this Contract will maintain that policy in full force and effect[2] (and will authorise the insurer to disclose to (*name 2*) any information regarding that policy that (he)/(she) may ask for).

---

1 Other provisions could be added. For example: increasing the cover periodically; an undertaking not to charge or assign the policy; remedies available if the insured fails to pay the premiums, etc.
2 This envisages that the obligation will cease on termination of the contract or shortly afterwards. The legal adviser should ensure that there are provisions to this effect in the clauses relating to the consequences of termination.

49 LIVING EXPENSES

(a) To be paid from joint account[1]

The following living expenses will be paid out of the parties' joint account: mortgage payments; rent; buildings insurance; contents insurance; water; gas; electricity; telephone; groceries; cleaning materials; general toiletries; television and video rental; television licence; holidays; joint recreation; car insurance; car maintenance . . .[2]

---

1 This clause assumes that reference is made elsewhere in the contract to a joint bank or building society account. See Precedent 5(b) at p 114 above.
2 Delete and add as appropriate

(b) To be paid in proportion to the parties' respective incomes

Except for any expenses that are solely attributable to one or the other of them, the parties agree to share all living expenses[1] in proportion to their respective incomes or in such other proportions as they may from time to time agree.

---

1 It would be wise to define 'living expenses'. See (d) below.

(c) Fixed percentages

(*Name 1*) will pay   per cent of the parties' living expenses[1] and (*name 2*) will pay the other   per cent.

---

1 It may be sensible to define 'living expenses'. See (d) below.

(d) One party pays all

1 For as long as the parties are living together (*name 1*) will pay all their living expenses.

2 'Living expenses' include, but are not restricted to: mortgage payments; rent; buildings insurance; contents insurance; water; gas; electricity; telephone; groceries; cleaning materials; toiletries; television and video rental; holidays; joint recreation (etc).

(e) Defined areas of responsibility

1 (*Name 1*) will be primarily responsible for paying the following living expenses: (*set out details*).

2 (*Name 2*) will be primarily responsible for paying the following living expenses: (*set out details*).

3 Both parties will contribute equally towards the payment of the following living expenses: (*set out details*).

50 MARRIAGE

(a) Contract to continue on marriage[1]

1 The parties intend that their respective rights and responsibilities contained in this Contract will not be varied or affected in any way if they marry each other.

2 The parties also intend that, if their marriage is subsequently dissolved or annulled, the provisions of this Contract should be one of the matters to which the court should have regard in deciding whether and how to exercise its powers.[2]

3 Despite the provisions above, nothing in this Contract constitutes an agreement by either party to marry the other.[3]

Warning

1 The effect of this clause is to turn a cohabitation contract into an antenuptial agreement or marriage contract. In its memorandum of May 1991 'Maintenance and Capital Provision on Divorce', The Law Society's Family Law Committee considers marriage contracts and recommends that legislation should be introduced to make them enforceable. See p 103 above, and p 229 below.

  At present the court's jurisdiction under the Matrimonial Causes Act 1973 to make property adjustment orders and to order maintenance cannot be ousted by a private agreement between the parties, and it would be contrary to public policy to enforce such an agreement (*Sutton v Sutton* [1984] 1 All ER 168).

2 In exercising its powers under ss 23, 24 and 24A of the Matrimonial Causes Act 1973, the court should have regard to all the circumstances of the case, including 'the conduct of each of the parties, if that conduct is such that it would in the opinion of the court be inequitable to disregard it' (s 25(2)(g)). Arguably, the execution of a private agreement would be 'conduct' in a wider sense.

3 The Law Reform (Miscellaneous Provisions) Act 1970, s 1, provides that an agreement between two persons to marry one another does not have effect as a contract giving rise to legal rights.

(b) Contract ceases to apply on marriage[1]

This Contract will cease to have effect if and when the parties marry each other.

---

1 See footnotes to (a) above.

Mediation (*see* Precedent 27 (b) and (c) at p 124 above).

51 MEDICAL INSURANCE

1 (*Name 1*) will take out and maintain in full force and effect for as long as he has an obligation to do so under this Contract[1] medical insurance with (*company*) for (*name 2*).

2 (*Name 1*) will take out and maintain in full force and effect medical insurance with (*company*) for the parties' children until each child reaches the age of (*18*).

3 Despite the above, (*name 1's*) obligation to take out and maintain medical insurance for (*name 2*) (*and the children*) will continue only for as long as such insurance is available under the scheme operated by (his)/(her) company, business or employer and will be limited to the coverage provided under that scheme.

---

1 If this obligation is to cease on the termination of the contract, words to that effect should be included in the clause relating to consequences of termination.

Modification (*see* Precedent 79 at p 153 below).

52 MORTGAGE PAYMENTS[1]

(*Name 1*) will pay   per cent and (*name 2*) will pay   per cent of the mortgage payments (and these payments will not affect the parties' respective beneficial interests in the property).[2]

---

1 For other permutations, see Precedent 49 (a) to (e) (p 134 above) relating to living expenses and adapt accordingly. For example: where payments are to be made from a joint account or where they paid in proportion to the parties' respective incomes or when one party pays all the mortgage payments.
2 Include or exclude the words in brackets as appropriate.

---

53 NON-DISCLOSURE OF CONTRACT TO THIRD PARTIES

Neither party will disclose any part of this Contract to any third party unless compelled to do so by legal process, or unless disclosure is necessary in order to protect or enforce the terms of this Contract.

54 PENSIONS AND DEATH-IN-SERVICE BENEFITS

Each party will:

1 nominate the other to receive (per cent of) the pension and death-in-service benefits payable under any pension scheme of which he or she may from time to time be a member;

2 at the other's request provide written evidence that such nomination has been received and recorded by the trustees of the pension scheme to which it relates.

55 PRESENT PROPERTY: SEPARATE

1 The property listed in Schedule (*number*) belongs to (*name 1*) and will at all times remain (his)/(her) separate property.

2 The property listed in Schedule (*number*) belongs to (*name 2*) and will at all times remain (his)/(her) separate property.

3 Neither party will acquire any right or title to or interest in the other's separate property simply by virtue of the parties' cohabitation.[1]

---

1 See Precedent 61 at p 141 below.

---

56 PRESENT PROPERTY AND DEBTS: SEPARATE[1]

1 The property listed in Part 1 of Schedule (*number*) belongs to (*name 1*) and will at all times remain (his)/(her) separate property.

2 The debts listed in Part 2 of Schedule (*number*) have been incurred by (*name 1*) and (he)/(she) will at all times remain solely liable for their repayment.

3 [*As in 1 above, but in respect of name 2.*]

4 [*As in 2 above, but in respect of name 2.*]

---

1 See also Precedent 24 at p 122 above and Precedent 78 at p 153 below.

---

57 PROPER LAW[1]

This Contract will be governed and interpreted in accordance with the law of (England and Wales).

---

1 'Where there is an express statement by the parties of their intention to select the law of contract, it is difficult to see what qualifications are possible, provided that the intention expressed is bona fide and legal, and provided there is no reason for avoiding the choice on the ground of public policy' (*Vita Food Products v Unus Shipping Co* [1939] 1 All ER 513 at 521, per Lord Wright).

---

58 RECITALS

(a) Cohabitation[1]

The parties (intend to)[2] live together.

[*OR*]

The parties have been living together since (*date*).

---

1 In old case law, which is still binding as precedent but would probably not be applied nowadays, a distinction was drawn between agreements which were entered into before cohabitation and those entered into during or after cohabitation. A contract entered into by a couple intending to cohabit would be illegal on the grounds that it promotes sexual immorality (*Walker v Perkins* [1764] 1 Wm Bl 517). By contrast, if the couple were living together or were separated the immorality would already exist or would have ceased (*Annandale v Harris* [1727] 2 P Wms 432).

2 Note that the words 'intend to', when incorporated in a recital, have been interpreted as a covenant. 'Where words of recital or reference manifested a clear intention that the parties should do certain acts, the courts have from these inferred a covenant to do such acts' (*Aspdin v Austin* [1844] 5 QB 671 at 683, per Lord Denman CJ). See, generally, G Dworkin *Odgers' Construction of Deeds and Statutes* (Sweet & Maxwell) 5th Edn at pp 159 to 160.

(b) Intention to create legal relations[1]

The parties intend that this Contract will be legally binding on them and their respective personal representatives and estates.

---

1 'As a rule when arrangements are made between close relations . . . there is a presumption against an intention of creating any legal relationship. This is not a presumption of law, but of fact' (*Jones v Padavatton* [1969] 1 WLR 328 at 332, per Salmon LJ.) In the absence of any statement to the contrary, a formal written contract should in itself rebut such presumption of fact. For a clause expressly stating that no legal relationship is created, see **(c)** below.

(c) Intention not to create legal relations[1]

The parties intend that this Contract will give rise to no legal rights and that no legal action will lie for its breach.

---

1 For contractual intention in social and domestic arrangements generally, see GH Treitel *The Law of Contract* (Sweet & Maxwell) 8th Edn at pp 151 to 153; see also *Balfour v Balfour* [1919] 2 KB 571.

(d) Purpose of this contract[1]

The purpose of this Contract is to define and regulate the respective rights and responsibilities of the parties both during and after their cohabitation.

---

1 Chris Barton *Cohabitation Contracts* (Gower, 1985), at p 55, mentions this as the first of a number of points to be considered by couples entering into a cohabitation contract.

(e) No duress or undue influence[1]

Each party is entering into this Contract freely and voluntarily and without coercion or pressure from the other party or anyone else.

---

1 A contract is voidable at common law if it was made under duress. Equity will also give relief against unconscionable bargains if one party has taken advantage of the fact that there is a marked inequality of bargaining power between the parties.

'The English Law gives relief to one who, without independent advice, enters into a contract upon terms which are unfair or transfers property for a consideration which is grossly inadequate, where his bargaining power is grievously impaired by reason of his own needs or desires, or by his own ignorance or infirmity, coupled with undue influence or pressures brought to bear on him by or for the benefit of the other' (*Lloyds Bank Ltd v Bundy* [1975] QB 326 at 339, per Lord Denning MR).

(f) Cohabitee under 18[1]

(*Name*) is a minor and understands that this Contract will be legally binding on (him)/(her) unless and until (he)/(she) repudiates it during (his)/(her) minority or within a reasonable time after (his)/(her) eighteenth birthday.

---

1 The status, in English law, of a cohabitation contract, is uncertain (see p 99). A fortiori, the status of a cohabitation contract made by a minor is highly uncertain. It is assumed that such a contract would be voidable at the minor's option before attaining 18 or within a reasonable time after attaining 18. For minors' contracts, see, generally, G H Treitel *The Law of Contract* (Sweet & Maxwell) 8th Edn at pp 481 to 501.

An intention to share assets equally was found by the Arizona Supreme Court in *Cook v Cook* 142 Ariz 573, 691 P 2d 664 [1984], where the man was 40 and the woman 17 when they began to live together.

(g) Recitals to be legally binding[1]

The parties warrant that these recitals are true and accurate and intend that they will be legally binding on them.

1 For the construction of recitals generally, see *Re Moon* [1886] 17 QBD 275 at 286.

(h) Independent legal advice[1]

Before signing this Contract each party received independent legal advice on its provisions and implications.

1 See, generally, 'Independent Legal Advice' at p 106 above. See also Precedents 4 and 47 at pp 81 and 133 above.

(i) Understanding the nature and effect of the contract[1]

Each party warrants that he or she understands the nature and effect of this Contract and is entering into it after careful consideration of all the facts, circumstances and implications.

1 A party must be capable of understanding the nature and effect of the contract that he or she is entering into (*Boughton v Knight (1873)* [1861–1873] All ER Rep 40). Capacity relates to the specific contract, not to contracts in general. A legal adviser should always make his or her client distinctly acquainted with the legal effect of any step the client may take (*Re a Solicitor, ex parte Incorporated Law Society* (1895) SJ 219).

59 RECITALS: PERSONAL INFORMATION ABOUT THE PARTIES[1]

1 (*Name*) was born on (*date*).

2 (*Name*) is employed as a (*job description*). [OR]
2 (*Name*) is a self-employed (*job description*). [OR]
2 (*Name*) is unemployed. [OR]
2 (*Name*) is a retired (*former job description*).

3 (*Name*) is (single)/(separated)/(divorced) (a widow/widower).

4 Details of (*name's*) current assets, liabilities and income are recorded in Schedule (*number*).

1 See, generally, 'Disclosure of Material Facts' at p 105 above.

60 RECITALS RELATING TO THE CHILD(REN)

1 The parties are the mother and father of (*child's name*) who was born on (*date*); (*child's name*) who was born on (*date*).

2 By a Parental Responsibility Agreement made between the parties and recorded in the Principal Registry of the Family Division on (*date*)[1] (*name 1*) has parental responsibility for (*child's or children's name(s)*) in addition to (his)/(her)/(their) mother.

3 (*Name 2*) is also the mother of (*number*) child(ren) by her (former marriage(s))/(relationship(s)) namely: (*child's name*) who was born on (*date*); (*child's name*) who was born on (*date*).

4 (*Name 1*) is also the father of (*number*) child(ren) by his (former marriage(s))/(relationship(s)) namely: (*child's name*) who was born on (*date*); (*child's name*) who was born on (*date*).

5 (*Child's or children's name(s)*) live with the parties.

---

1 A parental responsibility agreement will not take effect until the prescribed form, duly completed and signed, has been filed in the Principal Registry of the Family Division (The Parental Responsibility Agreement Regulations 1991, SI 1991/1478). For the prescribed form, see Chapter 3, Precedent 5 at p 180 below.

---

61 RELEASE OF RIGHTS (IF ANY) OVER THE OTHER'S SEPARATE PROPERTY

Each party releases, renounces and surrenders all (if any) rights that he or she may now or subsequently have to claim any right or title to or any share or interest in any property or income now or subsequently owned or acquired by the other party alone.

62 RELEASE OF RIGHT TO APPLY TO THE COURT FOR AN ORDER UNDER THE INHERITANCE (PROVISION FOR FAMILY AND DEPENDANTS) ACT 1975[1]

Each of the parties releases, renounces and surrenders to the other and the other's estate any right which he or she may have as a cohabitee[2] to apply to the court for an order under section 2 of the Inheritance (Provision for Family and Dependants) Act 1975 or any statutory modification or re-enactment of it.

1 Whether it is actually possible to 'contract out' in this way was left an open question in *Zamet v Hyman* [1961] 1 WLR 1442, CA, where a similar release was entered into for monetary consideration by an elderly woman who was shortly to be married. In any event, strict proof would be required to establish that when the parties signed the contract they 'fully understood its significance and after full, free and informed (and particularly informed) thought about it' (at p 1450, per Lord Evershed MR). Compare s 15 of the Act which applies only in divorce proceedings, etc.

2 See, generally, the Inheritance (Provision for Family and Dependants) Act 1975, ss 1(1)(e), 1(3) and 3(4). See also p 185 below.

63 RELIGIOUS UPBRINGING OF CHILDREN[1]

If the parties have a child or children, he, she or they will be brought up as members of (the Roman Catholic Church; the Jewish faith; the Church of England; the Methodist Church; *or as the case may be*).

1 Lenore J Weitzman *The Marriage Contract: Spouses, Lovers and the Law* (The Free Press, NY, 1981) at pp 436 to 437, states that only 41 per cent of the contracts she surveyed mentioned religion. When religion was discussed it was usually in the context of the parties' children, and rarely in the context of the parties inter se. One couple sought explicitly to exclude religion from their relationship: 'Both Matt and Sandy are agnostic and uncommitted to any religion. If one partner does become involved and committed at some future time, then the other party has the option to cancel the contract'.

For the religious upbringing of children generally, see H K Bevan *Child Law* (Butterworths, 1988) at pp 462 to 470.

64 REMEDIES FOR BREACH OF CONTRACT[1]

If either party breaches or fails to comply with any promise or provision contained in this Contract the other may be entitled to apply to the Court for an order awarding:

1 damages;
2 specific performance;
3 an injunction;
4 costs.

1 For the remedies for breach of contract, see, generally, G H Treitel *The Law of Contract* (Sweet & Maxwell) 8th Edn at Chapter 21.

The inclusion of a clause of this nature puts the parties on notice as to the possible consequences of their failure to comply with any of the specific provisions of the contract.

Lenore J Weitzman *The Marriage Contract* (above) at p 444, states that 44 per cent of the cohabitation contracts she studied included provision for the payment of damages when one party failed to keep his or her part of the bargain. The damages were of fixed sums and mostly arose in two types of violation: a breach of an agreement to be sexually monogamous, and a breach of an agreement to perform specific household chores. In weighing the merits of damages over specific performance she wryly observes that 'it is much easier to make someone pay a 25 dollar fine for not cooking dinner than to compel the same person to cook dinner'.

65 RENT

Each party will pay one half of the rent.

[OR] (*Name 1*) will pay   per cent of the rent and (*name 2*) will pay   per cent of the rent.

[OR] (*Name*) will pay the rent.

66 REVIEW: AD HOC REVIEW[1]

If for any reason either party is unhappy about any provision in this Contract he or she may request an ad hoc review of that provision after giving the other party at least (7) days' notice.

1 Lenore J Weitzman *The Marriage Contract* (above) at p 444, reveals that in a quarter of the contracts studied in her empirical study where a review was considered, an ad hoc review was permitted at the request of either party. However, she states, at p 285, that 'the (review) procedure should not encourage frequent or capricious changes. It is important that both parties regard the contract as a fixed and definite agreement that cannot easily be altered'.

67 REVIEW OF CONTRACT[1]

1 The parties will review the provisions of this Contract:
   (a) at least once every year (on or about the anniversary of the date of this Contract); and
   (b) whenever there is a major change in the personal circumstances of either or both of them.

2 Events giving rise to a major change in the personal circumstances of either or both of the parties include, but are not restricted to:[2]

   (a) engagement or marriage;

(b) childbirth;

(c) illness, injury or accident;

(d) unemployment, re-employment or retirement;

(e) inheritance or unexpected good fortune;

(f) bankruptcy.

3 The purpose of a review is to decide whether, in the light of the information available and the circumstances reasonably foreseeable at the time:

(a) any provision of this Contract should be deleted;

(b) any provision of this Contract should be varied;

(c) any provision should be added to this Contract;

(d) this Contract should be cancelled; or

(e) this Contract should be superseded by a new contract.

4 If as a result of a review any deletions, variations or additions are necessary or this Contract is to be cancelled or superseded such change must be recorded in an instrument in writing executed (as a deed) by both parties.

---

1 Lenore J Weitzman *The Marriage Contract* (above), at p 444, states that in her empirical survey of contracts, 56 per cent of the couples set a specific date for periodic reviews, ranging from every six months to every five years. In addition, 25 per cent of the couples allowed for ad hoc reviews at the request of either party. For a clause permitting an ad hoc review, see Precedent 66 (above).

2 In May 1991, The Law Society's Family Law Committee published a memorandum 'Maintenance and Capital Provision on Divorce', which (inter alia) recommended that legislation be introduced to make marriage contracts, or antenuptial agreements – as distinct from cohabitation contracts – enforceable. One of the procedural safeguards it recommended was a number of triggers to compel a review of the contract. It recognised, at para 3.51, that 'unfortunately, no such list of triggers could ever be completely comprehensive and this, therefore, means that the risk would still exist that the contract could become unrealistic or unfair'. It recommended that terms relating to a periodic review (for instance, at least every five years) should be included in all contracts.

---

68 REVOCATION CLAUSE

This Contract revokes and replaces any previous written or oral agreement between the parties.

69 SEPARATION

After the termination of this Contract neither party will:

(a) without invitation enter or occupy any premises owned or occupied by the other party;

(b) annoy, embarrass, or interfere with the other party and his or her relatives, friends, acquaintances, and business colleagues and contacts.

70 SEVERANCE[1]

If the court finds that any provision of this Contract is illegal, invalid, or otherwise unenforceable, such provision may be severed from this Contract without affecting its other provisions which will continue to have full force and effect.

(The inclusion of this clause does not imply that the parties or their legal advisers believe that any provision of this Contract may be illegal, invalid, or otherwise unenforceable.)

---

1 'The general rule is that, where you cannot sever the illegal from the legal part of a covenant, the contract is altogether void; but where you can sever them, whether the illegality be created by statute or by the common law, you may reject the bad part and retain the good' (*Pickering v Ilfracombe Railway Co* [1868] LR 3 CP 235 at 250, per Willes J).

  The illegal term must be capable of being separated from the remainder of the contract under what is generally known as 'the blue pencil rule'.

  Note two Californian cases. In *Jones v Daly* [1981] 176 Cal Rptr 130, the word 'lover' appeared in an intimate contract, and the court applied the *Marvin v Marvin* rule and held that the word 'lover' showed that sexual services were an inseparable part of the bargain. By contrast, in *Whorton v Dillingham* [1988] 202 Cal App 3d 447, it was held that the word 'lover' could be severed, and that the rest of the contract could remain intact. In this case, the agreement had been entered into by a gay couple. The plaintiff had agreed to be the defendant's chauffeur, secretary, business companion, bodyguard, companion and lover. The court held that the claimant's recovery would be limited to what could be described as the legitimate services, and that any value that might be attached to the sexual elements would be ignored.

71 SEXUAL RELATIONS[1]

Nothing in this Contract is to be interpreted as imposing an obligation on either party to have sexual relations with the other (or to abstain from having sexual relations with anyone else).[2]

---

1 This is a clause for the ultra cautious. One of the grounds on which it is considered that cohabitation contracts generally may be illegal is that they promote sexual immorality and are, accordingly, contrary to public policy. Principles decided in 18th and 19th century case-law are still binding precedents. It is unlikely, however, that a court would now strike down a typical cohabitation contract as immoral. 'The court's function is to apply the law, not personal prejudice. Only in a case where there is still a generally accepted moral code can the court refuse to enforce rights in such a way as to offend that generally accepted code' (*Stephens v Avery* [1988] 2 All ER 477 at 481, per Sir Nicolas Browne-Wilkinson V-C). See Scottish Law Commission 'Report on Family Law' (1992) at p 127, note 4, which expresses the opinion of the Faculty of Advocates. Indeed, one

Australian judge has said that 'the social judgments of today upon matters of "immorality" are as different from those of the last century as is the bikini from a bustle' (*Andrews v Parker* [1973] Qd R 93, per Stable J at p 104. See, generally, Chris Barton *Cohabitation Contracts* (Gower, 1985), at pp 38 to 42.

2 Lenore J Weitzman *The Marriage Contract* (above), at p 436, notes that out of 38 couples in a sample survey, 33 expected a sexually monogamous relationship, and only four couples expressly allowed sexual activity outside the contract relationship.

An agreement in which a woman promised to forbear from having sexual relations with any other person, but not requiring her to have sex with the other party, would not be invalidated as 'meretricious' (*Bower v Weisman* 674 F Supp 113 (SDNY 1987)).

72 SUPPORT

(a) Mutual support[1]

For as long as the parties are living together each will be responsible for supporting the other.

1 Lenore J Weitzman *The Marriage Contract*, (above) at p 430, states that a majority (57 per cent) of the contracts surveyed by her included specific provision in case of one partner's lay off, illness, disability or maternity leave. They typically agreed to continue treating the non-earning partner as 'a partner who is still making an equal contribution to the collective enterprise which must, of course, be defined more broadly than a mere economic partnership'.

See, generally, 'Support' at p 104 above.

(b) No obligation

Neither party is under any obligation to maintain, support or make any form of financial provision to or for the benefit of the other at any time during or after their cohabitation.

(c) No promises made

Neither party has agreed, promised or represented to the other that he or she will maintain, support or make any form of financial provision to or for the benefit of the other at any time during or after their cohabitation.

(d) Reservation of right

Nothing in this Contract deprives either party of the right voluntarily to maintain, support or make any other form of financial provision to or for the benefit of the other.

(e) Waiver of rights

Each party waives, releases and surrenders any right which he or she may now or subsequently have to claim or receive maintenance, support or any other form of financial provision from the other party at any time during or after their cohabitation.

73 SURNAME

(a) Each to retain their own[1]

Each party will retain his or her own surname.

---

1 Lenore J Weitzman *The Marriage Contract* (above), at p 435, reveals that in her survey of cohabitation contracts 47 per cent of the couples decided that both would assume the male's surname, and 41 per cent agreed that each party would retain his or her own surname.

(b) Both to be known by the same surname[1]

Both parties will use the surname (*surname*).

---

1 For a form of Change of Name Deed, see Chapter 5, Precedent 1 at p 230 below.

---

74 TERMINATING EVENT

(a) End of relationship[1]

Either party can terminate this Contract at any time simply by ceasing to live with the other party.

---

1 There is no fixed or uniform approach as to what constitutes a termination of a cohabitation contract. For a more comprehensive list of terminating events, see Precedent 75 below.

(b) Notice

Either party can terminate this Contract by giving the other party at least (2) weeks' notice in writing.

75 TERMINATING EVENTS

Without prejudice to any provisions of this Contract that come into force on or remain in force after its termination, this Contract will terminate when the earliest of these events occurs:

1 The death of a party.

2 The marriage of the parties to each other.[1]

3 The parties mutually agree on its termination and sign a written instrument cancelling this Contract.[2]

4 The expiration of a period of (4) weeks beginning on the date when one party gives to the other written notice of his or her wish to terminate this Contract.

5 If the parties have lived apart for a continuous period of at least (4) weeks and one party gives to the other written notice that this Contract is terminated.

6 If the Court grants an injunction under section 1 of the Domestic Violence and Matrimonial Proceedings Act 1976 or any statutory modification or re-enactment of it and (either party) [OR] (the party who applies for the injunction) gives to the other party written notice that this Contract is terminated.[3]

7 If one party excludes the other from (the property) without reasonable cause and the excluded party gives written notice to the excluding party that this Contract is terminated.

8 The Court or an Arbitrator orders that this Contract is terminated.

---

1 For a clause providing that the contract will continue on marriage, see Precedent 50(a) at p 135 above; for the consequences of termination on marriage, see Precedent 77 at p 152 below.

2 See Precedent 10 at p 116 above.

3 The Domestic Violence and Matrimonial Proceedings Act 1976, s 1, applies not only to the parties to a marriage but also to 'a man and a woman who are living together in the same household as husband and wife' (s 1(2)).

76 TERMINATION CONSEQUENCES

(a) General introductory clause

If this Contract is terminated for any reason other than the death of a party or the marriage of the parties to each other, the provisions of Schedule (*number*) will apply.

(b) Bank and building society accounts

(If this Contract is terminated (for any reason other than the death of a party or the marriage of the parties to each other)) the parties will:

1 immediately close all bank accounts and building society accounts held in their joint names;

2 immediately sever all plastic or other cards relating to the joint account(s) and return the pieces to the bank or building society;

3 immediately destroy all unused cheques;

4 immediately take whatever steps are necessary to ensure that their earnings and other income are no longer credited to any joint account;

5 on receiving the closing statements, divide the balances on all joint accounts equally between themselves;

6 continue to be jointly and severally liable for the repayment of all overdrafts, debts and interest payable in respect of the joint account(s);

7 punctually pay their respective share of all overdrafts, debts and interest, and each party indemnifies the other from and against all actions, demands, proceedings and losses arising from his or her failure to do so.

(c) Credit and charge cards

(If this Contract is terminated (for any reason other than the death of a party or the marriage of the parties to each other)) the parties will:

1 immediately close all joint credit and charge card accounts;

2 immediately close all credit and charge card accounts in the name of one party alone where the other party is an additional cardholder or authorised user;

3 immediately destroy all plastic or other cards relating to such accounts and return the destroyed cards to the creditor;

4 when they receive the closing statements, allocate the debts between themselves on the basis of who will retain each specific item obtained on credit or, where an item obtained on credit has been consumed, who consumed it or who ordered it;

5 punctually pay their respective share of all debts and interest payable on such accounts, and each party indemnifies the other against any consequences of his or her failure to do so.

(d) The dwelling: option to 'buy out' the other's share

(If this Contract is terminated (for any reason other than the death of a party or the marriage of the parties to each other)):

1 (*Name 1*) will have the option to purchase (*name 2's*) share of (*address*) or failing which any other principal residence jointly owned by the parties ('the property').

2 The property will be valued by the parties themselves at such figures as they agree.

3 If the parties are unable to agree a valuation of the property, it will be formally valued by a professionally qualified valuer, and if more than one formal valuation is obtained the average of the valuations will prevail.

4 The property will be valued on the basis that:

   (a) it is being sold with vacant possession at arm's length on the open market;
   (b) all fixtures, fittings, carpets and curtains which do not belong to (*name 2*) alone are included in the sale;
   (c) there is no discount for joint ownership.

5 The price that (*name 2*) will receive for (his)/(her) estate and interest in the property will be (his)/(her) share of the value of the property less (his)/(her) share of all mortgages and charges to which the property is subject.

6 In the absence of any alternative agreement between them, the parties will observe the following time limits:

   (a) within (2) weeks of the termination of this Contract the property will be valued and a redemption statement will be obtained in respect of every mortgage and charge to which the property is subject;
   (b) within (4) weeks of the termination of this Contract (*name 1*) will give (*name 2*) written notice of (his)/(her) intention to exercise this option;
   (c) within (8) weeks of the termination of this Contract (*name 1*) will complete (his)/(her) purchase of (*name 2's*) share.

7 If (*name 1*) is unable or unwilling to exercise this option within (4) weeks of the termination of this Contract or within such other time limit as (*name 2*) has agreed:

   (a) (his)/(her) option to purchase (*name 2's*) share will lapse;
   (b) (*name 2*) will have the option to purchase (*name 1's*) share of the property on the same terms mutatis mutandis and the following time-limits will apply in the absence of any alternative agreement between the parties;
   (c) within (2) weeks of the date on which (*name 1's*) option lapsed (*name 2*) will give (*name 1*) written notice of (his)/(her) intention to exercise this option;
   (d) within (4) weeks of the date on which (*name 1's*) option lapsed (*name 2*) will complete the purchase of (*name 1's*) share.

(e) Separate property

(If this Contract is terminated (for any reason other than the death of a party or the marriage of the parties to each other)) each party will keep his or her separate property (and each party will remain personally liable for his or her separate debts).

(f) Jointly owned goods and chattels[1]

If this Contract is terminated (for any reason other than the death of a party or the marriage of the parties to each other) all goods and chattels which the parties jointly own will be divided between them as they agree, and where they fail to agree on division those goods and chattels will be sold and the proceeds of sale will be divided equally between them.

---

1 For more comprehensive provisions relating to the division of chattels, see Precedent 84 at p 167 below.

(g) Support[1]

(If this Contract is terminated (for any reason other than the death of a party or the marriage of the parties to each other)) neither party will be under any continuing obligation to support or maintain the other party.

---

1 See, generally, 'Support', above at p 104.

(h) Lump sum payment[1]

(If this Contract is terminated (for any reason other than the death of a party or the marriage of the parties to each other)) within (4) weeks of the termination of this Contract (*name 1*) will pay to (*name 2*) the sum of £   to enable (him)/(her) (to establish a separate household) [*OR*] (in full and final settlement of any possible claim for support that may have arisen while the parties were living together.)

---

1 See, generally, 'Support', above at p 104.

(i) Miscellaneous cancellations

(If this Contract is terminated (for any reason other than the death of a party or the marriage of the parties to each other)) either party may:

1 cancel any nomination that names the other party as a potential recipient of any pension or other benefits arising on the nominator's death;

2 cancel any nomination that names the other party as the recipient of the benefits payable under any policy of insurance on the nominator's life;

3 revoke any (enduring) power of attorney which appoints the other party to be his or her attorney;

4 disclaim any appointment as the other party's attorney by giving the other party written notice of such disclaimer.

(j) Children

(If this Contract is terminated (for any reason other than the death of a party or the marriage of the parties to each other)) subject always to the ascertainable wishes and feelings of any child concerned considered in the light of his or her age and understanding:

1 the children of the parties' relationship ('the children') will live with (*name 2*);

2 the children can have contact with (*name 1*) and (his)/(her) family;

3 both parties will maintain the children according to their respective abilities to pay;

4 neither party will cause any of the children to be known by a new surname without the written consent of the other party or the leave of the court.

(k) The other's child(ren)[1]

If this Contract is terminated (for any reason other than the death of a party or the marriage of the parties to each other) neither party will be under any continuing obligation to support or maintain the other party's child or children.

---

1 But see the Children Act 1989, Sch 1, para 4(2).

---

77 TERMINATION OF CONTRACT ON MARRIAGE: CONSEQUENCES[1]

If this Contract is terminated on the marriage of the parties to each other:

1 the separate property and debts of each party will continue to be his or her separate property and debts;

2 any property that is jointly owned by the parties will continue to be jointly owned by them in the proportions or shares existing at the time of their marriage;

3 any debts for which the parties are jointly liable will continue to be their joint liability in the proportions or shares existing at the time of their marriage.

---

1 See footnotes to Precedent 50 at p 135 above.

---

78 TRANSFERS BETWEEN COHABITEES

1 Either party can at any time transfer his or her own separate property to the other party solely or jointly, conditionally or unconditionally.

2 Any such transfer must comply with the legal formalities governing the transfer of property of that nature.

3 If the nature of the property is such that no specific legal formalities govern its transfer then for the avoidance of doubt such transfer will be evidenced by an instrument in writing dated and signed by the transferor and transferee.

79 VARIATION OF CONTRACT[1]

(a) Clause

This Contract can only be varied by an instrument in writing executed (as a Deed)[2] by both parties.

---

1 See, generally, G H Treitel *The Law of Contract* (Sweet & Maxwell) 8th Edn at pp 172 to 174.
2 In *Berry v Berry* [1929] 2 KB 316, it was held that a separation agreement which had been made by deed (even though there was no legal requirement that it should be made by deed) could be varied by a subsequent agreement which was not a deed.

(b) Deed

THIS (DEED OF) VARIATION made on (*date*)
BETWEEN (1) (*name 1*) of (*address*) and (2) (*name 2*) also of (*address*).
WITNESSES as follows.

1 This (Deed)/(Variation) is supplemental to a Cohabitation Contract ('the contract') made between the parties on (*date*).
2 The parties now cancel and rescind Clause(s) (*number(s)*) of the contract.
3 The parties now add to the contract the Clauses set out in the Schedule.

THE SCHEDULE

(*insert new clauses*)

SIGNED as a Deed by (*name 1*) in the presence of: .

SIGNED as a Deed by (*name 2*) in the presence of: .

Wages for housework (*see* Precedent 39 at p 129 above).

80 WAIVER OF BREACH[1]

If either party fails to enforce any provision of this Contract at any time such acquiescence will not constitute a waiver of that provision or of the right at any other time to enforce that provision and all the other provisions of this Contract.

---

1 The right to rescind may be lost or limited by waiver or election. See, generally, G H Treitel *The Law of Contract* (Sweet & Maxwell) 8th Edn at p 709 et seq.

---

81 WHOLE AGREEMENT

1 This Contract contains the whole agreement between the parties and replaces any previous written or oral agreements between them.

2 The parties confirm that neither of them has entered into this Contract on the basis of any promises or representations which are not expressly included in this Contract.

82 WILLS[1]

Each party is aware of the rights[2] of the survivor if one of them should die, and each party intends to execute a will as soon as practicable.[3]

---

1 Lenore J Weitzman *The Marriage Contract: Spouses, Lovers and the Law* (The Free Press, NY, 1981), at p 443, states that in a sample survey of intimate contracts, 51 per cent contained provision for the making of wills. Usually such provision consisted of a simple statement to draft wills at a later date; eg 'Both parties agree to make wills within 90 days of signing this contract . . .' Of the wills studied, very few included provision for third parties, such as parents or siblings, but 42 per cent planned to leave part of their estate to their children.

2 The surviving cohabitee *may* be entitled to:
   (a) property passing by right of survivorship;
   (b) property passing under a statutory or non-statutory nomination;
   (c) claim under the Inheritance (Provision for Family and Dependants) Act 1975, or under the Fatal Accidents Act 1976.
   The surviving cohabitee has no rights on intestacy. See, generally, 'Surviving Cohabitee's Rights on Intestacy', Chapter 4, at p 184 below.
3 A will made pursuant to a contract to make a will in a particular form can be revoked, although the testator or his estate may be liable for breach of contract (*Schaefer v Schuhmann* [1972] AC 572.

Forms

83 COHABITATION CONTRACT

(a) Sharing everything

(i) Short form[1]

THIS COHABITATION CONTRACT is made on (*date*)
BETWEEN (1) (*name 1*) and (2) (*name 2*) both of (*address*).

THE PARTIES AGREE:

1 to combine their incomes for the purpose of living together as a family unit;

2 to support each other while they are living together;

3 that if they separate, each party will keep his or her own separate property; and

4 that if they separate, any property which they jointly own will be divided equally between them.[2]

SIGNED as a Deed by (*name 1*) in the presence of: .

SIGNED as a Deed by (*name 2*) in the presence of: .

---

1 A simple agreement along these lines was inferred by a Connecticut court in *Dosek v Dosek* (October 1978), Family Law Reporter 4, no 51; see Lenore J Weitzman *The Marriage Contract: Spouses, Lovers and the Law* (The Free Press, NY, 1981), at p 401. The couple had lived together for seven years. The woman had assumed the man's name and had borne his child. The court found that the couple had agreed (1) to combine their incomes for the purpose of living together as a family unit, and (2) in the event of a separation, to divide their assets equally.

2 Weitzman (above) at p 448, states that almost all (83 per cent) of the contracts studied in her survey provided for an equal division of community property. Many couples dealt with this division in one short sentence: 'Upon separation, each party will take his or her separate property and any jointly owned community property will be divided equally'.

(ii) Longer form

THIS COHABITATION CONTRACT is made on (*date*)

BETWEEN 'the parties' (1) (*name 1*) of (*address*) ('*name 1*') and (2) (*name 2*) (also) of (*address*) ('*name 2*').

IT IS AGREED that:

1 Recitals

1.1 (*Name 1*) was born on (*date*).
1.2 (*Name 1*) is (unmarried)/(separated)/(divorced)/(a widow/ widower).
1.3 (*Name 1*) is a (*job description*).
1.4 (*Name 1*) has a current net annual income of approximately £   from all sources.
1.5 (*Name 1*) has current net capital resources worth approximately £   .
1.6 (*Name 2*) was born on (*date*).
1.7 (*Name 2*) is (unmarried)/(separated)/(divorced)/(a widow/ widower).
1.8 (*Name 2*) is a (*job description*).
1.9 (*Name 2*) has a current net annual income of approximately £   from all sources.
1.10 (*Name 2*) has current net capital resources worth approximately £   .
1.11 The parties (intend to) live together.
1.12 The purpose of this Contract is to define and regulate the respective rights and responsibilities of the parties while they are living together and if they separate.
1.13 Each party has received independent legal advice on the provisions and implications of this Contract.
1.14 Each party has had an opportunity to examine the other party's financial records.
1.15 The parties intend that this Contract will be legally binding on them.

2 The house

2.1 The parties (intend to) live at (*address*) ('the house').
2.2 The parties (intend to) own the house as beneficial (joint tenants) [*OR*] (tenants in common in equal shares), regardless of the actual contributions made by either party towards its acquisition.

3 Separate property

3.1 The items listed in Schedule 1 belong to (*name 1*) and will continue to be (his)/(her) separate property.
3.2 The items listed in Schedule 2 belong to (*name 2*) and will continue to be (his)/(her) separate property.

4 Gifts

4.1   Nothing in this Contract regarding the separate property of each party deprives either party of the right to give to or receive from the other party any property and assets by way of gift transfer or legacy.

4.2   Any gift from one party to the other will be presumed to be an absolute gift unless it is expressly given on the condition that it will be returned to the giver on the termination of the parties' relationship.

4.3   Any gift, inheritance or unexpected good fortune received by either party will be and will remain the separate property of that party.

5 Income

The parties will pool and commingle their respective incomes from all sources, except for the income received from any assets which are specified as the separate property of one party, and will share equally all accumulations of and property acquired from their pooled incomes, regardless of the actual income earned or received by either party.

6 Support

For as long as the parties are living together each party will support the other.

7 Termination

This Contract will terminate:

7.1   if and when the parties marry each other, although nothing in this Contract constitutes an agreement by either party to marry the other; or, earlier

7.2   if and when the parties cease to live together.

8 Termination: consequences

If this Contract terminates because the parties cease to live together:

8.1   neither party will be under any continuing obligation to support the other;

8.2   the trust for sale on which the house is held may be enforced by either party;

8.3   all bank accounts, building society accounts, credit accounts and charge card accounts held in the parties' joint names will immediately be closed and the balances and debts will be divided equally between the parties;

8.4   each party will retain his or her separate property;

8.5 all goods and chattels which are jointly owned by the parties will be divided between them as they agree, and in default of agreement the goods and chattels will be sold and the proceeds of sale will be divided equally between the parties.

9 Dispute resolution

Any difference, disagreement or dispute arising out of or in connection with this Contract will be referred in the first instance to a Conciliator, without prejudice to the right of either party to apply subsequently to the Court for adjudication.

10 Variation

This Contract can only be varied by an instrument in writing executed as a Deed by both parties.

11 Whole agreement

This Contract contains the whole agreement between the parties and neither of them has entered into it on the basis of any promises or representations which are not expressly included in it.

12 Severability

If the Court finds that any provision of this Contract is illegal, invalid, or otherwise unenforceable, such provision may be severed from this Contract without affecting any other provisions which will continue to have full force and effect.

SCHEDULE 1

((*Name 1's*) separate property.)

SCHEDULE 2

((*Name 2's*) separate property.)

SIGNED as a Deed by (*name 1*) in the presence of: .

SIGNED as a Deed by (*name 2*) in the presence of: .

(b) Keeping everything separate

THIS COHABITATION CONTRACT is made on (*date*)
BETWEEN (1) 'the parties' (1) (*name 1*) of (*address*) (*name 1*) and (2) (*name 2*) (also) of (*address*) (*name 2*).

IT IS AGREED that:

1 Recitals

(Similar to the recitals in Precedent 83(a)(ii) at p 157 above.)

2 The house

2.1 The parties own (*address*) ('the house').
2.2 The parties bought the house on (*date*).
2.3 The purchase price of the house was (*price*).
2.4 The incidental costs of purchasing the house amounted to £
2.5 The house is mortgaged to (*lender*).
2.6 The mortgage advance was £
2.7 (*Name 1*) paid £   towards the purchase price and purchase costs.
2.8 (*Name 1*) will pay   per cent of the mortgage payments.
2.9 (*Name 1*) will pay   per cent of the sale costs.
2.10 (*Name 1*) will receive   per cent of the sale price less   per cent of the amount required to redeem the mortgage and less   per cent of the sale costs.
2.11 (*Name 2*) paid £   towards the purchase price and purchase costs.
2.12 (*Name 2*) will pay   per cent of the mortgage payments.
2.13 (*Name 2*) will pay   per cent of the sale costs.
2.14 (*Name 2*) will receive   per cent of the sale price less   per cent of the amount required to redeem the mortgage and less   per cent of the sale costs.

3 Bank accounts

3.1 Each party will maintain separate bank accounts and building society accounts and the money in each such account will remain the separate property of that party.
3.2 The parties do not intend to open a joint account.

4 Debts

4.1 Each party will remain personally liable for his or her current debts and any future debts incurred in his or her sole name.
4.2 The payment by one party of any part of the other's personal debts will in no way render the payer liable for or to make any further contribution in respect of those debts.

5 Separate property

5.1 The items listed in Schedule 1 belong to (*name 1*) and will continue to be (his)/(her) separate property.
5.2 The items listed in Schedule 2 belong to (*name 2*) and will continue to be (his)/(her) separate property.

5.3 The use by one party of any property belonging to the other party will not give rise to the joint ownership of that property.

5.4 Each party releases, renounces and surrenders all (if any) rights he or she may now or subsequently have to claim any right or title to or share or interest in any property and income which is now or subsequently owned or acquired by the other party alone.

6 Cars

Each party will permit and effect proper insurance to enable the other party to drive his or her car.

7 Gifts

(As in Precedent 83(a)(i), Clause 4 at p 158 above.)

8 Living expenses

The parties will contribute equally towards their joint living expenses which include, but are not restricted to, payments for water, gas, electricity, telephone, food, drink, cleaning, joint recreation and holidays.

9 Support

9.1 Except for the extent to which each party is liable to contribute towards the mortgage payments and their joint living expenses, neither party is under any obligation to support or maintain the other while they are living together and after they have ceased to live together.

9.2 Each party releases, renounces and surrenders to the other and the other's estate any right which he or she may have as a cohabitee to apply to the Court for an order under section 2 of the Inheritance (Provision for Family and Dependants) Act 1975 or any statutory modification or re-enactment of it.

10 Review

The parties will review the provisions of this Contract:

10.1 at least once every year; and

10.2 whenever there is a major change in the personal circumstances of either of them.

11 Variation

This Contract can only be varied by an instrument in writing executed as a Deed by both parties.

12 Termination

This Contract will terminate:

12.1 if and when the parties marry each other; or, earlier

12.2 if and when the parties cease to live together.

13 Termination consequences

If this Contract is terminated on the marriage of the parties to each other:

13.1 the separate property and debts of each party will continue to be his or her separate property and debts;

13.2 any property that is jointly owned by the parties will continue to be owned by them in the proportions or shares existing at the time of their marriage;

13.3 any debts for which the parties are jointly liable will continue to be their joint liability in the proportions or shares existing at the time of their marriage.

14 Whole agreement

(As in Precedent 83(a)(ii), Clause 11 at p 159 above.)

15 Severability

(As in Precedent 83(a)(ii), Clause 12 at p 159 above.)

SCHEDULE 1

((*Name 1's*) separate property.)

SCHEDULE 2

((*Name 2's*) separate property.)

SIGNED as a Deed by (*name 1*) in the presence of: .

SIGNED as a Deed by (*name 2*) in the presence of: .

(c) One party supporting the other

THIS COHABITATION CONTRACT is made on (*date*)
BETWEEN 'the parties' (1) (*name 1*) of (*address*) ('*name 1*') and (2) (*name 2*) (also) of (*address*) ('*name 2*').

IT IS AGREED that:

1 Recitals

(The same as, or similar to, those in Precedent 83(a) at p 157 above.)

2 Consideration

The promises made in this Contract by (*name 1*) are made in consideration of:

2.1   (*name 2*) giving up (his)/(her) present (job)/(accommodation) in order to live with (*name 1*); and

2.2   the releases given by (*name 2*).

3 The house

3.1   The parties (intend to) live together at (*address*) ('the house').

3.2   (*Name 1*) owns the house.

3.3   (*Name 2*) releases, renounces and surrenders all (if any) rights (he)/(she) may have to claim any right or title to or any share or interest in the house and its net proceeds of sale.

4 Living expenses

While the parties are living together (*name 1*) will pay:

4.1   the costs of financing, maintaining and running the house;

4.2   the bills for the utilities;

4.3   the grocery bills;

4.4   for their joint recreation and holidays.

5 Housekeeping allowance

5.1   While they are living together (*name 1*) will pay (*name 2*) a (weekly)/(monthly) allowance of £

5.2   The allowance will be adjusted at least once a year in order to bring it in line with the cost of living.

5.3   Any property that (*name 2*) acquires with the allowance and any accumulations of the allowance will belong to (*name 2*) absolutely.

6 Car

6.1   While they are living together (*name 1*) will provide (*name 2*) with the use of a car.

6.2   (*Name 1*) will pay all the expenses of running the car, including vehicle excise duty, insurance, maintenance, repairs, membership of the (AA)/(RAC) and petrol.

6.3   (*Name 1*) will retain the ownership of the car.

6.4   On the termination of this Contract (*name 2*) will deliver up possession of the car to (*name 1*) .

7 Credit

7.1   (*Name 1*) will nominate (*name 2*) to be an additional cardholder on (his)/(her) (*credit company*) account.

7.2   Between themselves (*name 2*) will be responsible for paying for all purchases on that account made solely for (his)/(her) own use, enjoyment and benefit and will be accountable for any interest attributable to those purchases.

8 Separate property

8.1   The items listed in Schedule 1 belong to (*name 1*) and will continue to be (his)/(her) separate property.

8.2   The items listed in Schedule 2 belong to (*name 2*) and will continue to be (his)/(her) separate property.

8.3   The use by one party of any property belonging to the other will not give rise to the joint ownership of that property.

8.4   Each party releases, renounces and surrenders all (if any) rights he or she may now or subsequently have to claim any right or title to or any share or interest in any property and income which now or subsequently belongs to the other party alone.

9 Gifts

9.1   Nothing in this Contract regarding the separate property of each party deprives either party of the right to give to or receive from the other party any property or assets by way of gift or transfer.

9.2   Any gift from one party to the other will be presumed to be an absolute gift unless it is expressly given on the understanding that it will be returned to the giver on the termination of the parties' relationship.

9.3   Any gift, inheritance or unexpected good fortune received by either party alone will be and will remain the separate property of that party.

10 Estate rights

10.1   (*Name 2*) acknowledges that (*name 1*) is under no obligation to make any financial provision for (him)/(her) or to confer any other benefits on (him)/(her) by Will or otherwise in the event of (his)/(her) death.

10.2   (*Name 1*) has not agreed, promised or represented to (*name 2*) that (he)/(she) will execute a Will or sign any other instrument which will make financial provision for or confer any benefit on (*name 2*) in the event of (his)/(her) death.

10.3   (*Name 2*) releases, renounces and surrenders to (*name 1*) and (his)/(her) estate any right which (he)/(she) may have as a cohabitee to apply to the Court for an order under section 2 of the Inheritance (Provision for Family and Dependants) Act 1975 or any statutory modification or re-enactment of it.

10.4   Nothing in this Contract constitutes a renunciation of the right of (*name 2*) (if entitled) to obtain a grant of representation to (*name 1's*) estate or a disclaimer by (*name 2*) of any benefits conferred on (him)/(her) by (*name 1*) in (his)/(her) Will or arising otherwise as a result of (his)/(her) death.

11 Confidentiality

(*Name 2*) promises never to use, disclose or divulge to the detriment or disadvantage of (*name 1*) any confidential information about (his)/(her) private life, family life or business affairs which may have come to (his)/(her) knowledge or attention during the course of their relationship.

12 Termination

This Contract will terminate when the parties cease to live together.

13 Termination: rights and obligations of (*name 1*)

When this Contract terminates (*name 1*) will:

13.1 be entitled to stop paying the (weekly)/(monthly) allowance to (*name 2*) ;
13.2 pay (*name 2*) a lump sum of £   to assist (him)/(her) to establish a separate household;
13.3 pay (*name 2*) an additional lump sum of £   in respect of every complete year which has elapsed between the date of this Contract and the date on which it terminates;
13.4 be entitled to deduct from these lump sum payments any unpaid balance on the (credit card) account which represents purchases made by (*name 2*) for (his)/(her) sole use, enjoyment or benefit together with any interest attributable to that unpaid balance;
13.5 make the above payments to (*name 2*) within a period of (4) weeks from the latest of the following dates, namely the date on which:

    (a) this Contract terminates;
    (b) (*name 2*) ceases to live in the house;
    (c) (*name 2*) removes all (his)/(her) belongings from the house;
    (d) (*name 2*) delivers up possession of the car to (him)/(her);
    (e) (*name 2*) returns the credit card to (him)/(her).

14 Termination: rights and obligations of (*name 2*)

When this Contract terminates (*name 2*) will:

14.1 leave the house;
14.2 remove all (his)/(her) belongings from the house;
14.3 deliver up possession of the car to (*name 1*);
14.4 return the credit card to (*name 1*);
14.5 be entitled to receive the payments less deductions mentioned in the preceding clause.

15 Separation

After this Contract has terminated neither party will:

15.1 without invitation enter or occupy any premises that are owned or occupied by the other party;

15.2 annoy, embarrass, interfere with or molest the other party and his or her relatives, friends, acquaintances, business colleagues and contacts.

16 Remedies

If either party breaches or fails to comply with any promise or provision contained in this Contract the other may be entitled to apply to the Court for an order awarding (inter alia):

16.1 damages;
16.2 specific performance;
16.3 an injunction;
16.4 costs.

17 Variation

This Contract can only be varied by an instrument in writing executed as a deed by both parties.

18 Whole agreement

This Contract contains the whole agreement between the parties and neither of them has entered into it on the basis of any promises or representations which are not expressly included in it.

19 Proper law

This Contract will be governed and interpreted in accordance with the law of England and Wales.

20 Severability

If the Court finds that any provision of this Contract is illegal, invalid or otherwise unenforceable, such provision may be severed from this Contract without affecting any other provisions which will continue to have full force and effect.

SCHEDULE 1

((*Name 1's*) separate property.)

SCHEDULE 2

((*Name 2's*) separate property.)

SIGNED as a Deed by (*name 1*) in the presence of: .

SIGNED as a Deed by (*name 2*) in the presence of: .

84 AGREEMENT RELATING TO PERSONAL CHATTELS ACQUIRED JOINTLY BY COHABITEES[1]

THIS AGREEMENT is made on (*date*)
BETWEEN 'the parties' (1) (*name 1*) of (*address*) ('*name 1*') and (2) (*name 2*) also of (*address*)('*name 2*').

THE PARTIES AGREE as follows:

1 They bought a (*description of item*) ('*the item*')[2] at/from (shop; seller; auctioneer, etc) on (*date*) for (*price*).

2 (*Name 1*) contributed £   and (*name 2*) contributed £   towards the purchase price.

3 The purpose of this Agreement is to establish what will happen to the (*item*) if one party dies or if the parties separate.

4 If the parties are living together and one of them dies the (*item*) will belong to the survivor absolutely.[3]

5 If the parties separate and neither of them wishes to keep the (*item*):

   (a) it will be sold; and
   (b) its net proceeds of sale will be divided between the parties (equally) [OR] (in the proportions that each of them contributed towards the purchase price).

6 If the parties separate and only one of them wishes to keep the (*item*):

   (a) it will be valued; and
   (b) the party who wishes to keep it will pay the other party (one half of its value) [OR] (the proportion of its value that the other party contributed towards the purchase price).

7 If the parties separate and both of them wish to keep the (*item*) and neither of them is willing to relinquish it to the other:

   (a) the (*item*) will be valued;
   (b) the parties will (toss a coin) [OR] (draw lots) [OR] (throw a dice);[4]
   (c) the winner will keep the (*item*); and
   (d) the winner will pay the loser (one half of its value) [OR] (the proportion of its value that the loser contributed towards the purchase price).

8 For the purposes of Clauses 6 and 7 of this Agreement:

   (a) the (*item*) will be valued informally by the parties themselves at such sum they agree;
   (b) in default of agreement between the parties the (*item*) will be valued

formally by one or more persons whom the parties reasonably believe to be qualified to value it;

(c)   if more than one formal valuation is obtained the average of the valuations will prevail;

(d)   the cost of a formal valuation which is requested jointly by the parties will be paid by the parties in equal shares and the cost of obtaining any other formal valuation will be paid by the party instructing the valuer.

9   Any difference, disagreement or dispute that arises out of or in connection with this Agreement will be referred in the first instance to (*name*), who will act as a mediator between the parties, without prejudice to the right of either party to apply subsequently to the Court for adjudication.[5]

10   Without prejudice to (his)/(her) role as mediator (*name*) may, at the parties' request, supervise and have conduct of any of the procedures set out in this Agreement.

11   (*Other clauses*).[6]

SIGNED as a Deed by (*name 1*) in the presence of: .

SIGNED as a Deed by (*name 2*) in the presence of: .

---

1   This Agreement could be adapted to provide for several joint purchases. It could also be incorporated into a 'cohabitation contract' proper.
2   Describe the item fully and accurately, and then give it a brief but appropriate definition: eg 'the cat'; 'the video'; 'the Rembrandt'.
3   Subject to the de minimis rules, the deceased's share may have to be brought into account for inheritance tax purposes.
4   For King Solomon's solution, see 1 Kings 3, 24 and 25.
5   See the Law of Property Act 1925, s 188(1).
6   Other clauses might include: provisions relating to payment; further assurance to effect the transfer; assumption of responsibility for future payments where the item is being acquired on HP, etc; indemnity for the other party.

---

85   AGREEMENT SETTING UP A JOINT ACCOUNT TO PAY HOUSING COSTS, ETC

THIS AGREEMENT is made on (*date*)
BETWEEN 'the parties' (1) (*name 1*) of (*address*) ('name 1') and (2) (*name 2*) (also) of (*address*) ('name 2').

IT IS AGREED that:

1   The parties (intend to) live together at (*address*) ('the property').

2   The parties (intend to) own the property as beneficial tenants in

common (in equal shares) [OR] (as to   per cent of the net proceeds of sale for (*name 1*) and   per cent for (*name 2*)).

3 On the (first) day of each month (*name 1*) will pay the sum of £   by standing order from (his)/(her) separate bank account.

4 On the (first) day of each month (*name 2*) will pay the sum of £   by standing order from (his)/(her) separate bank account.

5 The monthly sums paid by each party will be credited to the account held in their joint names at (*name and branch of bank or building society*) ('the joint account').

6 The monthly sums payable by each party will be revised in (September) each year and each revision will take into account:

    (a) any variation in the cost of living in the property during the preceding 12 months; and

    (b) any foreseeable variation in the cost of living in the property during the next 12 months.

7 The revised monthly sums will become payable on the (1 October) each year and before that date each party will instruct his or her bank to amend the standing order accordingly.

8 The following payments will be made from the joint account:

    (a) the mortgage payments;
    (b) the mortgage endowment policy premiums;
    (c) buildings and contents insurance;
    (d) water services charges;
    (e) gas bills;
    (f) electricity bills;
    (g) telephone bills;
    (h) Council Tax;
    (i) repairs and improvements to the property;
    (j) any other payments that the parties jointly authorise.

9 Either party can terminate this Agreement by giving the other party not less than (one month's) notice in writing.

10 When one party gives the other written notice of his or her intention to terminate this Agreement, the parties will immediately:

    (a) close the joint account;
    (b) cut into pieces all plastic and other cards relating to the joint account and return the pieces to the bank (or building society);
    (c) destroy all unused cheques on the joint account;
    (d) cancel the standing orders relating to their respective monthly sums.

11 When the joint account has been closed the parties will:

    (a) divide the balance on it between themselves (equally) [OR] (in the proportions that their respective monthly sums bear to each other);

(b) continue to be jointly and severally liable for any overdraft, debt, interest and bank charges incurred on the joint account;

(c) punctually pay their respective shares of any such overdraft, debt, interest and bank charges, and each party indemnifies the other against the consequences of the indemnifying party's failure to do so.

SIGNED as a Deed by (*name 1*) in the presence of: .

SIGNED as a Deed by (*name 2*) in the presence of: .

CHAPTER 3: CHILDREN

INDEX

PART 1: INTRODUCTORY TEXT

Introduction[1]

Where a child's father and mother were married to each other at the time of his or her birth, each of them has parental responsibility for the child.[2] Where a child's father and mother were not married to each other at the time of his or her birth, the mother has parental responsibility[3] but the father does not, unless he acquires it in accordance with the provisions of the Children Act 1989.[4]

An unmarried father can acquire parental responsibility for his child by:

1 marrying the child's mother;[5]
2 applying to the court for a parental responsibility order;[6]
3 entering into a parental responsibility agreement with the child's mother;[7]
4 being appointed as the child's guardian;[8] and
5 being awarded a residence order.[9]

---

1 See, generally, Hershman and McFarlane *Children: Law and Practice* (Family Law); Andrew Bainham *Children. The New Law* (Family Law, 1990); and Gillian Douglas *Children Act 1989: Transitional Arrangements Guide* (Family Law, 1991).
2 Children Act 1989, s 2(1). For the meaning of 'parental responsibility', see ibid, s 3.
3 Ibid, s 2(2)(a).
4 Ibid, s 2(2)(b).
5 Ibid, s 2(3) indirectly recognises the effect of the Legitimacy Act 1976, s 2.
6 Children Act 1989, s 4(1)(a).
7 Ibid, s 4(1)(b). See below. For the prescribed form of parental responsibility agreement, see Precedent 5 at p 180 below.
8 Children Act 1989, s 5. See below. For the appointment of a guardian by will, see Chapter 4, Precedents 12 and 13 at p 195 below. For the simple, informal appointment, see Precedent 1 at p 176 below.
9 Children Act 1989, ss 8 and 12. Possibly an unmarried father could also acquire parental responsibility by adopting his child.

Parental Responsibility Agreement

Where a child's father and mother were not married to each other at the time of the child's birth, the father and mother may, by an agreement known as a parental responsibility agreement, provide for the father to have parental responsibility for the child.[1] Section 4 of the Children Act 1989, which deals with parental responsibility agreements, implemented the recommendations of the Law Commission, who considered that there was a need for a simple, straightforward alternative to judicial proceedings in order to confer parental responsibility on an unmarried father.[2] The section also accords with the recommendation on parental responsibilities adopted by the Committee of Ministers of the Council of Europe in 1984.[3]

A parental responsibility agreement must be in the prescribed form.[4] It must also be recorded in the prescribed manner.[5] The completed, signed and witnessed agreement, together with two copies, must be filed in the Principal Registry of the Family Division.[6] When the agreement and copies have been filed, an officer of the Principal Registry will seal the two copies and send one to the child's mother and the other to the child's father.[7] The original agreement remains in the Principal Registry, where it is available for inspection by anyone during office hours.[8] The object of these procedures is to ensure that, as far as possible, both parents understand the importance and effects of the agreement.[9]

A parental responsibility agreement will come to an end when the child reaches the age of 18.[10] It can also be brought to an end by an order of the court.[11] Any person who has parental responsibility for the child can apply for such a court order,[12] and so can the child, provided that the court is satisfied that he or she has sufficient understanding to make the proposed application.[13]

---

1 Children Act 1989, s 4(1)(b).
2 Law Com No 172 'Family Law: Review of Child Law: Guardianship and Custody' (1988), at paras 2.17 to 2.21. For further background, see Law Com No 91 'Guardianship' (1985), at paras 4.20 to 4.24.
3 Council of Europe 'Parental Responsibilities' (Recommendation R(84)4), adopted by the Committee of Ministers on 28 February 1984.
4 Children Act 1989, s 4(2)(a). The agreement must be in the form set out in the Schedule to the Parental Responsibility Regulations 1991, SI 1991/1478, which came into force on 14 October 1991. For the prescribed form, see Precedent 5 at p 180 below.
5 Children Act 1989, s 4(2)(b); and SI 1991/1478, reg 3.
6 The address of the Principal Registry is Somerset House, Strand, London WC2R 1LP.
7 SI 1991/1478, reg 3(2).
8 Ibid, reg 3(3).
9 Law Com No 172, at para 2.19.
10 Children Act 1989, s 91(8).
11 Ibid, s 4(3).
12 Ibid, s 4(3)(a).
13 Ibid, s 4(3)(b) and (4).

Guardianship

Until the Children Act 1989 came into force,[1] a child's parent or guardian could only appoint a testamentary guardian by will or deed. In 1988 The Law Commission recommended that there should be a simpler method of appointing guardians, given the general desirability of encouraging parents to appoint guardians and an extremely common reluctance, particularly among young adults, to make wills.[2] A fortiori, a parent under 18 cannot execute a valid will, except in privileged circumstances.[3] The Children Act 1989 implemented this recommendation.[4] A guardian can only be appointed in accordance with the provisions of s 5 of that Act.[5] The court can appoint an individual[5] to be the child's guardian.[7] A parent who has parental responsibility for the child can appoint another individual to be the child's guardian in the event of his or her death;[8] and a guardian himself can appoint another individual to take his place as the child's guardian in the event of his death.[9] An appointment by a parent or guardian will only have effect if 'it is made in writing, is dated and is signed by the person making the appointment'.[10] An appointment can be made by two or more persons acting jointly.[11] Section 6 of the Children Act contains provisions relating to the revocation, disclaimer and termination of guardianship appointments.

---

1 The Act came into force on 14 October 1991.
2 Law Com No 172 'Family Law: Review of Child Law: Guardianship and Custody' (1988) at para 2.29.
3 Wills Act 1837, s 7 (as amended by the Family Law Reform Act 1969, s 3(1)(a)).
4 Children Act 1989, s 5(5).
5 Ibid, s 5(13). For the transitional provisions, see ibid, Sch 14, paras 12 to 14.
6 'Individual' is not defined in the Act; presumably, it excludes the holder of an office. Although an 'individual' must be appointed, a 'person' may disclaim (ibid, s 6(5)).
7 Ibid, s 5(1).
8 Ibid, s 5(3).
9 Ibid, s 5(4).
10 Ibid, s 5(5). For the appointment of a guardian by will, see Chapter 4, Precedent 12 at p 195 below. For the simple, informal appointment, see Precedent 1 at p 176 below.
11 Ibid, s 5(10). See Precedent 2 at p 176 below.

Child Maintenance Agreement[1]

The Child Support Act 1991 imposes, for the first time, a statutory duty on each parent to maintain his or her child.[2] The Act also revolutionises the means by which maintenance for children is assessed, collected and enforced.[3] Functions which until now have been exercised by the courts will gradually be transferred to the Child Support Agency,[4] a limb of the DSS, with a right of appeal to a child support appeal tribunal of similar constitution to a social security appeal tribunal.[5] Controversially, the Act requires unmarried mothers to co-operate with the Agency by disclosing details of the child's father, and failure to co-operate could result in a reduced benefit direction.[6] It is unclear at this stage what effect the Child Support Act 1991 will have on maintenance agreements. Although that Act envisages their continuance,[7] the existence of a maintenance agreement will not prevent a party to it, or anyone else, from applying to the Agency for a maintenance assessment.[8] Any provision in a maintenance agreement which purports to restrict the right to apply for a maintenance assessment is void.[9]

1 See Precedent 3 at p 178 below.
2 Child Support Act 1991, s 1. The Children Act 1989 did not directly impose a statutory duty to maintain, but read s 3(4) in conjunction with Sch 1, para 1(2). See, generally, Roger Bird *Child Maintenance – The Child Support Act 1991* (Family Law, 1993).
3 For maintenance assessment see the Child Support Act 1991, s 11 and Sch 1. For collection and enforcement, see ibid, ss 29 to 41.
4 The Child Support Agency is not actually mentioned in the Act. The powers to be exercised by the Agency are conferred on child support officers (ibid, s 13).
5 Ibid, ss 20 and 21, and Sch 3.
6 Ibid, ss 6 and 46.
7 Ibid, s 9(2).
8 Ibid, s 9(3).
9 Ibid, s 9(4).

PART 2: PRECEDENTS

1 INFORMAL APPOINTMENT OF A GUARDIAN BY ONE PARENT[1]

Children Act 1989, s 5

I (*name*) of (*address*) APPOINT (*name*) of (*address*) to be the Guardian of my (son)/(daughter) (*child's name*) in the event of my death.

Dated

Signed

---

1 Informal insofar as it is not contained in a will or deed. See, generally, 'Guardianship' above at p 173. The Children Act 1989, s 5(5) allows a parent or guardian to appoint a guardian provided that the appointment 'is made in writing, is dated and is signed by the person making the appointment'. This form of appointment would be particularly suitable for a parent under the age of 18, who, by virtue of the Wills Act 1837, s 7 (as amended), would not be able to execute a valid will. Note that legal aid (Green Form plus GF4) is still available for a lone parent wishing to make a will appointing a guardian (Legal Aid Advice and Assistance (Scope) Regulations 1989, SI 1989/550 (as amended), reg 4(2)(d)).

2 INFORMAL APPOINTMENT OF A GUARDIAN BY BOTH PARENTS[1]

Children Act 1989, s 5

WE (*father's name*) and (*mother's name*) of (*address*) JOINTLY APPOINT[2] (*name*) of (*address*) to be the Guardian of our (son)/(daughter) (*child's name*) in the event that both of us die before (he)/(she) reaches the age of eighteen.[3]

Dated

Signed

Signed

---

1 See, generally, the note on 'Guardianship' above at p 173. See also the footnote to Precedent 1 above.

2 Children Act 1989, s 5(10): 'Nothing in this section shall be taken to prevent an appointment under subsection (3) or (4) being made by two or more persons acting jointly'.

3 Unless it is brought to an end earlier in accordance with the provisions of s 6, the appointment of the guardian will continue until the child reaches 18 (ibid, s 91(8)).

3 CHILD MAINTENANCE AGREEMENT[1]

THIS MAINTENANCE AGREEMENT made on (*date*)
BETWEEN (1) (*father's name*) of (*address*) ('*name 1*') and (2) (*mother's name*) of (*address*) ('*name 2*')
WITNESSES as follows:

1 Recitals

1.1 On (*date*) (*name 2*) gave birth to a (son)/(daughter) whose name is (*child's name*) ('*name 3*').

1.2 (*Name 1*) acknowledges that he is (*name 3's*) father.

2 Maintenance agreement

(*Name 1*) agrees that:

2.1 he will pay to (*name 2*) maintenance for (*name 3's*) benefit;

2.2 the maintenance payable will start at £   a year;

2.3 the maintenance payable each year will be paid in 12 equal monthly instalments;

2.4 each instalment will be paid in advance by standing order on the (first) day of each month;

2.5 the first instalment will be paid on (*date*);

2.6 the maintenance payable will be reviewed in (April) each year when:

(a) the amount of maintenance payable until then will be multiplied by the extent to which the Retail Prices Index has changed during the year which ended on (31 March) immediately before the review; and

(b) the revised amount of maintenance payable will take effect with the payment of the instalment due on (1 May) immediately after the review and will continue to be payable at the same rate until it is reviewed again immediately after the payment of the instalment due on the following (1 April)

2.7 he will continue to pay maintenance in accordance with the terms of this Agreement until the date on which a maintenance assessment made under the Child Support Act 1991 with respect to (*name 3*):

(a) takes effect;[2] or

(b) would, if a maintenance assessment had been made, cease to have effect.[3]

3 Right to apply for maintenance assessment

The existence of this Agreement does not prevent either party, or any other person, from applying to the Secretary of State for a maintenance assessment to be made with respect to (*name 3*).[4]

SIGNED as a Deed by (*name 1*) in the presence of: .

SIGNED as a Deed by (*name 2*) in the presence of: .

---

1 See, generally, 'Child Maintenance Agreement', at p 174 above. See, generally, Roger Bird *Child Maintenance – The Child Support Act 1991* (Family Law, 1993) 2nd Edn.
2 For the effective date of the maintenance assessment, see the Child Support Act 1991, Sch 1, para 11. A maintenance assessment will take effect on such date as may be determined in accordance with regulations made by the Secretary of State (which date may be earlier than the date on which the assessment is made).
3 For the termination of maintenance assessments, see the Child Support Act 1991, Sch 1, para 16.
4 Ibid, s 9(3).

---

4 CHANGE OF NAME DEED MADE BY A MOTHER ON BEHALF OF HER CHILD: NOT INTENDED FOR ENROLMENT[1]

THIS CHANGE OF NAME DEED made on (*date*)
BY me (*mother's name*) of (*address*).
WITNESSES that:

1 I am

1.1 the mother of (*child's forename(s) and old surname*) ('*child*')[2] who was born on (*date*); and
1.2 the only person who has parental responsibility for (*child*).[3]

2 On (*child's*) behalf:

2.1 I completely renounce and abandon the use of (his)/(her) surname (*old surname*); and
2.2 I now adopt and assume for (him)/(her) the surname (*new surname*); and
2.3 I ask and authorise all persons at all times when addressing, describing and identifying (*child*) to use (his)/(her) new surname (*new surname*).

3 From now onwards (*child*) will be known as (*child's forename(s) and new surname*):

3.1 in all deeds, documents, forms, records and other written instruments; and

3.2 in all actions and proceedings; and

3.3 in all dealings and transactions; and

3.4 on all occasions.

SIGNED as a Deed by me (*mother's name*) on behalf of my (son)/(daughter) (*child's forename(s) and new surname*) in the presence of:

---

1 For changing a child's name generally, see Nasreen Pearce *Name-changing: A Practical Guide* (Fourmat Publishing, 1970) at Chapter 3. See also 'Change of Name' at Chapter 5, p 228 below.

2 Insert the child's usual forename for future reference in the deed.

3 See Children Act 1989, s 2(2). If the mother is not the only person having parental responsibility, see ibid, ss 13 and 33(7), and Form CHA11 in Appendix 1 to the Family Proceedings Rules 1991, SI 1991/1247.

5 PARENTAL RESPONSIBILITY AGREEMENT

SCHEDULE – FORM OF AGREEMENT   Regulation 2

Parental Responsibility Agreement

Date Recorded

Section 4 (1) (b)   The Children Act 1989

▶ Please use black ink.

▶ The making of this agreement will seriously affect the legal position of both parents.
   You should both seek legal advice before completing this form.

▶ If there is more than one child, you should fill in a separate form for each child.

THE ▨▨▨ CHILDREN ▨▨▨ ACT ·

This is a parental responsibility agreement between

the child's mother

Name
Address

and

the child's father

Name
Address

We agree that the father of the child named below should have parental responsibility for [him] [her] in addition to the mother.

Name	Boy / Girl	Date of birth	Date of 18th birthday

Ending of the agreement

Once a parental responsibility agreement has been made it can only end :

- by an order of the court made on application of any person who has parental responsibility for the child.

- by an order of the court made on the application of the child with leave of the court.

- when the child reaches the age of 18.

Signed (mother)		Date	
Signature of witness		Date	
Signed (father)		Date	
Signature of witness		Date	

This agreement will not take effect until this form has been filed with the Principal Registry of the Family Division. Once this form has been completed and signed please take or send it and two copies to :

> The Principal Registry of the Family Division
> Somerset House
> Strand
> London WC2R 1LP

THE ▨▨▨ CHILDREN ▨▨▨ ACT

CHAPTER 4: WILLS

INDEX

Forms

PART 1: INTRODUCTORY TEXT

Introduction

About 600,000 people die every year in England and Wales.[1] On average, probate (which means that there must have been a will) is granted in respect of 27.5 per cent of these deaths. Letters of administration account for another 11 per cent, but in a substantial majority of cases (61.5 per cent) no formal steps are taken to wind up the deceased's estate.[2] In most of these cases, the estate is too small to justify any action, but there is still a large number of estates where no grant of representation is needed because all or most of the deceased's assets pass automatically to a surviving spouse or partner, completely outside the scope of the laws relating to testate and intestate succession.

There are several reasons why property does not pass under a will or intestacy. The most significant are where property held as joint tenants goes to the survivor *iure accrescendi*, and where a statutory[3] or non–statutory nomination[4] has been made in favour of a particular beneficiary or beneficiaries.[5]

1 There are roughly 565,000 deaths in England, and 35,000 in Wales.
2 These figures were taken from Law Com No 108 'Distribution on Intestacy', at para 1.3, and are attributed to the Judicial Statistics Annual Report 1986. In Scotland, which has approximately one-tenth of the population of Great Britain, the percentages are very similar. See M C Meston *The Succession (Scotland) Act 1964* (W Green & Son Ltd) 3rd Edn at p 11.
3 For example, under the Industrial and Provident Societies Act 1965, the Friendly Societies Act 1974, the Trade Union (Nominations) Regulations 1977, SI 1977/789.
4 For example pension schemes and death-in-service benefits (see Precedent 34 at p 220 below).
5 These assets may, nevertheless, form part of the deceased's 'net estate' for the purpose of an order under the Inheritance (Provision for Family and Dependants) Act 1975, ss 8 and 9.

Surviving Cohabitee's Rights on Intestacy

If a cohabitee dies without having left a valid will, that part of his estate which is not subject to any nomination or right of survivorship will be distributed in accordance with the law relating to intestate succession.[1] A surviving cohabitee is entitled to nothing under the intestacy rules, except, in extremely rare cases, a discretionary ex-gratia payment from the Crown if the estate falls to be administered as *bona vacantia*.[2] The Law Commission recently considered the position of the surviving partner, and recommended that cohabitees should continue to be excluded from having automatic rights of intestate succession.[3] It did, however, recommend an extension of the right of a cohabitee to apply to the court for discretionary provision out of the estate.[4]

---

1 The present law can be found in the Administration of Estates Act 1925 (as amended) and the Family Provision (Intestate Succession) Order 1987, SI 1987/799. Entitlement to apply for a grant of letters of administration is governed by the Non-Contentious Probate Rules 1987, SI 1987/2024, r 22.
2 Administration of Estates Act 1925, s 46(1)(vi). Depending on where the deceased lived, the estate will pass to the Crown, the Duchy of Lancaster or the Duchy of Cornwall. Similar provisions apply in Scotland where about 200 estates a year pass to the Crown as *ultimus haeres*. On behalf of the Crown the Queen's and Lord Treasurer's Remembrancer makes roughly 25 concessionary grants each year (usually to 'relatives' who have no intestate succession rights, or close friends and neighbours who rendered substantial services to the deceased without payment).
3 Law Com No 187 'Distribution on Intestacy', at para 58. The Scottish Law Commission came to the same conclusion (Scot Law Com No 135, 'Report on Family Law' (May 1992), at paras 16.24 to 16.45).
4 Law Com No 187 (above), at paras 59 to 61: Scot Law Com No 135, at paras 16.31 to 16.36. See the note below.

Inheritance (Provision for Family and Dependants) Act 1975[1]

A surviving cohabitee may be entitled to apply to the court for an order under s 2 of the Inheritance (Provision for Family and Dependants) Act 1975, on the grounds that the disposition of the deceased's estate fails to make reasonable financial provision for him or her.[2] The applicant must prove that he or she was being maintained, either wholly or partly, by the deceased immediately before the death otherwise than for full valuable consideration,[3] and that the deceased was making a substantial con-tribution in money or money's worth towards the applicant's reasonable needs.[4] The present interpretation of dependence has been criticised as being too restrictive.[5] The Act confers *locus standi* on those who did not give the deceased valuable services in return for the maintenance provided, and denies relief to those who gave full value for their money or their keep.[6] The Law Commission has recommended that if he or she had been living with the deceased as husband or wife for a period of at least two years immediately before the death, the surviving cohabitee should be able to apply for relief without having to prove actual dependence.[7]

1 See generally Tyler/Oughton *Family Provision* (Professional Books Ltd, 1984) 2nd Edn.

2 Inheritance (Provision for Family and Dependants) Act 1975, s 1(1).

3 Ibid, s 1(1)(e). This subsection is not exclusive to cohabitees (*Re Wilkinson (deceased) Neale v Newell* [1978] 1 All ER 221).

4 Ibid, s 1(3).

5 Law Com No 187, 'Distribution on Intestacy' (1989), at paras 59 to 62.

6 See the dicta of Butler-Sloss LJ in *Bishop v Plumley* [1991] 1 All ER 236 at 242d, and Stephenson LJ in *Jelley v Iliffe* [1981] 2 All ER 29 at 36d.

7 Law Com No 187 (above), paras 58 to 62. The criteria would be the same as those under the Fatal Accidents Act 1976.

Wills

In principle there should be no difference between the contents of the wills of a married couple and those of an unmarried couple, and in practice there is little difference.[1] However, the law itself distinguishes between married and unmarried couples in this area in a number of ways. Among them are the following.

1 *Wills Act 1837, s 15* states that a gift to a beneficiary is void if the will is witnessed by the beneficiary or his or her spouse.[2] However, if a cohabitee were to witness a will conferring a benefit on his or her partner, the gift would be valid.

2 *Wills Act 1837, s 18* (as amended) provides that, except in certain circumstances, a will is revoked by the subsequent marriage of the testator.[3] Subsequent cohabitation outside marriage will not revoke an existing will.

3 *Wills Act 1837, s 18A* (as added)[4] provides that on the dissolution or annulment of a marriage, a will takes effect as if the appointment of the former spouse as an executor or trustee were omitted, and any devise or bequest to the former spouse lapses.[5] These provisions apply automatically, unless a contrary intention appears by the will. The section does not apply on the termination of the relationship of an unmarried couple.[6]

4 *Administration of Justice Act 1982, s 22* states a presumption. Unless a contrary intention is shown, it is presumed that where a testator gives property to his spouse in terms which in themselves would give an absolute interest to the spouse, but also purports to give his issue an interest in the same property, the gift to the spouse is absolute notwithstanding the purported gift to the issue. The presumption does not apply in the case of an unmarried couple. So, if the testator were to say, 'I give all my property to (*cohabitee*) and after her death to my children', the surviving partner would receive only a life interest, not an absolute interest.[7]

5 *Inheritance Tax Act 1984, s 18*. Generally speaking, transfers of value between spouses are wholly exempt.[8] This exemption does not apply to unmarried couples.

1 Except in the context of inheritance tax planning.

2 This was the problem in the well-known negligence case *Ross v Caunters* [1980] Ch 297.

3 The main exception is where the will is expressly made in expectation of marriage (see Precedents 3 and 4 at p 191 below). There is, incidentally, no similar provision in Scots Law: a subsequent marriage does not revoke a will, but a child who is born subsequently can invoke the *conditio si testator sine liberis decesserit* for the purpose of having the will reduced.

4 Added by the Administration of Justice Act 1982, ss 18(2) and 73(6), with effect from 1 January 1983.

5 It is unfortunate that s 18A did not provide that for all the purposes of the testator's will the former spouse should be treated as having predeceased him (*Re Sinclair* [1985] Ch 446). The Law Commission has published an informal consultation paper: 'The Effect of Divorce on Wills' (November 1992).

6 A new will or codicil should be executed (see Precedent 35 at p 221 below).

7 This presumption was recommended by the Law Reform Committee in its 19th Report, 'Interpretation of Wills', Cmnd 5301, at paras 60 to 62. It applies mainly to 'home-made' wills.

8 If the transferor/deceased is domiciled in the United Kingdom and the spouse is domiciled outside the UK, the exemption applies only to the first £55,000. This figure has not been increased since 1982.

Describing the Partner

A testator should describe his partner clearly, accurately and unambiguously. The best course of action is simply to state the partner's full and correct forenames and surname (and any alias) and his or her address. To abbreviate any later references in the will, the partner's forename, or some other concise and accurate description, can be placed in brackets immediately after the first occurrence of the full name. For example: DIANA FRANCES SPENCER ('Diana'); or, more traditionally, (hereinafter called 'Miss Spencer').

A description on its own – 'my partner', 'my cohabitee', 'my boyfriend' – must never be used, but where it is stated in addition to the full and correct name it will probably be innocuous. Several reported decisions reveal a tendency among some unmarried couples to refer to each other as 'my husband' or 'my wife'.[1] When it comes to making their wills, these terms should be avoided for the obvious reason that they have led, and could continue to lead, to litigation. However, in most cases where the inaccurate or euphemistic expression 'my wife' has been used in addition to the partner's full and correct name, the courts have applied the *falsa demonstratio* rule,[2] and the gift has not been invalidated.

1 For example: *Re Smalley* [1929] 2 Ch 112; and *Re Lynch* [1943] 1 All ER 168.

2 In this context the full maxim is *falsa demonstratio non nocet dummodo constet de persona* (a false description does no harm provided that it is clear who the person is). The ambiguity can be cured by extrinsic evidence.

'Cohabitation' and Wills

Prima facie, the words used in a will are given their ordinary, grammatical meaning.[1] The ordinary meaning of 'cohabitation' is 'living together as husband and wife' which, in fact, is its dictionary definition.[2] However, it is the testator's privilege to be able to use 'his own dictionary' and make words mean whatever he wishes.[3] 'He can make "black" mean "white" if he makes the dictionary sufficiently clear in his will'.[4] If by 'cohabitation' the testator means something other than 'living together as husband and wife' he must say so – clearly.[5]

References in a will to 'cohabitation' are likely to occur in two sets of circumstances. First, in the context of the testator's own relationship, where a gift to the surviving partner is made subject to the condition precedent that the couple are still living together when the testator dies.[6] The second, and more usual, occurrence is where a life interest is given to the surviving partner and it is expressed to be determinable on cohabitation.[7] The under-lying purpose is usually economic. If the survivor enters into a new relationship, the testator – or his estate – will no longer be responsible for maintaining her or him.

Where a life interest is determinable on cohabitation, the very act of cohabiting, whatever that may be, will operate as a disqualification. The burden of proof is on those who are seeking to disqualify. It is notoriously difficult to establish whether or not a couple are cohabiting.[8] Often the couple are uncertain themselves. There is no certificate or court order to evidence that split second when their status changed; when courtship ended and cohabitation began; and, by extension, when a life interest terminated. Partners could simply be sharing accommodation. Alternatively, they could be living together 'as husband and wife'.[9] By referring to 'cohabitation' in his will the testator is asking someone – primarily the executors and trustees, but perhaps also the remaindermen, the surviving partner, and the court – to make a value judgment as to which incidents of a normal husband and wife relationship are to be treated as essential, and which incidents can be discarded as superfluous. In order to shield the trustees it has become common practice to impose a discretionary trust, which probably makes their evidential burden lighter, extends their immunities, and circumscribes the scope for any appeal against their decision.[10] Although a discretionary trust has its uses, the testator must still make his intentions clear to the trustees, perhaps by way of an off-the-record memorandum. But neither the trust nor the memorandum will resolve the underlying difficulties in answering the question, 'are this couple cohabiting?'.

---

1 *Gorringe v Mahlstedt* [1907] AC 225 at 227.
2 Shorter Oxford English Dictionary. The word 'cohabitation' first appeared in the English language in the 1530s.
3 *Re Lynch* [1943] 1 All ER 168.

4 Parry and Clark *The Law of Succession* (Sweet & Maxwell) 9th Edn at p 414: a view which would have been endorsed by Humpty Dumpty. 'When *I* use a word', Humpty Dumpty said in a rather scornful tone, 'it means just what I choose it to mean – neither more nor less' (Lewis Carroll *Alice Through the Looking-Glass*, Chapter 6).

5 For some alternative definitions, see Precedent 31 at p 217 below.

6 For an example and further comment, see Precedent 23 at p 204 below.

7 For examples, see Precedents 16 and 28(g) at pp 198 and 208 below.

8 For the criteria recommended by the Department of Social Security ('DSS') to its adjudication officers, see the current edition of John Mesher's book *CPAG's Income Support, The Social Fund and Family Credit: The Legislation* (Sweet & Maxwell). The six criteria are, briefly: (1) members of the same household; (2) stability; (3) financial support; (4) sexual relationship; (5) children; and (6) public acknowledgment.

9 See the dicta of Webster J in *Robson v Secretary of State for Social Services* [1982] FLR 232 at 236.

10 For an 80 year discretionary trust, see Precedent 28(i) (at p 209 below); for a two year discretionary trust, see Precedent 28(j) (at p 211 below); for a life interest subject to the trustees' power of revocation, see Precedent 28(h) (at p 208 below).

PART 2: PRECEDENTS

Clauses

1 COMBINED COMMENCEMENT AND REVOCATION CLAUSE[1]

I (*name*)[2] of (*address*) DECLARE that this is my Will[3] and that it revokes[4] my earlier Wills.[5]

---

1 For separate commencement and revocation clauses, see Precedent 2 below.
2 The testator's full and correct forenames and surname should be stated. If any assets are registered in another name, it may be sensible to add after the full and correct name '(also known as   )'. This would facilitate the inclusion of the other name in the grant of representation. See, generally, the Non-Contentious Probate Rules 1987, SI 1987/2024, r 9.
3 The words 'last will', which are often used, are probably of no significance.
4 It is usual practice to revoke all earlier wills, even when it is clear that there are none to revoke.
5 It is submitted that the widely used expression 'testamentary dispositions' is less likely to be understood by an ordinary layman. The use of that expression 'may be thought unnecessary now that national service has been abolished and the possibility of there being a testamentary disposition by a testator while he is a soldier, sailor or airman and in actual military service is remote' (*Williams on Wills* (Butterworths) 5th Edn, Vol 2, at p 1231(c)). The words 'and codicils' are probably also unnecessary, as the codicils are merely additions to the earlier wills. The nomination of a beneficiary under a pension scheme is not a 'testamentary disposition' (*Re Danish Bacon Co* [1971] 1 WLR 248).

---

2 COMMENCEMENT INCLUDING DATE: SEPARATE REVOCATION CLAUSE[1]

THIS WILL is made on (*date*)[2] by me (*name*)[3] of (*address*).

1 I REVOKE my earlier Wills.[4]

---

1 For a combined commencement and revocation clause, see Precedent 1 above.
2 If the date is not included in the commencement it is usually stated in the testimonium at the end of the will.
3 See Precedent 1, footnote 2 above.
4 See Precedent 1, footnotes 4 and 5 above.

3 WILL IN EXPECTATION OF MARRIAGE[1]

THIS WILL will not be revoked by my expected marriage to (*cohabitee*).

---

1 Except in certain cases, a will is revoked by the testator's marriage (Wills Act 1837, s 18(1), as amended). Section 18(3) states that 'where it appears from a will that at the time it was made the testator was expecting to be married to a particular person and that he intended that the will should not be revoked by the marriage, the will shall not be revoked by his marriage to that person'. Until s 18 was substituted by the Administration of Justice Act 1982, such wills were known as 'wills in contemplation of marriage', by virtue of the wording of the Law of Property Act 1925, s 177.

---

4 WILL IN EXPECTATION OF MARRIAGE: SOME PROVISIONS APPLYING BEFORE MARRIAGE AND OTHERS ON MARRIAGE[1]

1 THIS WILL will not be revoked by my expected marriage to (*cohabitee*).

2 PART I[2] of this Will applies at all times.

3 PART II will apply until my expected marriage is solemnised.

4 PART III will apply when my expected marriage has been solemnised.

PART I
(*Insert the provisions which will apply regardless of whether or not the marriage has been solemnised, for example funeral wishes, specific bequests, trustee powers, etc.*)

PART II
(*Insert provisions which apply immediately.*)

PART III
(*Insert the provisions which will apply on the solemnisation of the expected marriage.*)

---

1 For wills made in expectation of marriage, see Precedent 3, footnote 1 above.
2 Division into 'parts' may be considered preferable to division into 'schedules' as it enables each clause of the will to continue in numerical order (*cf* Matrimonial Causes Act 1973, etc).

---

5 DECLARATION OF MUTUALITY[1]

I HAVE AGREED with (*cohabitee*) that if I survive (him)/(her) I will not revoke or change this Will.

1 **Warning** A 'mutual will' is made when testators contractually agree that neither of them will revoke or alter his will. If, after the first death, the survivor revokes the mutual will, Equity will enforce the original agreement by imposing a constructive trust on the survivor's death. The advantages of a mutual will are that the survivor's ability to renege on the agreement is curtailed, and the survivor is free to enjoy the assets without being subject to a trust. The disadvantages are: (a) the will is revoked on marriage; (b) it is very difficult to identify the assets which are subject to the constructive trust; and (c) the agreement can be frustrated by lifetime alienation or dissipation of the assets. A mutual will, made by an unmarried person, may be contrary to public policy because it acts in restraint of marriage (*Robinson v Ommanney* [1883] 23 Ch D 285, CA).

　　See, generally, *Williams on Wills* (Butterworths, 1987) 6th Edn, Vol 1, at Chapter 3; A J Oakley *Constructive Trusts* (Sweet & Maxwell, 1987) 2nd Edn; Law Reform Committee's 22nd Report (1980), 'The making and revocation of wills', at paras 3.50 to 3.52; and the articles by Professor C E F Rickett, 'Mutual Wills and the Law of Restitution' (1989) 105 LQR 534, and 'Extending Equity's Reach through the Mutual Wills Doctrine' (1991) MLR 581.

6 DECLARATION OF NON-MUTUALITY[1]

ALTHOUGH (*cohabitee*) and I are making Wills in similar terms they are not 'Mutual Wills' and each of us can alter or revoke his or her Will at any time.

1 See footnotes to Precedent 5 above. It is important to distinguish between 'mutual wills' in the lay sense and 'mutual wills' in the legal sense. There is often some confusion (see Anne Barlow *Living Together: A Guide to the Law* (Fourmat Publishing, 1992), at p 11).

7 SURVIVORSHIP CLAUSE:[1]

(a) General applicability

ANYONE who does not survive me by (14) days[2] will be treated as having died before me for all the purposes of this Will.

1 According to The Law Commission 'it is the current practice to incorporate a survivorship clause into wills' (Law Com No 187, 'Distribution on Intestacy' (1989), at para 57). Compare the Scottish Law Commission's (1990) 'Report on Succession', Scot Law Com No 124, at 64, note 1, which states that research found that about eight per cent of testators included such a provision, and that the survival period required was usually one month.

　　The object of a survivorship clause is to stop the assets of both partners passing to the parents or relatives of the second to die in cases of not quite simultaneous death, usually in accidents. See also the statutory presumption that where uncertainty exists as to the order in which two or more persons have died, 'the younger shall be deemed to have survived the elder' (Law of Property Act 1925, s 184). There may also be inheritance tax advantages in including a survivorship clause in a will (Inheritance Tax Act 1984, s 92).

2 Law Com No 187 (above), para 57 states: 'We consider that an appropriate length for
such a survivorship clause is 14 days. Any longer might lead to unacceptable delays in
the administration of estates'. Compare the Scottish Law Commission's Report (above),
Part V, which recommends a survivorship period of 'at least five days' unless the will
specifies some other period. The Scottish recommendation follows sections 2–104 and
2–601 of the Uniform Probate Code (USA) which provides a survivorship period of 120
hours.

(b) Specific to cohabitee[1]

IF (*cohabitee*) does not survive me by (14) days (he)/(she) will be treated as
having died before me for all the purposes of this Will.

1 See Precedent 7(a), footnotes 1 and 2 above.

8 FUNERAL WISHES[1]

IF possible and practicable I would like:

- any part of my body which may be of use to others to be made available
  for treatment or transplantation;[2]
- my (kidneys)/(corneas)/(heart)/(lungs)/(liver)/(pancreas) to be used for
  transplantation;[2]
- (*name of firm*) to be my funeral directors;
- an obituary notice to be inserted in (*name of newspaper, journal, etc*);
- my funeral service to be conducted in accordance with the (rites)/(usages)
  of (*name of faith or denomination*);
- my funeral service to be held at (*location*);
- there to be no religious formalities at my funeral;
- (*hymns, songs, tunes, music etc*) to be played or sung at my funeral;
- (*scriptural, poetry or other readings*) to be read at my funeral;
- family flowers only;
- donations, if desired, to be made to (*Charity*);
- to be cremated;
- my ashes to be scattered (in the grounds of the Crematorium [OR]
  (*wherever*);
- my ashes to be interred in (*location*);
- to be buried;
- to be buried in (*location*) [OR] (wherever is most convenient)/(at sea);[3]
- a headstone to be placed on my grave;
- (*cohabitee*) to decide what wording should be inscribed on the headstone;
- refreshments to be provided for those attending my funeral;
- my funeral arrangements to be as simple (and inexpensive) as possible;
- (*cohabitee*) to decide on any other funeral arrangements;

- the expenses incurred in carrying out these wishes (and *cohabitee's* wishes) to be paid out of my estate.

---

1 A binding disposition of the body of the deceased cannot be made by will so as to oust the executors' rights and duties as to its disposal. Many precedent books suggest that it is unnecessary or even undesirable to incorporate funeral wishes in a will. The main arguments for *excluding* such wishes include:

(a) the will might not be found until it is too late;
(b) the wishes are generally not binding; and
(c) it adds to the cost of preparing the will, or having to prepare another will or codicil if the testator changes his mind about any of these wishes.

Reasons for *including* funeral wishes in a will include:

(a) they require the testator to make his wishes known;
(b) others are relieved of the duty of making such decisions;
(c) there is less likelihood of conflict between executors, relatives, beneficiaries, etc;
(d) such wishes are usually honoured and rarely changed; and
(e) expenditure can be formally authorised.

2 This sub-clause is based on the wording of the standard 'Donor Card'.
3 Those with an appetite for black comedy might enjoy the Scottish case *Herron v Diack and Newlands* 1973 SLT (Sh Ct) 27 which involved an unsuccessful burial at sea.

---

9 APPOINTMENT OF COHABITEE AS EXECUTOR[1]

I APPOINT (*cohabitee*) of (*address*) to be the Executor of this Will but if (he)/(she) dies before me or is unwilling or unable to act as Executor I APPOINT (*name*) of (*address*) (and (*name*) of (*address*)) to be the Executor(s) (and Trustees)[2] of this Will instead.

---

1 If the cohabitee is also the universal beneficiary use Precedent 10 (below) instead.
2 It is only necessary to appoint trustees where there is or could be an ongoing trust.

---

10 APPOINTMENT OF COHABITEE AS SOLE EXECUTOR AND UNIVERSAL BENEFICIARY[1]

IF (he)/(she) survives me by (14) days[2] I GIVE all of my estate[3] to (*cohabitee*) of (*address*) AND APPOINT (him)/(her) to be my Executor[4] but if (he)/(she) fails to survive me by (14) days the following clauses will apply.[5]

---

1 The sole executor and universal beneficiary must be an adult.
2 A survivorship clause is not essential but advisable.
3 For the meaning of 'estate' see, generally, *Williams on Wills* (Sweet & Maxwell, 1987) 6th Edn.
4 As the sole executor and universal beneficiary has all the powers needed to administer the

estate, no further powers or provisions are necessary. There is no continuing trust, so there is no need to appoint the executor as a trustee.

5 It is virtually essential to include substitutionary gifts, appointments and provisions.

11 APPOINTMENT OF EXECUTORS AND TRUSTEES INCLUDING A PROFESSIONAL CHARGING CLAUSE[1]

1 I APPOINT (*name*) of (*address*) and (*name*) of (*address*)[2] to be the Executors and Trustees of this Will.

2 In this Will 'my trustees' means my personal representatives and the persons who at any time are the trustees of any trusts created by this Will.

3 A professionally qualified trustee can charge and be paid in priority to the gifts in this Will for all the work done by him or his firm in obtaining probate, administering my estate, and acting as a trustee, even though some of the work could have been done by a person who is not professionally qualified.[3]

1 It seems logical to include a professional charging clause (where appropriate) in the appointment itself. This generally happens where trust corporations are appointed.
2 The maximum number that can be appointed is four (Trustee Act 1925, s 34; Supreme Court Act 1981, s 114(1)).
3 A trustee cannot profit from his trust. Accordingly, unless it is expressly authorised, a trustee cannot receive payment for his services. A professional charging clause is strictly construed, and a solicitor/trustee who is authorised to make 'professional charges' will not be entitled to charge for work done other than in his capacity as a solicitor. Amounts due under a charging clause rank as general legacies, not as administration expenses; so where the estate has been exhausted by specific legacies the charges will not be paid at all. See, generally, the Law Reform Committee's Twenty Third Report, 'The Powers and Duties of Trustees' (1982), at paras 3.42 to 3.55.

12 APPOINTMENT OF GUARDIANS[1]

I APPOINT (*name*) of (*address*) (and (*name*) of (*address*))[2] to be the Guardian(s) of my children under eighteen.[3]

1 A guardian can only be appointed in accordance with the provisions of s 5 of the Children Act 1989 (s 5(13)). See, generally, 'Guardianship' at p 173 above.
2 More than one person may have parental responsibility for the same child at the same time (ibid, s 2(5)).
3 Unless it is brought to an end earlier, the appointment of a guardian continues until the child reaches the age of 18 (ibid, s 91(8)).

13 APPOINTMENT OF GUARDIAN AND SUBSTITUTE GUARDIAN[1]

I APPOINT (*name*) of (*address*) to be the Guardian of my children under eighteen but if this appointment fails for any reason[2] I APPOINT (*name*) of (*address*) to be the Guardian instead.

---

1 A guardian can only be appointed in accordance with the provisions of Children Act 1989, s 5(13). See, generally, 'Guardianship' at p 173 above.

2 For example the guardian could predecease the testator; the guardian could die before the child reached 18; the guardian could disclaim; or the appointment could be brought to an end by order of the court. See, generally, ibid, s 6(5), (6) and (7).

---

14 GUARDIANSHIP

(a) Statement of wishes concerning children under 18[1]

IT IS MY WISH that, as far as circumstances and finances permit, my children will be:

- kept together;
- allowed to retain their present surname(s);[2]
- encouraged to keep in contact with their (grandparents, uncles, aunts, cousins, godparents, etc as the case may be);[3]
- brought up in the (Christian) faith;[4]
- educated at (a single sex)/(an independent) school;
- (*other wishes, as appropriate*).

---

1 The wishes of the parent are only permitted to prevail if they are not inconsistent with other considerations relating to the child's welfare (*Ward v Laverty* [1925] AC 101). See also Children Act 1989, s 1.

2 See, generally, Nasreen Pearce, *Name-changing, A Practical Guide* (Fourmat Publishing, 1990) at Chapter 3.

3 For 'contact orders', see Children Act 1989, s 8(1).

4 'In accordance with the *Gillick* principle, the parent's wishes over religious upbringing yield to the child's right to make his own decision once he has reached sufficient intellect and understanding to be capable of doing so' (H K Bevan *Child Law* (Butterworths, 1989), at para 11.06).

(b) Trustees' power to lend capital to guardians[1]

MY TRUSTEES can at any time raise capital from my residuary estate and lend it to the Guardian(s) of any child of mine:

- on such terms and conditions (including repayment, interest, and security) as they consider appropriate in the circumstances;

- even if they exhaust my residuary estate in the process;
- even if one of the Guardians is also a trustee of this Will;
- without being liable for any loss incurred;
- but only if they consider that doing so would be better for the child than not doing so.

---

1 If the children are the beneficiaries under the will, the cost of looking after them will generally be met (so far as funds are available) by the trustees under their statutory powers of maintenance and advancement. There may be circumstances in which it would be helpful for the trustees to have power to lend capital to the guardians, for example the guardians may need to acquire a larger house in order to accommodate the children. For potential inheritance tax difficulties with such a power, see *Butterworth's Wills, Probate and Administration Service* (Butterworths) at para 371.

---

15 ABSOLUTE GIFT OF (A SHARE OF) A HOUSE

1 I GIVE to (*cohabitee*) my (share of the) property known as (*address*) or failing which the property that is my principal residence at the time of my death ('the property').[1]

2 IF when I die:
  (a) there is any doubt as to which of two or more properties is my principal residence the decision of my Trustees will be final;[2]
  (b) the property is subject to a binding but uncompleted contract of sale then this gift will take effect as a gift of (my share of) its net proceeds of sale;[3]
  (c) the property has been sold then I GIVE to (*cohabitee*) the sum of pounds (£   ) (free of tax) instead.

3 THIS GIFT is subject to any legal or equitable charge affecting the property immediately before my death AND I GIVE to (*cohabitee*) (free of tax) the full benefit of and all sums payable under any policies of insurance on my life which have been given as security for the repayment of such charges.[4]

[OR]

3 ANY legal or equitable charge affecting the property immediately before my death will (if not automatically discharged by any policies of insurance on my life given as security for this purpose) be paid and discharged from my residuary estate in exoneration of the property.[4]

4 THIS GIFT will bear its own share of any tax which is payable on or by reason of my death.[5]

[OR]

4 ANY tax attributable to the property which is payable on or by reason of my death will be paid and discharged from my residuary estate in exoneration of the property.[5]

5 ALL expenses incurred in transferring the property to (*cohabitee*) and registering (his)/(her) title at the Land Registry will be paid by (*cohabitee*).[6]

[OR]

5 ALL expenses incurred in transferring the property to (*cohabitee*) and registering (his)/(her) title at the Land Registry will be paid from my residuary estate.[6]

---

1 A specific devise or specific legacy will fail by ademption if its subject matter has ceased to form part of the testator's estate at the time of his death. If the testator sells the property, the disappointed devisee is not entitled to the traceable net proceeds of sale (*Re Bagot* [1862] 31 LJ Ch 772 at 774).

2 If there is any doubt about which of two or more residences is 'the principal residence', it may be considered preferable that the surviving partner should choose, rather than the trustees. For example: 'If (*address*) has been sold in my lifetime and if there is any doubt as to which of two or more properties is my principal residence at the time of my death this gift will apply only to the one property that (*cohabitee*) selects within (6 weeks) of my death'. Compare the prior rights of a surviving spouse on an intestacy in the dwelling house in Scottish Law (Succession (Scotland) Act 1964, s 8(1)).

3 A binding contract for sale will effect an ademption (*Farrar v Earl of Winterton* [1842] 5 Beav 1).

4 In the absence of any provision to the contrary the specific devisee would be primarily liable for any money charged on the property (Administration of Estates Act 1925, s 35).

5 See, generally, *Butterworth's Wills, Probate and Administration Service* (Butterworths), Volume 1, at paras 1031 to 1065, 'Tax Free or Not Tax Free'.

6 In the absence of a direction to the contrary the expense incurred in vesting a specific devise in the devisee is borne by the devisee personally (*Re Grosvenor* [1916] 2 Ch 375).

---

16 LIFE OR LESSER INTEREST IN (A SHARE OF) A DWELLING AND ITS NET PROCEEDS OF SALE[1]

1 I GIVE my (share of the) property known as (*address*) or failing which the property that is my principal residence at the time of my death[2] to my Trustees on trust for sale.

2 MY TRUSTEES can invest the net proceeds of sale of that property as freely as if it were their own money and can purchase and improve any replacement property or a share in any replacement property for (*cohabitee*) to live in.[3]

3 ANY property which is subject to these trusts is referred to as 'the property', and the property and any cash or investments representing it are referred to as 'the property fund'.

4 MY TRUSTEES will let (*cohabitee*) live in the property on the terms mentioned below and will pay any income from the property fund to (him)/(her) during (his)/(her) lifetime until (he)/(she) cohabits[4] ('the termination of these trusts').

5 UNTIL the termination of these trusts (*cohabitee*) can live in the property rent-free on the terms that (he)/(she):

(a) pays the outgoings;
(b) keeps it in reasonable repair and condition;
(c) keeps it insured to its full reinstatement value;
(d) complies with the covenants and conditions to which it is subject.

6 MY TRUSTEES will not:

(a) exercise their trust for sale without reasonable cause before the termination of these trusts;
(b) be personally liable for the failure of (*cohabitee*) to comply with any of the obligations imposed on (him)/(her);
(c) be personally liable for paying any income from the property fund to (*cohabitee*) after the termination of these trusts unless they have knowledge of the event causing the termination.

7 SUBJECT to these provisions my Trustees will hold the property fund (as part of my residuary estate)/(on trust for   )/ (for   ).

---

1 Contrast this clause with a clause giving the surviving partner a life or lesser interest in the whole of the estate (Precedent 28(f) at p 208 below) and a clause conferring mere occupation rights that do not extend to an interest in the proceeds of sale (Precedent 17 below).
2 This wording is designed to avoid the problem of abatement.
3 For the powers of trustees to purchase and improve land for occupation by a beneficiary, see the footnotes to Precedent 29(a) at p 213 below.
4 For difficulties which arise when a life interest is terminable on cohabitation, see p 188 and Precedent 31 at p 217 below.

---

17 OCCUPATION RIGHTS RESTRICTED TO A PARTICULAR PROPERTY: VARIATION LIFTING THAT RESTRICTION

1 I GIVE my (share of the) property known as (*address*) or failing which the property that is my principal residence at the time of my death ('the property') to my Trustees on trust for sale.

2 MY TRUSTEES will let (*cohabitee*) live in the property for as long as (he)/(she) wishes on the terms that (he)/(she):
(a) pays the outgoings;
(b) keeps it in reasonable repair and condition;
(c) keeps it insured to its full reinstatement value;
(d) complies with the covenants and conditions to which it is subject.

(IF (*cohabitee*) wishes to live elsewhere my Trustees can sell the property and apply the proceeds in or towards the purchase of another property or a share in another property which will be held on exactly the same trusts as the property itself (but if the purchase price of the other property or a share in it is less than the net proceeds of sale of the property itself the surplus cash will immediately (form part of my residuary estate)/(be paid by my Trustees to))).

3 MY TRUSTEES will not:

(a) require (*cohabitee*) to pay an occupation rent;
(b) require (*cohabitee*) to share the property with anyone else;
(c) be personally liable for the failure of (*cohabitee*) to comply with any of the obligations imposed on (him)/(her);
(d) exercise their trust for sale without reasonable cause unless or until (*cohabitee*) ceases to occupy the property on a permanent basis[1] or fails to comply with any of the obligations imposed on (him)/(her).

4 SUBJECT to these provisions my Trustees will hold (my share of) the property and its net proceeds of sale (as part of my residuary estate)/(on trust for   )/(for   ).

---

1 For consideration of the meaning of expressions such as 'permanently ceases to reside', see *Re Coxen* [1948] 2 All ER 492 at 500.

---

18 HOUSE SETTLED ON COHABITEE FOR LIFE UNDER THE SETTLED LAND ACT 1925[1]

1 I APPOINT my Trustees to be trustees for the purpose of the Settled Land Act 1925.

2 I GIVE my property known as (*address*) or failing which the property that is my principal residence at the time of my death ('the property') to (*cohabitee*) for (his)/(her) life.

3 (*COHABITEE*) will be responsible for:

(a) paying all the outgoings on the property;
(b) keeping the property in reasonable repair, decoration and condition;[2]
(c) keeping the property insured to its full reinstatement value with an insurance company of which my Trustees approve;
(d) complying with all the covenants and conditions to which the property is subject.

4 CAPITAL may be invested or applied (with my Trustees' consent) in any investment authorised by my Will in respect of my residuary estate including the purchase of land outside England and Wales.[3]

5 AFTER the death of (*cohabitee*) I GIVE the property or the capital representing it to (*name*).

1 This clause may be considered appropriate where the testator wishes to give the surviving cohabitee a life interest, but is anxious to ensure that the survivor is not at the mercy of trustees for sale. As tenant for life the survivor has all the powers of trustees for sale, and can direct the application of the proceeds of sale towards the purchase of another property.

2 *Re Cartwright* [1889] 41 Ch D 532.

3 'Capital money . . . shall not be applied in the purchase of land out of England and Wales, unless the settlement expressly authorises the same' (Settled Land Act 1925, s 73(2)).

19 OPTION TO PURCHASE (A SHARE OF) DWELLING[1]

1 I GIVE to:

(a) my Trustees my (share of the) property known as (*address*) or failing which the property that is my principal residence at the time of my death ('the property') on trust for sale;

(b) (*cohabitee*) the option to purchase the property from my Trustees at the price and on the terms and conditions stated below.

2 THE PROPERTY will be valued on the basis that:

(a) it is being sold at arm's length on the open market with vacant possession;

(b) all the fixtures and fittings and carpets and curtains are included in the sale;

(c) there is no discount for joint ownership.[2]

3 THE PRICE will be (75 per cent of) the value of (my share of) the property.

4 FROM the date of my death, within a period of:

(a) (4) weeks the property will be valued by a professionally qualified valuer appointed by my Trustees;

(b) (6) weeks my Trustees will give written notice of this option to (*cohabitee*);

(c) (8) weeks (*cohabitee*) will give written notice to my Trustees exercising this option;

(d) (12) weeks (*cohabitee*) will complete the purchase of the property.

5 MY TRUSTEES can:

(a) compromise on the price if (*cohabitee*) obtains a valuation of the property which differs from that obtained by them;

(b) let (*cohabitee*) live in the property rent free until it is sold provided that (he)/(she) pays all the outgoings and keeps it insured to its full reinstatement value;

(c) enforce their trust for sale after the end of the period of (12) weeks from the date of my death;

(d) extend any of the time-limits set out in this clause if they consider that such an extension is reasonable in the circumstances.

6 MY ESTATE will pay:

   (a) the cost of obtaining the valuation;

   (b) the costs of transferring the property to (*cohabitee*); including Stamp Duty, Land Registry fees and legal fees;

   (c) any Inheritance Tax payable because the price is less than the open market value.

7 THIS OPTION:

   (a) is personal to (*cohabitee*) and cannot be exercised by anyone else;

   (b) can be exercised by (*cohabitee*) even though (he)/(she) is one of my Trustees;

   (c) will lapse if it has not been exercised by (*cohabitee*) within (8) weeks from the date of my death or within such later period as my Trustees consider to be reasonable in the circumstances.

8 SUBJECT to these provisions my Trustees will hold (my share of) the net proceeds of sale of the property (as part of my residuary estate)/(on trust for   )/(for   ).

---

1 An option to purchase can be very useful. It allows the surviving partner to buy the whole property and, where the testator permits his partner to purchase at an undervalue, there is an added incentive to buy. It frees the property from an ongoing trust for sale, and it releases cash for distribution to other beneficiaries. Note the Law of Property (Miscellaneous Provisions) Act 1989, s 2.

2 See *Wight and Another v CIR Lands Tribunal* (1982) 264 EG 935, which related to the valuation of a property held as tenants in common. It was held that for capital transfer tax purposes the discount for joint ownership should be 15 per cent, rather than the 10 per cent which had become customary following the earlier decision in *Cust v CIR* (1917) 91 EG 11.

---

20 BEQUEST OF PERSONAL CHATTELS

I GIVE free of tax to (*cohabitee*) all my personal chattels (as defined in the Administration of Estates Act 1925)[1] that have not been specifically bequeathed to others.

---

1 'Personal chattels' means carriages, horses, stable furniture and effects (not used for business purposes), motor cars and accessories (not used for business purposes), garden effects, domestic animals, plate, plated articles, linen, china, glass, books, pictures, prints, furniture, jewellery, articles of household or personal use or ornament, musical and scientific instruments and apparatus, wines, liquors and consumable stores, but do not include any chattels used at the death of the intestate for business purposes nor money or securities for money' (s 55(1)x).

   The same definition, with the addition of the words 'including wearing apparel' is used in Statutory Will Forms 1925, Form 2.

   Although it dates from an age when the car had not quite supplanted the horse, this is still considered to be the most satisfactory definition of 'personal chattels', and is used almost without exception. It may need to be adapted slightly to suit the testator's requirements. For example ' . . . and this gift includes any car and accessories used for business purposes'.

21 BEQUEST OF PERSONAL CHATTELS: COHABITEE TO CHOOSE

1 I GIVE free of tax to (*cohabitee*) such of my personal chattels (as defined in the Administration of Estates Act 1925)[1] that have not been specifically bequeathed to others as (he)/(she) may choose within the period of (6) weeks beginning with the date of my death.

2 Any personal chattels that (he)/(she) has not chosen within that period will form part of my residuary estate.

1 For definition of personal chattels, see Precedent 20, footnote (above).

22 SPECIFIC BEQUEST

(a) Jewellery[1]

I GIVE all my jewellery including watches[2] to my daughter (*name*) free of tax (and my Trustees can let her wear my jewellery when she reaches the age of (14)).

1 Unless they are particularly valuable, it is usually preferable that specific chattels vest in a minor immediately, rather than be made contingent on the child reaching 18. Strictly speaking, the chattels should be kept until the child is 18 and can give a valid receipt for them.
2 D T Davies *Will Precedents and Inheritance Tax* (Butterworths) 4th Edn at p 176, contains a more comprehensive definition: 'all my jewellery and all other articles of a like nature including tiaras, rings, necklaces, earrings, brooches, pendants, bracelets and watches'.

(b) Car on hire purchase, etc[1]

I GIVE to (*cohabitee*) (free of tax) any car I own or lawfully have in my possession at the time of my death.

IF the car is subject to a hire purchase or conditional sale agreement . . .[2] I GIVE to (*cohabitee*) all my rights under that agreement on condition that (he)/(she) pays all sums, performs all obligations and indemnifies my estate against all liabilities arising under it.

[*OR*]

. . . my Trustees will do what they can to complete the purchase of the car and to transfer it to (*cohabitee*) at the expense of my residuary estate.

---

1 Although this clause relates to a car, the same principles would apply in respect of other goods being acquired on HP. Clauses of this nature are fraught with difficulties and, wherever possible, the practitioner should inspect the HP, etc, agreement. For comments and precedents on goods subject to a credit sale agreement and leasing agreement, see *Butterworth's Wills, Probate and Administration Service* (Butterworths) Vol 1, para 736.
2 The ownership of goods under an HP agreement is not vested in the testator (compare credit sale agreements).

---

23 COHABITATION AS A CONDITION PRECEDENT:[1] PECUNIARY LEGACY[2]

IF (*cohabitee*) and I are still living together at the time of my death, I GIVE (him)/(her) the sum of   pounds (£   ) free of tax.

---

1 Wills Act 1837, s 18A, contains provisions relating to the effect on wills of a decree of dissolution or annulment of marriage. Nothing comparable exists in respect of the end of an unmarried couple's relationship. If the couple split up, it is imperative that they review their wills as soon as possible. For example, see Precedent 35 at p 221 below. If a testator specifically wishes to make a gift to the cohabitee conditional on their still living together, he should appoint independent executors who could apply to the court for directions if there were any problems over compliance with the condition precedent.
2 The pecuniary legacy is merely an illustration of the condition precedent. The same rules would apply in respect of other gifts. If the cohabitee does not satisfy the condition specified, the pecuniary legacy will fail.

---

24 PECUNIARY LEGACY: INDEX-LINKED[1]

1 I GIVE to (*cohabitee*) the sum of £   free of tax ('this legacy').

2 This legacy will be index-linked by reference to the extent by which the Retail Prices Index has changed between the month in which I sign this Will and the month in which I die.

3 If the Retail Prices Index no longer exists at the time of my death my Trustees may apply whatever formula they consider appropriate to ensure that the value of this legacy is the same at my death as it was when I signed this Will.[2]

---

1 The Retail Prices Index ('RPI') is designed to measure the changes in the prices of goods and services purchased by householders from their net income, and is, therefore,

indicative of the purchasing power of money. The figures are published by the Department of Employment monthly.

2 This sub-clause is probably unnecessarily cautious. The original 'Cost-of-Living Index' was introduced in 1914, and was superseded by the RPI in June 1947. A new base for the RPI was set in January 1987.

25 RELEASE OF DEBT[1]

I RELEASE (*cohabitee*) free of tax from any debt and the interest on any debt which (he)/(she) may owe me at the time of my death.

1 The release of a debt constitutes a pecuniary legacy to the debtor (*A-G v Holbrook* (1823) 3 Y & J 114). If the debtor dies before the testator, the release will lapse like any other legacy, unless the will contains express provisions against lapse, for example: ' . . . but if (he)/(she) dies before me (his)/(her) personal representatives will have the benefit of this release'. Cohabitees often make loans to each other, with varying degrees of formality, and it is sensible to ascertain exactly what the testator's wishes are in order to avoid any misunderstanding. A declaration in the will that moneys advanced by the testator were gifts, not loans, to the cohabitee would, in theory, produce the same result, but there are constructional difficulties in such a declaration. The clause would 'speak' from the date of the will, rather than from the date of death.

26 LUMP SUM TO BUY AN ANNUITY[1]

I GIVE free of tax to (*cohabitee*) the sum that my Trustees consider sufficient to enable (him)/(her) to purchase from a reputable insurance company a gross annuity of £   payable quarterly from the date of my death AND I HOPE that (*cohabitee*) will use the sum to purchase such an annuity.

1 This is probably the easiest way of providing the surviving cohabitee with an annuity. More complicated provisions, including index-linking, can be found in the standard will precedent books. If the surviving cohabitee is or is likely to be receiving income-related benefits from the DSS, the notional capital rule under reg 51 of the Income Support (General Regulations) 1987, SI 1987/1967, must be considered.

27 ADMINISTRATION TRUSTS AND DEFINITION OF RESIDUARY ESTATE[1]

I GIVE all (the rest)[2] of my estate to my Trustees on trust to:

1 sell or retain;

2 pay my debts, funeral expenses, executorship expenses,[3] and any

Inheritance Tax (that is not charged on or primarily payable out of other property);[4] and

3 hold what remains ('my residuary estate') on the following trusts.

1 It may be considered preferable to separate the administration trusts from the trusts of residue. Compare, Statutory Will Forms 1925, Form 8 'Administration Trusts'.
2 The words 'the rest' should be included if this clause is preceded by a legacy or legacies.
3 The words 'executorship expenses' seem to be more fashionable than the expression 'testamentary expenses'. There is no difference between their meanings. 'I cannot distinguish between executorship expenses and testamentary expenses' (*Sharp v Lush* [1879] 48 LJ Ch 231 at 232, per Jessel MR).
4 In the absence of a direction to the contrary, the residue will bear the inheritance tax. The testator may prefer to state 'pay . . . any Inheritance Tax attributable to property which I hold as a joint tenant'.

28 RESIDUARY ESTATE

(a) Cohabitee entitled absolutely[1]

MY TRUSTEES will pay or transfer my residuary estate to (*cohabitee*) absolutely.

IF (*cohabitee*) dies before me, my Trustees will pay or transfer my residuary estate to (or hold it on trust for) . . .[2]

1 This clause assumes that 'my residuary estate' has already been defined (see Precedent 27 above).
2 It is advisable to include a gift over.

(b) Cohabitee and other adults equally entitled: no gifts over[1]

MY TRUSTEES will pay or transfer my residuary estate to (*cohabitee*) and (*name*) and (*name*) in equal shares or to the survivor of them absolutely.

1 This clause assumes that 'my residuary estate' has already been defined. The words 'pay or transer' are probably preferable to, and less misleading than, 'hold on trust for' where there is no on-going trust.

(c) Cohabitee and testator's children given specified shares: provisions for their 'separate families'

MY TRUSTEES will divide my residuary estate into (*number*) equal shares which they will hold as follows:

1 *(number)* shares ('the *(cohabitee's family name)* Fund') for *(cohabitee)*;

2 *(number)* shares ('the *(testator's family name)* Fund') for my children *(name)* and *(name)* in equal shares or for the survivor absolutely;

3 if *(cohabitee)* dies before me my Trustees will hold the *(cohabitee's family name)* Fund for (his)/(her) children *(name)* and *(name)* in equal shares or for the survivor absolutely;

4 if any of my children or *(cohabitee's)* children dies before me leaving a child or children living at my death, that child or those children on reaching the age of (18) will take, and if more than one in equal shares, the share of my residuary estate which his, her or their parent would have taken if he or she had survived me;

5 if the trusts affecting either Fund completely fail that Fund will be added to the other Fund.

---

1 This clause assumes that 'my residuary estate' has already been defined. It is designed to cover 'funds' of equal or unequal size.

(d) The 'slice system'[1]

MY TRUSTEES will pay or transfer to *(cohabitee)*:

1 (75) per cent of the first (£100,000) of my residuary estate; and
2 (50) per cent of my residuary estate in so far as it exceeds (£100,000).[2]

IN DEFAULT of and subject to this gift my Trustees will hold my residuary estate (on trust) for *(names)*.

---

1 For a general discussion on the advantages and disadvantages of the 'slice system', see the Scottish Law Commission's 'Report on Succession' (1990), Scot Law Com No 124, at pp 22 and 146.
2 The percentages and figures can be adapted to suit the testator's requirements; those quoted are merely illustrative. The clause can be adapted to provide alternatives where the testator is survived by the cohabitee and issue, and where the testator dies without issue and is survived by the cohabitee. For example: 'If I die without issue and *(cohabitee)* survives me . . .'; and 'If I die leaving issue and *(cohabitee)* survives me . . .'.

(e) Cohabitee's entitlement based on the duration of the relationship[1]

MY TRUSTEES will pay or transfer to *(cohabitee)* (10) per cent of my residuary estate[2] for each complete year which has elapsed between *(date)* [OR] (the date of this Will)[3] and the date of my death[4] and no apportionment will be made in respect of any period of less than a year.

IN DEFAULT of and subject to this gift my Trustees will hold my residuary estate (on trust) for *(names)*.

1 The same concept could be applied to a pecuniary legacy.
2 The percentage can be adapted to suit the testator's requirements.
3 If any date other than the date of the will is stated it must be precise: eg day, month, year.
4 If it is considered necessary, the following words could be added: ' . . . so that if I die on or after (*date*), (*cohabitee*) will be entitled to all of my residuary estate . . .'

(f) Life interest

1 MY TRUSTEES will hold my residuary estate on trust to pay its income[1] to (*cohabitee*) during (his)/(her) lifetime.

2 AFTER the death of (*cohabitee*) my Trustees will hold the capital and income of my residuary estate on trust for those of my children who survive me[2] and reach the age of (18) and if more than one in equal shares.

3 IF any of my children dies before me[2] or before reaching the age of (18) leaving a child or children who do reach that age that child or those children equally will take the share of my residuary estate that his, her or their parent would otherwise have taken.

1 The income may be insufficient for the surviving partner's needs. Consider whether the trustees should have power to advance capital or make loans.
2 Note that the interests of the remaindermen are contingent on their surviving the testator, not the life tenant. If the alternative is preferred, delete the word 'me' and replace it with the life tenant's name or description.

(g) Life interest determinable on cohabitation[1]

1 MY TRUSTEES will hold my residuary estate on trust to pay its income to (*cohabitee*) during (his)/(her) lifetime until (he)/(she) cohabits.[2]

2 SUBJECT to the above trust my Trustees will hold my residuary estate (on trust) for

1 For a brief discussion of the definition of 'cohabits' and the evidential problems experienced in trying to establish whether a couple are cohabiting, see p 188.
   For alternative provisions in respect of the residuary estate, consider a revocable life interest (Precedent 28(h) below), and a discretionary trust (Precedents 28(i) and (j) below).
2 It is considered that the word 'marries' in the expression 'until (he)/(she) marries or cohabits (whichever happens first)' is probably otiose.

(h) Revocable life interest[1]

1 MY TRUSTEES will hold my residuary estate on trust to pay the income from it to (*cohabitee*) during (his)/(her) lifetime subject to the powers and provisions that follow.

2 MY TRUSTEES can revoke the life interest of (*cohabitee*) and hold my residuary estate as if (he)/(she) had died on the date of revocation.

3 THE REVOCATION can only be made:

(a) by my Trustees, provided that they are at least two in number or a trust corporation;

(b) by deed.

4 THE REVOCATION can be made:

(a) in respect of (*cohabitee's*) interest in all of my residuary estate or any asset comprised in it;

(b) before Probate of this Will has been granted;

(c) before the administration of my estate has been completed;

(d) at any time during the lifetime of (*cohabitee*).

5 IN EXERCISING their power of revocation:

(a) my Trustees will have absolute discretion;

(b) my Trustees can have regard to, or disregard, any wishes I may have communicated to them;

(c) the decision of my Trustees will be final and binding.

6 MY TRUSTEES can:

(a) appoint any person, professional trustee or trust corporation to be a new trustee of all or any part of my residuary estate and, where appropriate, provide for their remuneration;

(b) provided that they are at least two in number or a trust corporation, execute any deed or deeds extinguishing or restricting the future exercise of their power of revocation.

7 SUBJECT to the above trusts, powers and provisions my Trustees will hold the capital and income of my residuary estate (on trust) for

---

1 A revocable life interest is one of the devices used by some practitioners to overcome some of the difficulties that arise when a testator wishes to give his partner a life interest, but also wishes it to terminate as soon as she enters into a new relationship. See, generally, p 188. It is not entirely clear how successful such a clause is in practical and human terms.

(i) 80-year discretionary trust[1]

1 MY TRUSTEES will hold the capital and income of my residuary estate on trust for any one or more of the Beneficiaries whom they appoint.

2 THE BENEFICIARIES are:

(a) (*cohabitee*);

(b) anyone with whom I am living at the time of my death;

(c) my (husband)/(wife), if any;

(d) my former (husband)/(wife), if any;

(e) my children and remoter issue;

(f) my parents;

(g) my brothers and sisters and their children and remoter issue;

(h) the children and remoter issue of (*cohabitee*), anyone with whom I am living at the time of my death, my (husband)/(wife) and my former (husband)/(wife).

3 THE APPOINTMENT(S) can only be made:

(a) by my Trustees, provided that they are at least two in number or a trust corporation;

(b) by deed;

(c) within the period of 80 years (less 3 days) beginning with the date of my death ('the 80-year period');

(d) so as to avoid infringing the rules about remoteness, and for the purposes of these trusts the perpetuity period will be the 80-year period.

4 THE APPOINTMENT(S) can be made:

(a) as one appointment or as several appointments;

(b) at any time during the 80-year period;

(c) before Probate of this Will has been granted;

(d) before the administration of my estate has been completed;

(e) revocably or irrevocably;

(f) even though one or more of my Trustees stands to benefit personally from the appointment(s).

5 IN MAKING any appointment my Trustees:

(a) have total discretion;

(b) have the same powers that they would have if my residuary estate belonged to them personally;

(c) may have regard to, or disregard, any wishes I may have communicated to them;

(d) are under no obligation to ensure equality among the Beneficiaries or any class of Beneficiaries;

(e) can create interests that are free from any trust;

(f) can create any kind of trust;

(g) can stipulate any age or date at which a Beneficiary may be entitled;

(h) can confer any powers and discretions they think fit;

(i) can impose any restrictions, limitations, terms and conditions they think fit;

(j) can make any provisions they think fit;

(k) will not invalidate any earlier payment or application of any part(s) of the capital or income of my residuary estate.

6 MY TRUSTEES can:

(a) appoint any person, professional trustee or trust corporation to be a new trustee of the whole or any part of my residuary estate and, where appropriate, provide for their remuneration;

(b) provided that they are at least two in number or a trust corporation, execute at any time(s) a deed or deeds extinguishing or restricting the future exercise of their powers.

7 IN DEFAULT of any appointment and subject to any appointment the following provisions apply.

8 DURING the 80-year period my Trustees:

(a) will pay all or any part of the income of my residuary estate to any one or more of the Beneficiaries or apply it for his, her or their benefit, education, maintenance and support in whatever manner they think fit;

(b) can pay or apply any accumulations of income from past years as if they were the income of the present year.

9 DESPITE the preceding sub-clause my Trustees can, during the first 21 years after my death, accumulate all or any part of the income of my residuary estate by investing it and, if they do so, those accumulations can be added to the capital of my residuary estate.

10 AT THE END of the 80-year period my Trustees will hold the capital and income of my residuary estate for my children and remoter issue who are alive at that time and if more than one in equal shares according to their stocks, so that no issue whose parent is still alive will be entitled.

---

1 Discretionary trusts allow the trustees great flexibility, enabling them to react to changing family and tax circumstances. In the context of cohabitation they are occasionally used for the purpose of varying the financial provision made for the surviving partner according to any changes in his or her personal circumstances. The trustees have extremely wide-ranging powers. It is essential to establish whether the testator really wishes to leave his family's welfare and finances in the hands of trustees on a long-term basis.

A discretionary trust gives no qualifying interest in possession for the purposes of the Inheritance Tax Act 1984, s 58. No inheritance tax arises on the death of any of the potential beneficiaries, but the trust is subject to a 10-yearly charge and exit charges (ibid, ss 64 and 65).

For a full discussion of the tax implications and the advantages and disadvantages of these trusts, see D T Davies *Will Precedents and Inheritance Tax* (Butterworths) 4th Edn and *Butterworth's Wills, Probate and Administration Service* (Butterworths).

(j) Two-year discretionary trust[1]

1 MY TRUSTEES will hold the capital and income of my residuary estate on trust for any one or more of the Beneficiaries whom they appoint.

2 THE BENEFICIARIES are:

(a) (*cohabitee*);
(b) anyone with whom I am living at the time of my death;
(c) my (husband)/(wife), if any;
(d) my former (husband)/(wife), if any;
(e) my children and remoter issue;
(f) my parents;
(g) my brothers and sisters and their children and remoter issue;
(h) the children and remoter issue of (*cohabitee*), anyone with whom I am living at the time of my death, my (husband)/(wife) and my former (husband)/(wife).

3 THE APPOINTMENT(S) can only be made:

(a) by my Trustees, provided that they are at least two in number or a trust corporation;
(b) by deed;
(c) within the period of two years (less 3 days) beginning with the date of my death ('the two-year period');
(d) so as to avoid infringing the rules about remoteness, and for the purposes of these trusts the perpetuity period will be 80 years from the date of my death.

4 THE APPOINTMENT(S) can be made:

(a) as one appointment or as several appointments;
(b) at any time during the two-year period;
(c) before Probate of this Will has been granted;
(d) before the administration of my estate has been completed;
(e) revocably or irrevocably;
(f) even though one or more of my Trustees stands to benefit personally from the appointment(s).

5 IN MAKING any appointment my Trustees:

(a) have total discretion;
(b) have the same powers that they would have if my residuary estate belonged to them personally;
(c) may have regard to, or disregard, any wishes I may have communicated to them;
(d) are under no obligation to ensure equality among the Beneficiaries or any class of Beneficiaries;
(e) can create interests that are free from any trust;
(f) can create any kind of trust;
(g) can stipulate any age or date at which a Beneficiary may be entitled;
(h) can confer any powers and discretions they think fit;
(i) can impose any restrictions, limitations, terms and conditions they think fit;
(j) can make any provisions they think fit;

(k) will not invalidate any earlier payment or application of any part(s) of the capital or income of my residuary estate.

6 MY TRUSTEES can:

(a) appoint any person, professional trustee or trust corporation to be a new trustee of the whole or any part of my residuary estate and, where appropriate, provide for their remuneration;

(b) provided that they are at least two in number or a trust corporation, execute at any time(s) a deed or deeds extinguishing or restricting the future exercise of their powers.

7 IN DEFAULT of any appointment and subject to any appointment the following provisions apply.

8 DURING the two-year period my Trustees:

(a) will pay all or any part of the income of my residuary estate to any one or more of the Beneficiaries or apply it for his, her or their benefit, education, maintenance and support in whatever manner they think fit;

(b) can accumulate the income;

(c) can add accumulations of income to the capital of my residuary estate.

9 AT THE END of the two-year period my Trustees will hold the capital and income of my residuary estate (on trust) for . . .

---

1 A two-year discretionary trust is widely used as an inheritance tax planning device, and takes advantage of the provisions of the Inheritance Tax Act 1984, s 144. For a fuller discussion see *Butterworth's Wills, Probate and Administration Service* (Butterworths) at para A967.

In the context of cohabitation a 'mini discretionary trust' might be regarded as a useful 'wait and see' vehicle, where the testator wishes to make provision for the surviving partner, but also wishes to withdraw such provision as soon as the survivor has entered into a new, stable relationship.

The testator should make his wishes clear to his trustees, preferably in a written 'off-the-record' memorandum.

The interaction of 'mini discretionary trusts' and the Inheritance (Provision for Family and Dependants) Act 1975 has not yet been fully explored by the courts.

---

29 TRUSTEES' POWERS

(a) Investment[1]

(MY TRUSTEES can) invest as freely as if the assets of my residuary estate were their own and can acquire assets which produce no income[2] and can purchase[3] and improve[4] any property for the purpose of providing a home for a beneficiary.[5]

1 For a discussion of the present powers and duties of trustees in respect of investments, and for criticisms and recommendations for reform, see The Law Reform Committee's 23rd Report (1982), Cmnd 8733, at paras 3.1 to 3.25.
2 Assets which produce no income are not 'investments', and are, therefore, unauthorised (*Re Wragg* [1919] 2 Ch 58).
3 See the Law of Property Act 1925, s 28(1) and the Settled Land Act 1925, s 73(1)(x). In the absence of either of these powers or express authorisation, trustees cannot purchase land.
4 A very limited power to raise money for improvements is conferred by the Landlord and Tenant Act 1927, s 13.
5 A power to invest in the purchase of land does not automatically authorise the trustees to acquire a vacant freehold house for occupation by the testator's family; because it produces no income it is not an investment (*Re Power* [1947] Ch 572). The Law Reform Committee (above) considered that 'legislation is required to reverse the decision in Re Power' (at para 3.5).

(b) Delegation of investment management[1]

(MY TRUSTEES can) delegate their powers of investing, managing and administering trust assets to any person or company (whether UK resident or not) and allow trust assets to be held in the name of that person or company as their nominee on whatever terms (including remuneration) they think appropriate.

1 For existing powers see the Trustee Act 1925 (as amended), ss 23(1) and 25. For criticisms and recommendations for reform, see The Law Reform Committee's 23rd Report (1982), Cmnd 8733, at paras 4.1 to 4.8, and pp 65 and 66. Note also The Law Commission's Consultation Paper No 118, 'The Law of Trusts: Delegation by Individual Trustees' (1991).

(c) Maintenance[1]

(MY TRUSTEES can) apply all or any part of the income of that share of my residuary estate to which a beneficiary is or may in future be entitled for that beneficiary's maintenance, education or benefit in whatever manner they in their absolute discretion think fit, regardless of whether other funds are available for these purposes, and regardless of whether anyone has a legal duty to provide for that beneficiary's maintenance or education.[2]

1 The statutory power to apply income for maintenance and to accumulate surplus income during a minority is contained in the Trustee Act 1925, s 31. The Law Reform Committee recommended that the section should not be changed (23rd Report (1982), Cmnd 8733, at para 4.40). It is submitted that the standard will clauses which refer to this section and amend it are unintelligible to the ordinary testator.
2 If necessary, the clause could prohibit any payment being made while the father has anything to do with the child's education or upbringing (*Re Borwicks Settlement* [1916] 2 Ch 304).

(d) Advancement[1]

(MY TRUSTEES can) apply all[2] or any part of the capital of that share of my residuary estate to which a beneficiary is or may in future be entitled for that beneficiary's advancement or benefit[3] in whatever manner they in their absolute discretion think fit.[4]

1 The statutory power of advancement is contained in the Trustee Act 1925, s 32. It is submitted that the widely used type of clause which refers to the section and amends it is unintelligible to the ordinary testator.
2 Ibid, s 32(1), proviso (a), restricts the money paid or applied to 'one-half of the presumptive or vested share or interest'. The Law Reform Committee's 23rd Report (1982), Cmnd 8733, at para 4.41 recommended no change to s 32.
3 'Advancement' suggests establishing the beneficiary in life. The wider-term 'benefit' includes (inter alia) payments for the beneficiary's maintenance or education. The trustees must have good reason for making the advance, and must see that its purpose is carried out (*Re Pauling* (No 1) [1965] Ch 303).
4 Trustee Act 1925, s 32(1), proviso (b), which requires that the advances be brought into account, will apply unless specifically excluded.

(e) Insurance[1]

(MY TRUSTEES can):

1 insure any asset in my estate against any insurable risk[2] and for any amount[3] even though a beneficiary is absolutely entitled to it;[4]

2 pay insurance premiums out of income or capital[5] in whatever manner they think fit;

3 use any insurance money they receive to restore the asset or alternatively treat that money as if it were the net proceeds of sale of the asset insured.

1 For the existing statutory powers, see the Trustee Act 1925, s 19. For criticisms and recommendations for reform, see The Law Reform Committee's 23rd Report (1982), Cmnd 8733, at paras 4.29 to 4.36, and p 66.
2 The statutory power is restricted to 'loss or damage by fire' (Trustee Act 1925, s 19(1)).
3 The statutory power is limited to an amount 'not exceeding three fourth parts of the full value of the building or property' (ibid, s 19(1)).
4 Ibid, s 19(2) excludes the trustees' statutory power of insurance where they hold on a bare trust.
5 The statutory power is exercised at the expense of income (ibid, s 19(1)).

(f) Appropriation[1]

(MY TRUSTEES can) appropriate any part of my estate in its then actual condition or state of investment in or towards the satisfaction of any legacy, interest or share in my estate without having to obtain any consent and regardless of whether they are acting as personal representatives or trustees.[2]

1 See, generally, the Administration of Estates Act 1925, s 41.
2 The statutory power applies only to personal representatives. It does not apply to trustees. For comment and proposed reform see The Law Reform Committee's 23rd Report (1982), Cmnd 8733, at para 4.41.

(g) Exclusion of apportionment rules[1]

(MY TRUSTEES can) disregard the statutory and equitable rules relating to the apportionment of income, and can treat any payment in the nature of income as income arising at the time when it is received, regardless of the period to which it relates.

1 For the statutory and equitable rules relating to conversion and apportionment, see general texts on equity and trusts. For criticisms and recommendations for reform see The Law Reform Committee's 23rd Report (1982), Cmnd 8733, at paras 3.20 to 3.41, and p 64.

(h) Remuneration[1]

(MY TRUSTEES can) if they are professionally qualified trustees or a trust corporation[2] charge and be paid for all the work they do in obtaining probate, administering my estate and acting as trustees, even though some of that work could have been done by a person who is not professionally qualified.

1 See Precedent 11, footnote 3 at p 195 above.
2 Although no specific power is required to appoint a trust corporation as a trustee, such a corporation will only take on the trusteeship if it has power to charge. Express authorisation to charge is not required where the Public Trustee takes on the appointment (Public Trustee Act 1906, s 5).

30 STATEMENT FOR THE PURPOSES OF THE INHERITANCE (PROVISION FOR FAMILY AND DEPENDANTS) ACT 1975[1]

I HAVE NOT MADE (greater)/(any) provision[2] in this Will for (*cohabitee*) (not through any lack of love or affection for (him)/(her) but) because:

(a) I consider that (he)/(she) already has adequate financial resources;[3]
(b) (he)/(she) is not maintained by me or financially dependent on me;[4]
(c) our relationship has been of a comparatively short duration;[5]
(d) I believe that my (children) have a greater claim on my estate;
(e) (*other reasons, if any*).[6]

1 For the admissibility as evidence of statements made by the deceased, see the Inheritance (Provision for Family and Dependants) Act 1975, s 21. If the statement is defamatory,

objectionable, or distressing to 'the family' it will be excluded from the probate (*In the Estate of Hall* [1943] 2 All ER 159).

2 For anyone other than a spouse 'reasonable financial provision' means 'such financial provision as it would be reasonable in all the circumstances of the case for the applicant to receive for his maintenance' (Inheritance (Provision for Family and Dependants) Act 1975, 1(2)(b)).

3 See ibid, s 3.

4 See ibid, s 2(3). However, the situation could change between the date of the will and the testator's death.

5 See ibid, s 3(4). Likewise, the situation could change between the date of the will and the testator's death.

6 For example: there could be a nomination in the cohabitee's favour; various assets could pass to the cohabitee by the *ius accrescendi*; the testator may have made lifetime gifts to the cohabitee; the cohabitee may have expectations under the will of someone else; the origin of the deceased's assets may be relevant; the couple might even have signed a cohabitation contract waiving the right to apply to the court for an order under the act. See Chapter 2, Precedent 30 at p 125 above. See also Precedent 40, clause 10 at pp 226 below.

31 THE WORD 'COHABITS' IN WILLS

(a) Definitions[1]

For the purposes of this Will 'cohabitation' exists where a man and a woman who are not married to each other live together in the same household as husband and wife, and 'cohabits' will be interpreted accordingly.[2] [OR]

For the purposes of this Will 'cohabitation' exists where a man and a woman who are not married to each other live together in the same household as husband and wife for a period of (*number*) months in any (*number*) month period, and 'cohabits' will be interpreted accordingly.[3] [OR]

For the purposes of this Will (*cohabitee*) will be treated as cohabiting if (he)/(she) lives in the same household with a person of either sex who is not a blood relative of (his)/(hers) or mine.[4] [OR]

For the purposes of this Will 'cohabits' means 'has sexual relations'.[5]

1 See, generally, p 188. See also, Chris Barton *Cohabitation Contracts* (Gower, 1985) at pp 2 to 5 on definitions and terminology.

2 This definition is based partly on the wording of the Domestic Violence and Matrimonial Proceedings Act 1976, s 1(2) and the Social Security Act 1986, s 20(11).

3 This definition is based partly on the Solicitors' Family Law Association *Precedents for Consent Orders* (3rd Edn), Precedent 32. *Cf* Barton, above, at p 3: 'sharing a bedroom during at least four nights per week during at least three consecutive months with someone of the opposite sex'.

4 *Cf* Jill Bowler, Jacqui Jackson and Eileen Loughridge *Living Together Precedents* (Waterlow, 1989) at p 47: '(His)/(Her) cohabiting with a person of either sex not being a member of (his)/(her) or my immediate family (but this condition shall not preclude normal short term visits by friends or relatives).'

5 *Cf* the euphemistic expression '*dum casta vixerit*'. It is submitted that some testators would construe 'cohabits' in exactly this way.

(b) Miscellaneous[1]

- For the purposes of deciding whether or not (*cohabitee*) is cohabiting, my Trustees may have regard to the criteria applied by the Department of Social Security for the purposes of deciding whether or not a claimant is cohabiting.[2]
- The fact that (*cohabitee*) is living in the same household with someone who is not (his)/(her) or my blood relative will give rise to a presumption that they are cohabiting and the burden of proving that (he)/(she) is not cohabiting will lie with (*cohabitee*).
- My Trustees will not be liable for paying the income from (my residuary estate) to (*cohabitee*) after (his)/(her) interest in it has terminated unless they have knowledge of the event causing the termination.[3]
- The decision of my Trustees as to whether or not (*cohabitee*) is cohabiting will be final and binding.[4]

---

1 See, generally, p 188.
2 For the criteria recommended by the DSS to its adjudication officers, see the current edition of John Mesher *CPAG's Income Support, The Social Fund and Family Credit* (Sweet & Maxwell).
3 The Trustee Act 1925, s 61 provides that 'if it appears to the court that a trustee . . . is or may be personally liable for any breach of trust . . . but has acted honestly and reasonably, and ought fairly to be excused . . . the court may relieve him either wholly or partly from personal liability'. This relief may also be extended to executors.
4 Any clause in a will which purports to make the trustees' decision final and binding is invalid (*Re Wynn* [1952] 1 All ER 341). The reason for this is that the court exercises a general controlling influence over all trustees, and a clause which attempts to oust its jurisdiction is thereby repugnant and contrary to public policy.

---

32 TESTIMONIUM[1]

AS WITNESS my hand on (*date*)

[*OR*]

SIGNED by me on (*date*).

---

1 The testimonium will be needed if the date does not appear in the commencement of the will.

33 ATTESTATION CLAUSE[1]

SIGNED by (*testator*) in our joint presence and then by us in (his)/(hers).

---

1 The formal requirements for the execution of a valid will are set out in the Wills Act 1837, s 9 (as substituted by the Administration of Justice Act 1982, s 17). This section ends with the statement that 'no form of attestation shall be necessary'.

   This clause is for use in normal cases. For attestation clauses where the testator is unable to read or write, or is visually handicapped, or when another person signs on the testator's behalf, see the standard will precedent books.

Forms

34 PENSION SCHEME: REQUEST TO TRUSTEES[1]

(Full Name and Address of Member)

To: The Trustees,   *(date)*
The *(name)* Pension Scheme,
(address)

Dear Sirs,

Statement of wishes concerning death benefits

Although I am aware that you have an absolute discretion in respect of the payment of any lump sum and other benefits on my death, I would be grateful if you could have regard to my wishes, as stated below, until you receive a further statement from me.

I would like the following people to receive the following shares:

Name   Relationship   Address   Percentage

Yours faithfully,

(member's signature)[2]

---

1 It would be sensible to check the terms of the scheme to see whether or not such a nomination is possible.
   As this is a 'non-statutory' nomination, the benefits do not form part of the deceased's estate for the purposes of an order under the Inheritance (Provision for Family and Dependants) Act 1975 (s 8(1)). See also *Re Cairnes* [1983] FLR 225.
2 A nomination of this kind is not a 'testamentary disposition' (*Re Danish Bacon Co Staff Pension Fund* [1971] 1 All ER 486).
   The member should send the letter to the trustees in a sealed envelope stating his full name, the date, and the words 'Statement of Wishes relating to the *(name)* Pension Scheme'.

35 CODICIL 'DISINHERITING' FORMER COHABITEE[1]

THIS (SECOND) CODICIL is made by me (*testator*) of (*address*) on (*date*) and is supplemental to my Will dated (*date*) (and the Codicil(s) to it dated).

1 I REVOKE the appointment of (*cohabitee*) as an Executor and Trustee of my Will.

2 I REVOKE every devise, bequest, legacy, benefit and privilege given to or conferred on (*cohabitee*) in my Will.

3 I INTEND that my Will will be interpreted and take effect as if (*cohabitee*) had died before me.[2]

4 I CONFIRM my Will (and Codicil(s)) in all other respects.

SIGNED by (*testator*) in our joint presence and then by us in (his)/(hers).

---

1 For unmarried couples there is no equivalent to the Wills Act 1837, s 18A, which describes the effect on a will of a decree of dissolution or annulment of marriage. Therefore, if cohabitees split up, it is vitally important that they should review their respective wills immediately. A codicil of this nature should only be executed if the will contains suitable alternative appointments and gifts unless, of course, the testator consciously wishes to bring about a potential intestacy or partial intestacy. A codicil of this nature could also be executed by a married person in the throes of a divorce but where no decree of the court has yet been made.
2 Cf *Re Sinclair* [1985] Ch 446.

---

36 WILL: UNMARRIED MOTHER LEAVING HER ENTIRE ESTATE TO HER CHILD UNDER 18

THIS WILL is made on (*date*) by me (*testatrix*) of (*address*).

1 I REVOKE my earlier Wills.

2 I WOULD LIKE to be (cremated).

3 I APPOINT my parents (*name*) and (*name*) of (*address*) ('my Trustees') to be my Executors and Trustees and the Guardians of my (son)/(daughter) (*child's name*).[1]

4 I GIVE all my estate to my Trustees on trust to:

    (a) sell or retain;
    (b) pay my debts, funeral expenses and executorship expenses; and
    (c) hold what remains ('my residuary estate') as follows.

5 MY TRUSTEES will hold my residuary estate on trust for my

(son)/(daughter) (*child's name*) if and when (he)/(she) reaches the age of (18).

6 IF my (son)/(daughter) dies before me or before (he)/(she) reaches (18) leaving issue, my Trustees will hold my residuary estate on trust for such issue who reach (18) and if more than one in equal shares.[2]

7 IF all of the above trusts fail, my Trustees will pay or transfer my residuary estate to my parents in equal shares or to the survivor of them absolutely.

8 MY TRUSTEES can:

(a) invest as freely as if the assets of my residuary estate were their own and can acquire assets which produce no income and can purchase and improve any property for the purpose of providing a home for a beneficiary;

(b) apply all or any part of the income of that share of my residuary estate to which a beneficiary is or may in future be entitled for that beneficiary's maintenance, education or benefit in whatever manner they in their absolute discretion think fit, regardless of whether other funds are available for these purposes, and regardless of whether anyone has a legal duty to provide for that beneficiary's maintenance or education;[3]

(c) apply all or any part of the capital of that share of my residuary estate to which a beneficiary is or may in future be entitled for that beneficiary's advancement or benefit in whatever manner they in their absolute discretion think fit.

SIGNED by (*testatrix*) in our joint presence and then by us in hers.

---

1 It is assumed that the child's father has not acquired parental responsibility. See, generally, the Children Act 1989, s 4.

2 Although the reference to the testatrix's grandchildren may seem completely inappropriate, it would not be possible in these circumstances to rely on the provisions of the Wills Act 1837, s 33. In order for that section to apply, the son or daughter would have to die before the testatrix, leaving issue living at her death. Furthermore, the gift over to the parents, which is probably sensible, could be construed as 'a contrary intention' for the purposes of s 33.

3 For example, a maintenance assessment may have been made under the Child Support Act 1991, requiring the absent parent to make periodical payments.

---

37 WILL: CHILDLESS COUPLE: ALL TO THE SURVIVING PARTNER: GIFT OVER TO THEIR RESPECTIVE PARENTS

THIS WILL is made on (*date*) by me (*testator*) of (*address*).

1 I REVOKE my earlier Wills.

2 I WOULD LIKE:

  (a) any part of my body which may be of use to others to be made available for treatment or transplantation;
  (b) to be cremated;
  (c) donations to be made to (*Charity*).

3 IF (he)/(she) survives me by (7) days I GIVE my estate to (*cohabitee*) of (*address*) AND I APPOINT (him)/(her) to be my Executor, but if (he)/(she) fails to survive me by (7) days the following clauses will apply.

4 I APPOINT (*name*) of (*address*) and (*name*) of (*address*) ('my Trustees') to be the Executors and Trustees of this Will.

5 I GIVE my estate to my Trustees on trust to:

  (a) sell or retain;
  (b) pay my debts, funeral expenses, executorship expenses and Inheritance Tax; and
  (c) hold what remains ('my residuary estate') as follows.

6 MY TRUSTEES will divide my residuary estate into two equal shares and if the trusts of one of these shares fail, that share will be added to the other share.

7 MY TRUSTEES will pay or transfer one share to my parents (*name*) and (*name*) of (*address*) equally or to the survivor of them.

8 MY TRUSTEES will pay or transfer the other share to (*cohabitee's*) parents (*name*) and (*name*) of (*address*) equally or to the survivor of them.

SIGNED by (*testator*) in our joint presence and then by us in (his)/(hers).

38 WILL: COUPLE WITH MINOR CHILDREN: BOTH PARENTS HAVE PARENTAL RESPONSIBILITY: ALL TO THE SURVIVING PARTNER: GIFT OVER TO CHILDREN: FURTHER GIFT OVER IN CASE OF A FAMILY CATASTROPHE

THIS WILL is made on (*date*) by me (*testator*) of (*address*).

1 I REVOKE my earlier Wills.

2 I WOULD LIKE to be (cremated).[1]

3 IF (he)/(she) survives me by (7) days I GIVE my estate to (*cohabitee*) of (address) AND I APPOINT (him)/(her) to be my Executor, but if (he)/(she) fails to survive me by (7) days the following clauses will apply.

4 I APPOINT (*name*) of (*address*) and (*name*) of (*address*) ('my Trustees') to be the Executors and Trustees of this Will.

5 I APPOINT (*name*) of (*address*) to be the Guardian of my children.

6 I GIVE all my estate to my Trustees on trust to:

(a) sell or retain;

(b) pay my debts, funeral expenses, executorship expenses and Inheritance Tax; and

(c) hold what remains ('my residuary estate') as follows.

7 MY TRUSTEES will hold my residuary estate on trust for my children who survive me and reach the age of (18) and if more than one in equal shares.

8 IF a child of mine dies before me or before reaching (18) leaving a child or children who do reach that age that child or those children equally will take the share of my residuary estate that his, her or their parent would otherwise have taken.

9 IF all the above trusts fail my Trustees will divide my residuary estate into two equal shares and if the trusts of one of these shares fail that share will be added to the other share.

10 MY TRUSTEES will pay or transfer one share:

(a) to my parents (*name*) and (*name*) equally or to the survivor of them; or

(b) if both of my parents die before me, to my brothers and sisters (*names*) equally or to the survivor of them.

11 MY TRUSTEES will pay or transfer the other share:

(a) to (*cohabitee's*) parents (*name*) and (*name*) equally or to the survivor of them; or

(b) if both of (*cohabitee's*) parents die before me, to (his)/(her) brothers and sisters (*names*) equally or to the survivor of them.

12 (*Trustees' powers.*)

SIGNED by (*testator*) in our joint presence and then by us in (his)/(hers).

---

1 If this is the woman's will, and the man does not have parental responsibility for the child(ren), insert a guardianship appointment at this stage. For example, 'I APPOINT (*cohabitee*) to be the Guardian of our children'.

---

39 WILL: OLDER UNMARRIED COUPLE: LIFE INTEREST TO THE SURVIVOR

THIS WILL is made on (*date*) by me (*testator*) of (*address*).

1 I REVOKE my earlier Wills.

2 I WOULD LIKE to be cremated.

3 I APPOINT *(name)* of *(address)* and *(name)* of *(address)* ('my Trustees') to be my Executors and Trustees.

4 I GIVE all my personal chattels (as defined in the Administration of Estates Act 1925) to *(cohabitee)* free of tax.

5 I GIVE the rest of my estate to my Trustees on trust to:

   (a) sell or retain;
   (b) pay my debts, funeral expenses, executorship expenses and Inheritance Tax; and
   (c) hold what remains ('my residuary estate') as follows.

6 MY TRUSTEES will hold my residuary estate on trust to pay its income to *(cohabitee)* during (his)/(her) lifetime.

7 AFTER the death of *(cohabitee)* my Trustees will pay or transfer the capital and income of my residuary estate to those of my children *(name)*, *(name)* and *(name)* who survive me and if more than one in equal shares.

8 IF any of my children dies before me leaving a child or children living at my death that child or those children equally on reaching the age of (18) will take the share of my residuary estate that his, her or their parent would otherwise have taken.

9 *(Trustees' powers, including a clause excluding the operation of the apportionment rules.)*

SIGNED by *(testator)* in our joint presence and then by us in (his)/(hers).

40 WILL: OLDER UNMARRIED COUPLE: LIMITED PROVISION FOR THE SURVIVING PARTNER: RESIDUE TO THE TESTATOR'S CHILDREN

THIS WILL is made on *(date)* by me *(testator)* of *(address)*.

1 I REVOKE my earlier Wills.

2 I WOULD LIKE:

   (a) to be cremated;
   (b) my ashes to be scattered;
   (c) *(cohabitee)* to decide what other funeral arrangements should be made;
   (d) the expenses incurred in carrying out these wishes to be paid out of my estate.

3 I APPOINT my children *(name)* of *(address)* and *(name)* of *(address)* ('my Trustees') to be the Executors and Trustees of this Will.

4 I GIVE to (*cohabitee*) free of tax all my personal chattels (as defined in the Administration of Estates Act 1925) and without imposing an obligation or creating a trust I would like (him)/(her), either by Will or lifetime gifts, to pass on to my children and grandchildren any articles which have particular associations with my family.

5 I GIVE to (*cohabitee*)   pounds (£   ) free of tax.

6 I RELEASE (*cohabitee*), free of tax, from any sum of money that (he)/(she) may owe me at the time of my death.

7 I GIVE the rest of my estate to my Trustees on trust to:

(a) sell or retain;
(b) pay my debts, funeral expenses, executorship expenses and Inheritance Tax including the tax attributable to property that I hold as a joint tenant; and
(c) hold what remains ('my residuary estate') as follows.

8 MY TRUSTEES will pay or transfer my residuary estate to my children (*name*) and (*name*) equally or to the survivor of them but if either of them dies before me leaving a child or children who reach the age of (18) that child or those children equally will take the share of my residuary estate that (his)/(her)/(their) parent would otherwise have taken.

9 (*Trustees' powers.*)

10 I HAVE NOT MADE greater provision for (*cohabitee*) in this Will because:

(a) the house and bank accounts that we hold as joint tenants will automatically pass to (him)/(her) by right of survivorship;
(b) I am satisfied that (he)/(she) has adequate resources to enable (him)/(her) to live comfortably for the rest of (his)/(her) life;
(c) of the possibility that if I had left the whole of my estate to (him)/(her) my family could be disinherited and (his)/(her) family commensurately enriched.

SIGNED by (*testator*) in our joint presence and then by us in (his)/(hers).

CHAPTER 5: MISCELLANEOUS DOCUMENTS

INDEX

PART 1: INTRODUCTORY TEXT

Change of Name[1]

A person can be called by whatever name he or she chooses.[2] No formalities are necessary, and a name can be acquired simply by habit and repute.[3] At some stage somebody is likely to require evidence of the change of name, and so it is usual practice to document a change of name by means of one of the more formal procedures, such as executing a deed or making a statutory declaration.[4] As far as children are concerned, where a residence order[5] or care order[6] is in force, nobody can cause the child to be known by a new surname without the leave of the court or the written consent of every person who has parental responsibility for the child.[7] Where a change of name deed is to be enrolled in the Central Office of the Supreme Court, the enrolment regulations distinguish between children who have attained the age of 16, and those who have not.[8] A child of 16 or over can either execute the deed poll himself or endorse his consent on the deed executed by his parent or guardian on his behalf.[9] Where a child is under 16 the deed poll must be executed by his parent or guardian, and the application for enrolment must be supported by an affidavit showing that the change of name is for the child's benefit.[10]

---

1 See, generally, Nasreen Pearce *Name-changing: A Practical Guide* (Fourmat Publishing, 1990).
2 Provided he does not do so for any fraudulent purpose or in order to deceive and inflict economic loss on another (*Du Boulay v Du Boulay* (1869) LR 2 PC 430; *Cowley v Cowley* [1901] AC 450).
3 *Dancer v Dancer* [1949] P 147.
4 Other methods include Notarial Instrument, Royal Licence, and even a private Act of Parliament.
5 Defined in the Children Act 1989, s 8(1).
6 Defined in ibid, ss 31(11) and 105(1).
7 Ibid, ss 13(1) and 33(7).
8 Enrolment of Deeds (Change of Name) Regulations 1983, SI 1983/680, r 8.
9 Ibid, r 8(3).
10 Ibid, r 8(5). See also the Practice Direction of 24 May 1976 [1977] 1 WLR 1065.

Contractual Licence[1]

A contractual licence is permission granted by the owner of property allowing another person to be on or in the property. The licence need not assume any particular form, and can be written or oral, but there must be an intention to create legal relations, and there must also be consideration.[2] For several years, landlords used the device of the contractual licence as a means of circumventing the operation of the Rent Acts. This contrivance was defeated by the decision of the House of Lords in *Street v Mountford*.[3] At the end of his judgment in that case Lord Templeman stated that: 'henceforth the courts which deal with these problems will, save in exceptional circumstances, only be concerned to inquire whether as a result of an agreement relating to residential accommodation the occupier is a lodger or a tenant'.[4]

It is submitted that a cohabitee sharing residential accommodation with his or her partner is usually neither a lodger nor a tenant, and would presumably fall within that residual category of 'exceptional circumstances'. Where a licensee shares accommodation with the licensor in his or her only or principal home, the licence is an excluded licence for the purposes of the Protection from Eviction Act 1977.[5]

---

1 See, generally, Jean Warburton *Sharing Residential Accommodation* (Sweet & Maxwell, 1990) at pp 24 to 35.
2 *Horrocks v Forray* [1976] 1 WLR 230, 236.
3 [1985] AC 809.
4 Ibid at 827E.
5 Protection from Eviction Act 1977, s 3A(2) (inserted by the Housing Act 1988, s 31).

Antenuptial agreement[1]

Until the Married Women's Property Act 1882 came into force 'the wife's existence was merged in that of her husband, and whatever property she might be possessed of upon her marriage or became possessed of during the marriage belonged, by the *ius mariti*, to him'.[2] An antenuptial settlement, whereby the bride-to-be transferred her property to trustees to hold on her behalf, was commonly used in wealthier families as a means of protecting a woman's assets.[3] As soon as married women became entitled to hold property in their own right, the need for such settlements diminished.

The increasing incidence of divorce and the effects of the court's redistributive powers on divorce have led to the emergence of 'antenuptial agreements' or 'marriage contracts', which are designed to protect the separate property of either or both the spouses on the dissolution of their marriage. At present such agreements are not valid in English law, perhaps because they have a tendency to oust the jurisdiction of the court. In response to public demand, the Law Society's Family Law Committee has recommended that legislation be introduced to make such agreements enforceable.[4]

---

1 See Precedent 4 at p 235 below.
2 Montague Lush *The Law of Husband and Wife* (Stevens & Sons, 1884), at p 98.
3 Subject to the doctrine of 'fraud on the marital rights' (see Lush (above), at pp 64 and 65).
4 The Law Society's Legal Practice Directorate: Memorandum (May 1991), 'Maintenance and Capital Provision on Divorce', at pp 22 to 28.

PART 2: PRECEDENTS

1 CHANGE OF NAME DEED: NOT INTENDED FOR ENROLMENT[1]

THIS CHANGE OF NAME DEED made on (*date*)
BY me (*forename(s) and new surname*) of (*address*) formerly known as (*forename(s) and old surname*)
WITNESSES that:

1 I now completely renounce and abandon the use of my former surname (*old surname*).

2 I now adopt and assume the surname (*new surname*).

3 I ask and authorise all persons at all times to address, describe and identify me by using the surname (*new surname*).

4 From now onwards I will use and sign the name (*forename(s)* and *new surname*):

   (a) in all deeds, documents, forms, records and other written instruments;
   (b) in all actions and proceedings;
   (c) in all dealings and transactions; and
   (d) on all occasions.

SIGNED as a Deed by (*forename(s) and new surname*) formerly known as (*forename(s) and old surname*) in the presence of:

---

1 See, generally, Nasreen Pearce *Name-changing: A Practical Guide* (Fourmat Publishing, 1990). For enrolment in the Central Office of the Supreme Court, see the Enrolment of Deeds (Change of Name) Regulations 1983, SI 1983/680.

   A change of name deed is commonly referred to as a 'deed poll'. Historically, a deed was either 'indented' or 'poll'. A deed indented was made by more than one party; more than one copy was made; each copy was cut or indented so that its indentations corresponded with the indentations in the other copy or copies. A deed poll was made by only one party, and was 'polled' or cut evenly without any indentations. For a change of name deed made by a mother on behalf of her child, see Chapter 3, Precedent 4 at p 178 above.

2 CONTRACTUAL LICENCE[1]

THIS LICENCE is made on (*date*)
BETWEEN 'the parties' (1) (*name 1*) of (*address*) ('*name 1*') and (2) (*name 2*) (also) of (*address*) ('*name 2*').

IT IS AGREED that:

1 Recitals

1.1 The parties (intend to) live together at (*address*) ('the property').
1.2 The property is owned by (*name 1*) (and is mortgaged to (*lender*)).[2]
1.3 The parties intend that this licence will be legally binding on them.[3]
1.4 This licence is made in consideration of the mutual concessions it contains and for other good and valuable consideration, the sufficiency of which each of the parties acknowledges.[4]

2 Licence

(*Name 1*) allows (*name 2*) to:

2.1 live with (him)/(her) in the property; and
2.2 use (his)/(her) furniture and fittings in the property; and
2.3 use the garage, parking space and garden belonging to the property.

3 Payment

On the first day of each month (*name 2*) will pay to (*name 1*) the sum of £   , or such other sum as the parties may from time to time agree, as a contribution towards (his)/(her) living and accommodation expenses.

4 Terms and conditions

(*Name 2*) will:

4.1 keep the property reasonably clean and tidy;
4.2 not intentionally damage the property or any part of it or any furniture and fittings in it;
4.3 not remove any of the furniture and fittings from the property;
4.4 not allow anyone else to stay overnight in the property without first obtaining the consent of (*name 1*);
4.5 consent to the sale of the property by (*name 1*), (his)/(her) personal representatives, trustee in bankruptcy or mortgagee, and vacate the property before completion of the sale;
4.6 not do anything that may annoy or cause a nuisance to (*name 1*) or the owners or occupiers of the premises nearby; and
4.7 not do anything that could render the insurance on the property void or voidable or could result in an increase in the insurance premium.

5 Licence revocable without notice

(*Name 1*) can revoke this licence at any time without having to give notice to (*name 2*) in advance if (*name 2*):

5.1 fails to pay (his)/(her) contribution towards (his)/(her) living and accommodation expenses when it is due; or

5.2 fails to comply with any of the terms and conditions of this licence.

6 Termination of licence

Subject to the above, this licence will come to an end when the first of the following events occurs:

6.1 the expiration of (one month's) written notice given by either party to the other; or

6.2 (*name 2*) vacates the property with the intention of never resuming residence in it; or

6.3 (two months) after (*name 1's*) death; or

6.4 when the property is sold.

7 The nature of this licence

(*Name 2*) acknowledges that:

7.1 this licence is not a lease;

7.2 this licence does not create any kind of tenancy;[5]

7.3 (he)/(she) has no exclusive right to occupy the property or any part of it;

7.4 (his)/(her) occupation of the property and use of its furniture and fittings will not give rise to joint ownership of the property or its furniture and fittings;

7.5 regardless of the contributions (he)/(she) makes towards (his)/(her) living and accommodation expenses (he)/(she) will not acquire any legal estate or beneficial interest in the property;

7.6 this licence is personal to (him)/(her) and cannot be transferred to anyone else; and

7.7 (he)/(she) understands the nature and effect of this licence and is entering into it freely and voluntarily after receiving legal advice on its provisions and implications.

SIGNED as a Deed by (*name 1*) in the presence of: .

SIGNED as a Deed by (*name 2*) in the presence of: .

---

1 See, generally, Jean Warburton *Sharing Residential Property* (Sweet & Maxwell, 1990) at pp 24 to 35.

2 The mortgagee will probably require the licensee to execute a deed postponing his or her rights in the property and undertaking not to assert an overriding interest against the mortgagee (*Williams & Glyn's Bank v Boland* [1981] AC 487).

3 *Horrocks v Forray* [1976] 1 WLR 230 at 236, per Megaw LJ.
4 Ibid.
5 'To constitute a tenancy the occupier must be granted exclusive possession for a fixed periodic term certain in consideration of a premium or periodical payments' (*Street v Mountford* [1985] AC 809 at 818E, per Lord Templeman).

---

3 SEPARATION AGREEMENT

THIS SEPARATION AGREEMENT is made on (*date*)
BETWEEN 'the parties' (1) (*name 1*) of (*address*) ('*name 1*') and (2) (*name 2*) of (*address*) ('*name 2*').

IT IS AGREED that:

1 Recitals

1.1 The parties lived together from (*date*) to (*date*).
1.2 The parties are now living apart.
1.3 The parties have (two) children, namely (*name 3*) who was born on (*date*) and (*name 4*) who was born on (*date*) ('the children').
1.4 Both of the parties have parental responsibility for the children.
1.5 The parties wish to effect an agreement which will dispose of any financial claims that either of them may have against the other and which will make provision for the future welfare and support of the children.
1.6 Each party has fully disclosed his or her financial situation to the other and each party is generally aware of the other's financial situation.
1.7 Each party is entering into this Agreement freely and voluntarily after receiving independent legal advice on its provisions and implications.
1.8 The parties intend that this Agreement will be legally binding on them.

2 Separation

The parties will (continue to) live separately and apart from each other.

3 Non-interference

Neither party will annoy or interfere with the other or his or her relatives, friends, colleagues or business contacts.

4 Confidentiality

Neither party will disclose, divulge or use to the detriment or disadvantage of the other any confidential information about the other's private life, family life, financial affairs or business interests which may have come to his or her knowledge during the course of their relationship, unless such disclosure is required in legal proceedings or for the purpose of making a maintenance assessment under the Child Support Act 1991 ('a maintenance assessment').

5 Children

5.1 The provisions of this Clause will at all times be subject to the ascertainable wishes and feelings of the children themselves, considered in the light of their respective ages and understanding.

5.2 The children will live with (*name 2*).

5.3 The children will be entitled to spend at least (two weekends) with (*name 1*) each month.

5.4 The children will be entitled to spend at least (two weeks) with (*name 1*) during the summer holidays each year.

5.5 The children will be entitled to spend Christmas Eve, Christmas Day and Boxing Day with (*name 1*) each alternate year.

5.6 The children will be entitled to maintain contact with (*name 1's*) parents, brothers and sisters.

5.7 All major decisions affecting the children's education, upbringing, health, welfare and the administration of their property will be made by the parties jointly.

5.8 Neither party will cause or allow the children to be known by a new surname or removed from the United Kingdom without the consent of the other party or the leave of the court.

5.9 Each party is responsible for maintaining the children.

5.10 From the date of this Agreement (*name 1*) will pay to (*name 2*) for the benefit of both of the children the sum of £   a month or such other sum as the parties may from time to time agree.

5.11 (*Name 1*) will continue to pay maintenance to (*name 2*) for the children's benefit in accordance with the terms of this Clause until a maintenance assessment takes effect or until such time as a maintenance assessment, if it had been made, would cease to have effect.

5.12 Regardless of the terms of this Clause, either party can at any time apply to the Child Support Agency for a maintenance assessment to be made in respect of either or both of the children.

6 Property

6.1 Within a period of (4) weeks from the date of this Agreement (*name 1*) will transfer to (*name 2*) (his)/(her) legal estate and beneficial interest in the property known as (*address*) ('the property') subject to the mortgage in favour of (*lender*).

6.2 (*Name 2*) will be responsible for the payment of the mortgage and all the other outgoings on the property.

6.3 (*Name 2*) will ensure that all future accounts relating to the outgoings are addressed to (him)/(her).

7 Personal chattels

7.1 The parties have already divided between them all of the personal chattels which formerly belonged to them jointly.

7.2 Each party is now the absolute owner of the personal chattels in his or her possession free from any claim, right or title of the other.

8 Debts

8.1 The parties have divided between them all the debts for which they are jointly and severally liable.

8.2 (*Name 1*) has assumed responsibility for the payment of the following debts:

[*name and address of creditor*]   [*amount outstanding*].

8.3 (*Name 2*) has assumed responsibility for the payment of the following debts:

[*name and address of creditor*]   [*amount outstanding*].

8.4 Each party promises to pay the debts for which he or she has assumed responsibility and will indemnify the other against all costs, claims, proceedings and demands arising in respect of those debts.

9 Conciliation

Any difference, disagreement or dispute arising out of or in connection with this Agreement will be referred in the first instance to the Family Conciliation Service without prejudice to the right of either party subsequently to apply to the court for adjudication or to the Child Support Agency for a maintenance assessment to be made or reviewed.

10 Variation

This Agreement can only be varied by an instrument in writing executed as a Deed by both parties.

SIGNED as a Deed by (*name 1*) in the presence of: .

SIGNED as a Deed by (*name 2*) in the presence of: .

4 ANTENUPTIAL AGREEMENT

THIS ANTENUPTIAL AGREEMENT made on (*date*)
BETWEEN: 'the parties' (1) ('*name*') of (*address*) ('*name 1*'); and (2) (*name*) also of (*address*) ('*name 2*')
WITNESSES as follows:

1 Recitals

1.1 The parties intend to marry each other within the next year.

1.2 Both of the parties are domiciled in England and Wales.

1.3 (*Name 1*) was born on (*date*) and has been previously married and divorced.

1.4 (*Name 1*) has (2) children namely (*children's names*) both of whom are over the age of eighteen years.

1.5 (*Name 2*) was born on (*date*) and has been previously married and divorced.

1.6 (*Name 2*) has (3) children namely (*children's names*) all of whom are over the age of eighteen years.

1.7 (*Name 1*) has disclosed to (*name 2*) full details of the income, earning capacity, property and other financial resources, and the financial needs, obligations and responsibilities which (he) (she) has now and is likely to have in the foreseeable future and such disclosure is set out in the First Schedule to this Agreement.

1.8 (*Name 2*) has disclosed to (*name 1*) full details of the income, earning capacity, property and other financial resources, and the financial needs, obligations and responsibilities which (he) (she) has now and is likely to have in the foreseeable future and such disclosure is set out in the Second Schedule to this Agreement.

1.9 Each of the parties has received separate, independent legal advice on his and her rights in the absence of this Agreement and on the manner in which those rights are or may be affected or extinguished by this Agreement.

1.10 Both of the parties fully understand the nature and effect of this Agreement and are entering into it after considering all the facts, circumstances and implications.

1.11 Each of the parties is entering into this Agreement freely and voluntarily, without coercion or pressure of any kind from the other party or from any third person.

1.12 Both of the parties intend that this Agreement will be legally binding on them.

1.13 Except where there is specific provision to the contrary in this Agreement, both parties wish and agree that their intended marriage shall not in any way change the legal rights and interests in and to any property of any kind which each separately owns now or may own in the future.

1.14 Both of the parties are and wish to remain financially independent of each other.

2 Present property

The parties agree that all property presently owned by either of them and any income derived from it and any increase in its value will continue to be that party's separate property despite their intended marriage.

3 Future property

The parties agree that any property acquired by either of them solely in the future and any income derived from it and any increase in its value will be that party's separate property.

4 No acquisition of beneficial interest

Each of the parties acknowledges that he or she will not acquire nor claim to have acquired any beneficial interest or any occupation rights (statutory or otherwise) in any property owned solely by the other now or in the future.

5 No claim for financial provision on dissolution

The parties agree that if either of them petitions the court for a decree of divorce, nullity of marriage, or judicial separation, neither of them will apply to the court for any order for financial provision which shall include, but is not limited to, any order requiring the other to:

5.1 pay maintenance pending suit;
5.2 make periodical payments for any term;
5.3 secure periodical payments for any term;
5.4 pay any lump sum;
5.5 secure the payment of any lump sum;
5.6 transfer any property; or
5.7 settle any property.

6 No claim for financial provision on death

The parties agree that if one of them dies the other will not apply to the court for an order under s 2 of the Inheritance (Provision for Family and Dependants) Act 1975 or any statutory modification or reenactment of it.

7 Support: no obligations created

If at any time either of the parties makes any financial provision to or for the benefit of the other:

7.1 the person making such provision will be under no obligation to make further provision; and
7.2 no obligation to provide for, maintain or support the other will have been created.

8 Debts

8.1 Each of the parties will remain solely liable for his or her present debts and any future debts which are incurred in his or her sole name.
8.2 The payment by one party of any part of the other's separate debts will in no way render the payer liable to make any further contribution in respect of such debts.

9 Exceptions

Nothing in this Agreement regarding the separate property and assets of the parties:

9.1 deprives either party of the right to give or receive from the other any kind of property or asset by way of gift, legacy or transfer;

9.2 affects the rights of either party in respect of any property or assets which he or she or they may deliberately vest in themselves as beneficial joint tenants or beneficial tenants in common regardless of the actual contributions made by each of the parties towards the acquisition of such property or asset.

10 Interpretation

No provision in this Agreement is to be interpreted against either party merely because his or her solicitor drafted that provision.

11 Proper law

This Agreement will be governed and interpreted in accordance with the law of England and Wales.

12 Paragraph headings

The paragraph headings in this Agreement have been inserted simply for reference and convenience and do not alter, amend, affect, define, limit or extend the scope or substance of the provisions above which they appear.

13 Severance

If any court finds that any provision of this Agreement is illegal, invalid or otherwise unenforceable such provision may be struck out of this Agreement without affecting its other provisions which will continue to have full force and effect.

14 Variation

The provisions of this Agreement can only be varied or cancelled by a deed executed by the parties.

15 Execution of implementing instruments

Each of the parties will at any time at the other's request sign, execute, deliver, file and record any deed, document, papers, form or instrument which may be necessary, convenient or desirable in order to implement the provisions of this Agreement.

16 Costs of this agreement

16.1 The legal costs relating to the preparation and execution of this Agreement will be paid by (*name 2*).

16.2 The costs incurred by (*name 1*) in obtaining separate legal advice and assistance on the provisions and implications of this Agreement will be paid by (*name 1*).

THE SECOND SCHEDULE
(*NAME 2's*) PROPERTY

	Now	*In the foreseeable future*
Income		
Earning capacity		
Property		
Other financial resources		
Financial needs		
Financial obligations		
Financial responsibilities		

SIGNED as a Deed by (*name 1*) in the presence of: .

SIGNED as a Deed by (*name 2*) in the presence of: .

INDEX

References in the right-hand column are to page numbers.